Praise for *Off to the Side*:

"A story of art's triumph over human fallibility and perversity . . . Readers will find [in *Off to the Side*] lovely prose, an original mind and a plainspoken man."   —Jonathan Yardley, *The Washington Post Book World*

"Part memoir and part menu from a sixty-four-year-old writer who is part man and part beast . . . [and] a deeply spiritual, reverent, and grateful man."
     —Susan Salter Reynolds, *Los Angeles Times*

"As fine a portrait of the species American writer as we're ever likely to have . . . A wholly winning book."   —James Sallis, *The Boston Globe*

"Celebrating the body's coarse demands and the mind's highest aspirations, Jim Harrison's bighearted memoir is a tell-all about the 'delicious freedom' of attentiveness. . . . The literary equivalent of a bear hug, enveloped by a whiff of garlic, booze and the brimstone that accompanies unfettered thought."   —Chris Waddington, *Minneapolis Star-Tribune*

"A grand treat . . . Crotchety, hyperliterate, ribald, wine-stained, a lingual barnstormer, the crazy rogue uncle of American writing—this is Jim Harrison, folks, and *Off to the Side* is proof yet again of his cockeyed genius."
     —Jonathan Miles, *Men's Journal*

"This is a big book, the book of a life, and it treats all aspects of Harrison's life with honesty and craft in the telling. . . . This book captured my mind, remained with me for days after reading it; and for those for whom it is but an introduction to Harrison's work, rather than one of the elegant capstones, I am deeply happy for their good fortune."
     —Rick Bass, *Shambhala Sun*

"Reading Jim Harrison's memoir, *Off to the Side*, is a lot like sitting down with a garrulous and wise uncle to hear story after story late into the night. He's been around the block, for sure, but he's neither bragging nor complaining. The pleasure comes from total immersion in a life lived to the hilt."
     —Dan Cryer, *Newsday*

September 19, 2004

Dear Jennifer,

Happy Birthday. This is my
favorite of my recent reads. Enjoy!

Don

OFF TO THE SIDE

A Memoir

Jim Harrison

Grove Press
New York

In memory of Winfield Sprague Harrison and Norma Olivia Walgren

Some of the pieces included in II: Seven Obsessions have been previously published in slightly different form in Men's Journal. "Alcohol" appeared under the title "A Man's Guide to Drinking" in the October 2001 issue. "Stripping" appeared under the title "Naked Women Dancing" in the December 2001 issue. "Private Religion" appeared under the title "How Men Pray" in the February 2002 issue. "The Road" appeared under the title "The Road: A Love Story" in the May 2002 issue. "Nature and Natives" appeared under the title "The End of Nature" in the August 2002 issue.

Published simultaneously in Canada
Printed in the United States of America

FIRST GROVE PRESS EDITION

Library of Congress Cataloging-in-Publication Data

Harrison, Jim, 1937–
Off to the side : a memoir / Jim Harrison.
p. cm.
ISBN 0-8021-4030-0 (pbk.)
1. Harrison, Jim, 1937–   2. Authors, American—20th century—Biography.   I. Title.
PS3558.A67 Z465 2002
813'.54—dc21   2002026051

Grove Press
841 Broadway
New York, NY 10003

03 04 05 06 07   10 9 8 7 6 5 4 3 2 1

"Beware, o wanderer, the road is walking too."
—Rilke

INTRODUCTION

When mentally fragile I like to drive to a far city, say at least a few hundred miles from any of the three modest places my family lives, check in to a somewhat pathetic brand-name motel with the pleasant feeling that I wouldn't know a single soul in the local phone book. And that my own phone won't ring except in the case of a dire event because my wife is well aware of my motives for staying in the anonymous room. Here I have shorn myself of my support systems and there is a fairly good chance that in a day or two I'll discover the etiology of what ails me, keeping in mind that the overexamined life is also not worth living.

Most often nothing in particular ails me, or nothing that is immediately correctable, other than a need to step aside from my life for a day or two and walk in unknown country. Close after dawn and armed with a local map I take a stroll in empty fields, canyons, woods, but preferably near a creek or river because since childhood I've loved the sound they make. Moving water is forever in the present tense, a condition we rather achingly avoid. I've always favored undistinguished places for reasons of privacy. And the fact that you're in new country, however modest, raises the level of attention for perhaps genetic reasons. Who goes here? Not many.

It is in this manner that I've always come up with the ideas and images that engender my poetry, novellas, and novels. I would add road trips that aren't particularly directional and have lasted for weeks. On solo road trips you see with clarity pieces of your life unroll against the unconditioned and nonhabitual backdrop. You refuse to think about anything you've thought about before, a tactic that seems to freshen the neurons and synapses because new images arise from the past, also new images from the unlived life before you. It is a somewhat mortal game.

Of course your own life is your truest story and it blinds you unless it's heavily edited. You can immediately dismiss all the routines which, though comforting, own the banality of a greeting card. This shrinkage alone will get rid of nine-tenths of your life. I recall that in his book *The Practice of the Wild*, Gary Snyder notes the relative sameness of our biographies but that our dreams and visions can be quite unique. The dream that I could write a good poem, a good novel, or even a good movie for that matter, has devoured my life.

I'm not sure I'm particularly well equipped to tell the truth. What our parents and teachers taught us as truth usually dealt with moral abstractions or the illusory notion of coming to grips with what they loosely termed as reality. Certain things happened and certain things didn't happen, and then the not very agile jump to certain things are true and others false. The wild humor of ten-year-olds comes from the first reading between the lines of this paralyzing bullshit that is destined to suffocate most of them.

I have noticed that everyone speaks a slightly different language. I suspect this is one way a writer can draw us together in that there is an effortless reverence among the intelligent for language mastery. I have also become aware that people's speech is less vivid than earlier in my life in terms of rural life—plants, animals both farm and wild, trees, weather, land and water shapes, the sun, moon, and stars. But then this is altogether natural in that during my own lifetime the thirty percent urban and semi-urban and seventy percent rural population has been reversed, thus the drift away from earthbound metaphor and images.

Maybe the idea of our unique dreams and visions is a little antique, if not pretentious. "Obsession" is more contemporary, though the young man who felt his brain transfigured by Keats and Whitman at sixteen felt called to these professions as surely as he would have felt if a voice had boomed out on a spring night from the marsh behind the house. We are drenched in cynicism, psychologisms, explanations, but life is still there, its essence quite beyond spin, its cycle as surely set as it always has been. And just recently there is the delightful reminder that in our trillion or so cells, within each one, in fact, are thirty thousand indicators of what we are genetically. That's just the beginning of the story which despite a lifetime of reading and hearing answers remains a mystery.

There is the additional corrective that on any given day for any number of reasons you are bound to look at your past a little differently. There is a very old Zen saying that is especially poignant on this matter: "If you wish to balance your past you are painting it with a turtle hair paintbrush." I can imagine a mortally wounded caveman sitting on a rock precipice and admitting to himself with puzzlement, "The life I've already lived is my life," not the less true being so naked.

I

EARLY LIFE

FAMILY

Norma Olivia Walgren met Winfield Sprague Harrison in 1933 at
the River Gardens, a dance hall just north of Big Rapids, Michigan,
on the banks of the Muskegon River. When young we children were
somewhat embarrassed to hear the story of our parents' probably fe-
verish collision on a summer evening early in the Great Depression.
The river has to slide past until we ourselves are in love and bent on
mating with the scant ability to lift our eyelids high enough to see
that it happens to nearly everyone. Norma was a very strong and
somewhat irascible character and remained that way until her death
at eighty-five. Winfield was obsessively hardworking, playful but
melancholy. He must have been troubled at the time because he had
worked his way through Michigan Agricultural College, graduating
in 1932, but the convulsed economy only allowed him a job driving
a beer truck and he was lucky to get that. I think I was twelve and we
were trout fishing when he told me that I had nearly missed existing.
One hot summer day on a hangover he had taken an after-lunch nap
in the shade underneath the beer truck. His employer had driven by
with a friend, seen his abandoned truck with its valuable cargo, and
driven the truck off, a back tire slightly grazing my father's head.

A close call with nonexistence, a vaguely stimulating idea until
I think of the nonexistence of my brothers and sisters and my children. At the time, though, of first hearing the story while driving
home from the Pine River, it seemed part of the carelessness of adults
similar to my uncles drinking a case of beer while fishing and falling
off the dock into the lake at the cabin in a semi-stupor. My father's
younger brothers, Walter and Arthur, had had a long and tough time
in the South Pacific during World War II and their general behavior
was never up to my mother's high standards. My father's side of the

family was verbally witty and Walt and Artie's talk was full of sexual badinage, some of which puzzled me at the time. Of course their wives, Audrey and Barbara, were young and you could imagine how much passion got saved up during four years in the armed services on ships with thousands of other men all mooning for home.

For a boy forced to attend church and Sunday school every week there is the fuzzy paradox of Bible lessons not jibing with what he hears and sees. One part of him feels slightly priggish about the behavior of adults. Young people seem not to know that they are going to get old, but older people know that they are not going to become young again. And the other part of the boy is sunk in his growing knowledge of the natural world and farm life where the sexual lives of dogs, cats, chickens, pigs, and cows is an open book, not to speak of the tingly warmth he feels when there's a glance up a girl's skirt at school or when he sees by happenstance a lovely aunt's breast while she's squeezing in or out of a bathing suit at the cabin. I've always been a bit cynical about the existence of the Oedipus complex but having a number of attractive aunts can be tough and dreamy at the same time. Your sense of wrong and right is tenuous and you drift around in a goofy haze of instinctual curiosity with your hard little weenie an almost acceptable embarrassment. At the time I was amazed at my childhood friend David Kilmer, who would heroically pursue the quest. David was a doctor's son with an ample allowance and would bribe certain girls with a quarter for an inspection, or their somewhat retarded housemaid a couple of bucks for a peek. I recall he wasn't the least bit fixated, spending most of the time fishing, killing frogs and turtles, repairing an Evinrude outboard, riding his bike off a gangplank at the end of their long dock under the erroneous assumption that he would truly fly through the air. It was, however, my decision to quit looking at the photos of women in his father's medical books. A woman is included in the book only if something has gone "haywire," we agreed, and the photos weren't pretty.

There is a specific melancholy to hardship that accrues later as a collection of gestures, glances, and dire events. I don't remember anyone ever saying life is hard but it was hard to a child in other puzzling ways, say at Great-uncle Nelse's shack when we joined him in eating possum, beaver, and raccoon, and I asked my dad why Nelse ate such strange things and he said, "He came up short on beef." I do remember Nelse embracing the keg of herring we bought him for Christmas, the salt brine soaking through the slats enough so that the wood was grainy with crystals to the touch. Nelse had been unhappily in love, rejected in his twenties, and retreated to the woods forever.

It's not a matter of romanticizing farm life or distorting it for effect. It was merely the given, the donnée as the French would have it. Anyone's earliest memories tend to be sensuous so that when we lived with my grandparents in the Depression I was a child and what is left is remarkably vivid but spotty and nonlinear. When my dad finally got work he was more than happy to leave because my mother's father was a true Swede autocrat whose opinions on farming were at extreme odds with what my dad had learned in agricultural college.

Strange to say my sister Judith knew the most about my grandfather John but then she died at nineteen and took her knowledge with her. John had come from a fishing family in northern Sweden (my grandmother's people were from the Stockholm archipelago), emigrating at sixteen to the United States where he soon took the train west hoping to be a cowboy in Wyoming or South Dakota. This was 1890, the year of Wounded Knee, certainly a signal event of American history. Grandma Hulda had been raised in the Swedish colony of Davenport, Iowa. They were said to have met in Chicago. They married and with modest savings made a down payment on a small farm in northern Michigan. He went back south to buy a team of draft horses, riding with them on a freight train north to Big Rapids, then reining them home the twelve miles to the farm.

That's not much but as my mother said, "We were never hungry during the Great Depression," a pretty big item. When shortly before her death at ninety-seven Hulda said to me, "Don't ever go to Milwaukee. The streets are full of mud in Milwaukee," it was because the streets weren't paved when she was there. I do know that Hulda and John raised five daughters—Inez, Grace, Norma, Evelyn, and Marjorie—on a cash income that never reached a thousand dollars a year.

Maybe I had been ill, or maybe it was shortly after my left eye was blinded, but I can return at will to a summer dawn in an upstairs room where I was confined: in a corner were three old trunks from Sweden with stickers in that foreign language, and lined with pasted newspaper I think from Göteborg (Gothenburg). I hear the screen door of the pump shed slam and in the dim light I can see my grandfather heading to the barn with two pails of milk skimmed for the calves. The rooster won't stop crowing. There had been a little rain in the night and I can smell the damp garden, the strong winey smell of the grape arbor, the bacon grease from the kitchen below. My older brother, also named John, runs out the pump-shed door followed by my maiden great-aunt Anna carrying a pail of slop for the hogs. Both John and I loved to watch the pigs feeding at their trough. John swiped them a few pieces of ham once and proclaimed them "goddamned cannibals." Pigs eat with marvelously vivid energy. Anna turns now to the gathering chickens and John has retrieved ground-shell corn from the granary and he and Anna broadcast it out to the frantic chickens with Anna pausing to scratch her arms which are covered with psoriasis. Grandpa has finished milking and turned the cows and the two big draft horses out to pasture. He had never owned a tractor and pretends he doesn't want one. He carries the milk to the house and soon I hear the cream separator whirring. Sometimes I'm allowed to turn the crank and this whirling machine divides the cream and the skim milk fed to the calves and pigs. We eat the heavy thick cream on our cereal. In bad weather I'm allowed to fork down hay from the mow to the horses and cows. Across from the granary is an outside toilet called a privy. Later, when I'm in high school, I help my father install an indoor toilet for my grandparents. The family also collected money and bought them a television but old John put the television out in the pump shed saying it was too late to start something new.

In the front yard there is a tire swing hanging from a maple branch near a grove of lilacs. If you swing high enough you look down at the flowers as if you were a bird. Sweet mint grows in the ditch near the section road.

What have I forgotten? Waking to the animal sounds that seem to comfort one, easing the soul into consciousness. There were no alarm clocks in the house. This ancient cycle was so embedded that no reminders were needed. The body's clock sufficed and through the screen window and the skein of a mosquito or fly's whine and buzz there was a sow's untroubled grunt, the muffled squeal of a piglet, the neighbor's dog, the milk truck two miles away, a cow lowing, a horse stomping a sleepy foot, and the long-awaited rooster's crow which, though it might still be dark, dispelled the inevitable night demons.

What else have I forgotten? My young aunt bathing in a tin tub in the kitchen. Old John telling me not to drop stones on the pigs from the granary roof. Pigs don't forget. A farm boy lost his errant kicking foot to a sow. Some evenings they all read in silence, or there was the stink of the aunts doing each other's hair with Toni Home Permanents. Or reading with a pillow on the floor next to the woodstove, or next to the kitchen range fueled by wood. On the floor when they played the card game pinochle for hours, smelling the spittoon, the raw cheap whiskey, Guckenheimer's, they poured into their coffee with sugar. In the herring crock I favored the tail pieces. I collected the little wood boxes the salt cod came in. They fried with lard and put butter on everything. Salt-pork gravy. Churning sweet butter. The heaviness of the rye bread eaten with herring. The sip of my father's beer, the wet straps of his undershirt when he plowed with horses wearing an old fedora for the sun. Old John's cabled arms when he harnessed the horses. The long country funerals. The gush of blood at pig butchering. You could hear it.

A poor farmer didn't really want five daughters but that's what John and Hulda got. It was sad for the daughters who felt his disappointment. They worked like men but that likely wasn't enough in his autocratic mind. The only son died as an infant during the flu epidemic around World War I. This flu epidemic was unimaginable in that it killed millions, the majority of them children and the aged. On one of my frequent visits to Nebraska to research *Dalva* and *The Road Home* my friend Ted Kooser, a Nebraska poet, took me to a country graveyard that was beautifully overgrown with lilacs and roses and wildflowers in a grove of pines. One family lost six children within a month, all of the children they had. What was left for the parents? Not much, I'd guess. Forty years later I can still hear the voices of my father and sister, Judith, who died together in an auto accident when I was twenty-five. I'm sure the parents of the six at night while looking up at the moon and stars could hear the voices, or in the morning so many empty chairs must have driven them quite mad. Kooser told me that in the middle of this extended plague people took to burying their dead in the night. A night funeral does seem more appropriate when you are dealing with small caskets.

My father's side of the family could be even more lachrymose than the Swedes, but also more immediate. Once when I was about ten and rowing the boat while old John fished it began to sprinkle, then rain pretty steadily. After an hour or so of fairly good fishing while it rained and we became fully drenched, John finally said, "It's raining, Yimmy." I was always Yimmy rather than Jimmy.

This kind of thing was out of the question in my father's family. "It's goddamned raining," they'd say and pop another bottle of A&P two-dollar-a-case beer. If it was raining hard you might get something as extreme as, "It's raining like a double-cunted cow pissing on a flat rock." Of the five children, Lena, Winfield, David, Walter, and Arthur, only David was completely even-tempered. The father, Arthur, know as Carty, was said to have gotten in his last fistfight well into his sixties. He had been a farmer, logger, cook for other loggers, a rural mailman. Their farm pretty much went bust and the family moved near the village of Paris, Michigan, numbering a hundred or so people, to the ample house on a high riverbank. My grandma Amanda, or Mandy, was a melancholy soul of unsound health, and this seemed to color their family life so that the moods could alternate between morose Sundays and wild semi-drunken card games the night before.

Naturally, both sides of the family seemed utterly normal to me at the time but a great deal less so in retrospect. Most of us have perceived that there are specific classes in this country though there is admittedly more mobility than France and England. Fate has never ladled out hardship very evenly, and this frequently trips our often infantile sense of justice. Symmetry, balance, ultimate fairness seem to be abstractions remote to our occasionally naked sense of reality, as startling as walking out of a crisp and idealized civics class at a country school and into a lavish party of congressmen and lobbyists. If you've just spent ten hours digging ditches on a hot summer day you don't enter the tavern and begin to talk about the virtues of hard work and thrift, the beauty of Calvinism as a moral system. You want several mugs of beer.

On both sides of the family no job was too lowly when connected to survival. My mother and her two older sisters worked as servant girls in the town of Big Rapids, a dozen miles from the farm, otherwise they wouldn't have been able to attend high school. My father camped out in a tent for two years, including winter, digging on a pipeline in order to go to college. It is easy for some to romanticize plowing with horses, or the ritual of autumn hog butchering, but with the latter I don't recall meeting anyone who actually enjoyed killing a pig. It was simply a necessity to get pork on the table. I'm unsure if it built my character in my early teens to dig a well pit for five bucks but I wanted the five bucks and it only took a long day's work. Early in high school I worked as a night janitor and rather than thinking it was demeaning I recall the quiet that allowed me to think of the books I had been reading, whether Erskine Caldwell or Sherwood Anderson or the very confusing Stendhal, *The Red and the Black*. With five children in our family and my father's relatively low-paying job as a government agriculturist it was readily assumed that you had to earn your own spending money.

Of course in the evolutionary curve we tend to remember the hard lessons more clearly than the pleasant experiences, a simple fact of life that allows you to learn survival. If it was unpleasant seeing a favorite pig get its throat cut, then gutted and scalded, it was wonderful when the whole extended family got together for the sausage and sauerkraut making. It was wonderful to fish in every spare moment and later to hunt. When older you come to understand that you were very lucky that your father began taking you fishing at the age of five, and at seven after you lost your left eye it was unthinkable ever to be left behind. I've said elsewhere that I had never heard any comment from my father or uncles in regard to fishing and hunting as "manly" sports. They were simply a part of life. The value judgments about "manly" preoccupations seemed to come later when the country became predominantly urban and semi-urban and people became quite remote from the sources of their food. However, I'll readily admit that a great deal of savage stupidity and rank behavior have attached themselves to hunting and fishing whether at game farms or tournament killing, the mechanization of hunting by all-terrain vehicles, or the sheer hoggery of fishing tourists returning from Mexico with hundreds of pounds of fillets. Man has an inexhaustible ability to beshit his environment, with politicians well in the lead.

If I ever had golden years it was in Reed City from the recoverable ages of five to twelve, though my brainpan recoils at the word "golden." I suspect the repellency I feel for the banalities of our usage comes from my father who would go to strenuous lengths to avoid saying the same thing the same way, but then this was a time when verbal wit in ordinary situations was prized rather than viewed with suspicion except in television comedians. People not otherwise diverted added color to their speech in order to rise above flatness and be heard. I was amazed a few years ago while hunting on the property of a Hutterite colony in northern Montana to hear how developed and playful the speech patterns of the Hutterite children were without the dubious benefits of radio and television. If everything becomes a diversion what is left at the center? Maybe my grandfather when he put the Christmas-present television out in the cold pump shed was being prescient. I have closely noted that people who watch a great deal of TV never again seem able to adjust to the actual pace of life. The speed of the passing images apparently becomes the speed they aspire to and they seem to develop an impatience and boredom with anything else. Children become so saturated with TV and video games that Ritalin becomes the alternative, or so I've read.

Recently out a windowpane about the size of a TV screen at my studio at the Hard Luck Ranch in Arizona the leaves of the pyrocanthus tree moved in a slight wind with the birds having nearly finished the last of the wizened red berries on this, the first day of spring. In the distance beyond the bed of a dry arroyo the far bank facing the sun was quite solid with yellow Mexican poppies. Offscreen cow dogs were drinking water from a tub in the yard. Two grayish butterflies fluttered past from left to right. Five minutes later a female vermilion flycatcher landed on a phone pole. Ten minutes later a green hummingbird acted irritated with a group of sparrows. A few weeks before something dramatic actually happened. Through the bushes surrounding the screened porch I could see the rancher Bob Bergier in his white pickup dragging a dead cow from the corral up to the boneyard on the side of a rock-strewn hill. Twelve cow dogs followed, all firm disciples of cow death. The dogs pranced in delight, a truly big meal in the offing.

Of course these changes in cultural behavior and the invention of diversions are part of an economic system far beyond my ken. I think of it as a matter of swimming in an anemic, sterile, and crowded swimming pool stinking of chlorine compared to swimming in a lake back in the woods, the lake's edge rimmed with flowering lily pads upon which small turtles sit, a heron or two in tall pines or in the shallows, a few water snakes in the reed beds, and when you dive down you see fish resting motionless under upraised logs. Even the black depths look attractive compared to a swimming pool, like a rainy spring walk in the woods compared to a serial where people in New York or L.A. are shot or pummeled to the tune of witty quips.

* * *

I suppose antic verbal propensities passed from father to son are best thought of as learned rather than transmitted genetically, at least until such a far-fetched idea as the latter can be proven, though I find it impossible not to believe that there's something in Irish blood that favors their power with words. Notions of genealogy have always filled me with torpor but the idea of the genome is stupefying. We Americans are trained to think big, talk big, act big, love big, admire bigness but then the essential mystery is in the small. Even in botanical terms with trees it's not so much the stalwart roots which are but a vehicle for the thousands of tiny root hairs that draw in nutrition and moisture that ensure life. With humans, in terms of what is thought of high society, it is always sadly comic to see some layabout princeling talking about his ancestors. This is as obviously ludicrous as a young writer thinking that there could be some meaningful earned credential other than his writing, pure and simple.

What we think of our hometown is our first substantial map of the world. In a city it's the neighborhood. Reed City was containable with clear borders of fields and woods. Two blocks from our five-bedroom house (which cost $3,500) was the courthouse where my father had his office. Across from the courthouse was the Congregational Church where we were members, and from where I mainly remember the gloom of the message, the anxious boredom of sitting there to hear about things quite remote from any of my concerns.

Filling in the total map of where you live never stops. At one friend's house, Glenn "Icky" Preston, we would eat catsup sandwiches, and at another's, people who had come up all the way from Louisiana for our modest oil boom, supper was mostly a plate of beans. I was slow to learn that this was poverty. Our class took up a collection to buy the dump-picker's daughter, Gertie, shoes and socks when cold weather came. And one friend was called "Purple" because he had a heart defect that gave his skin a purplish cast. This was during the war years and immediately afterwards and the postdepression prosperity hadn't reached the hinterlands, though many men would drive south to Grand Rapids, rent a room, take a factory job, returning on weekends. And there were several middle-aged, tattered men in town who hadn't fully survived the mustard and other gas attacks during World War I. They were indigent, living in shacks, mowing lawns and shoveling snow, but this was considered a better life than being confined to a VA hospital. People also tended not to sequester their retarded and otherwise dysfunctional. My first real girlfriend, Mary Cooper, had a mentally impaired aunt named Josephine, a big lumbering woman who tagged along with us. I recall it only as a fact of life. Josephine would pick literal bushels of wildflowers and sometimes secrete small frogs down in her bra. Her toilet habits were those of a farm animal but then I was used to that.

The fact of World War II pervaded our lives. Some evenings there were air-raid alarms and when our fire chief, Percy Conrad, would start the siren all of the lights in town had to be turned off, presumably to make Reed City a less obvious target for bombers from Germany and Japan. The question of why these mortal enemies would select us as a target was never asked in my earshot. Only my brother John claimed to hear approaching bombers while the rest of us merely sat there on the front porch listening to the radio through the living room window.

The hardest part was when we drove over from Reed City to Paris to visit my father's parents and would sit there in a circle around their radio listening to the war news from Gabriel Heater who had a raw voice of doom that equaled Edward Murrow's. Since my uncles Arthur and Walter were in the Pacific I didn't pay attention to anything going on in Europe. You wonder what a child truly draws in in such circumstances other than the fear of those around him: old Carty stone-faced, but Mandy with eyes brimming with tears, Winfield and David straining to hear. (Lena lived with her husband, Bernard, way down in Detroit.) Even now names can own an unpleasant resonance from the memory of Gabriel Heater's voice, especially Guadalcanal, the Philippines. One war would have been more than enough for a child's imagination but two in different hemispheres fractionated the mind. My mother's carefully preserved *Life* magazines and our world globe helped but only modestly. Fear is deeper than knowledge and overwhelms our rationality. What if Walter and Arthur had their heads chopped off by a Japanese officer? How would we even have a funeral? What would become of their girlfriends, Audrey and Babe? People are killing each other like we do pigs, cows, and chickens. You chop a chicken's head off and it runs in circles for longer than you expect and then it flops over. Do people do this? Then the mind stopped here, the head buried against the sofa or mother. In this darkness that fails to be comforting there is the question, "What if we lose the war?" Reed City will be blown apart and we will be captives.

During the war my sister Judith was born and I remember having mixed feelings about the loss of attention from my mother. This sense of loss was vastly energized by a woeful accident where I lost the vision in my left eye in a quarrel with a neighbor girl near a cinder pile in a woodlot behind the town hospital. She had shoved a broken bottle in my face and my sight had leaked away with a lot of blood.

The consequences of her simple, violent gesture were long-range, to use a euphemism. When this area is touched upon in quiet moments the aftereffects of the accident can arrive in comic profusion: since the left eye is skewed people are puzzled about whether or not I'm looking at them, I was 4-F and unable to fight for my country in Vietnam, I'd get blindsided in football, I knock over grocery displays in abrupt left turns, also run walking partners into buildings on left turns, tennis was finally out of the question, parking and shooting are complicated and somewhat impaired though most of the cues for depth perception were learned by the time of my accident at age seven.

Trauma is trauma but much of the time for a child it can be leavened because there are fewer neurotic reasons to hold on to it. Quite suddenly the left side of my world vanished but the worst was the nearly monthlong stay in the hospital, that long because someone came down with whooping cough or scarlet fever and we were quarantined. It naturally was a children's ward and a girl with bad burns had died after three days. No one mentioned it to us but a kid with two fractured legs had overheard nurses talking in the night. I think my mother and father spent a lot of time with me but I recall the fear of having both eyes totally covered for a week or so. Even now I can bring back this haunted time by closing my good eye and looking at a big moon on a summer night with my bad, something I would try in the months after the injury. It is a concentrated but foggy light, quite beautiful in its way, and the practice immediately emphasizes the sounds one might hear, nighthawks, coyotes, a whippoorwill, in the spring the eerie call of the loon, the mating call of a woodcock, river sounds. This is an odd habit, looking at the moon with an essentially blind eye. You have the idea you can actually hear color, and between hearing and smell you construct a world that is further decorated by tasting and touching the night air. The old Ch'an monk Yuan-Wu said a thousand years ago, "Throughout the body are hands and eyes."

The compensatory joys were my uncles coming home from the war, the gradual joy perceived by my brother and me of having a baby sister, a curious creature indeed who could be filled with simultaneous ebullience and anger, a shrewd girl who in a gifted sentence could perfectly marry joy and melancholy.

Easily the biggest item of consolation was my father and his brothers building us a cabin on a remote lake fifteen miles from town where we were to spend most of our summers for the next half-dozen years. It was one thing to live in a town with a small river going through a close-by modest-sized wild area, and large wooded areas intermixed with farms bordering the town, but quite another thing to live in a cabin without electricity and plumbing, and the goodly-sized lake having only three or four cabins on it. Last year in order to check the accuracy of childhood memories I looked at a detailed county map and discovered the empty area behind the cabin was indeed fairly large, about twelve by fourteen miles with no human habitation; huge gulleys covered by bracken and the large stumps of white pines cut in the logging era, small bogs and lakes, some too shallow for fish, grand swamps, and ridges covered with birch, oak, maple, and beech. Whether alone or with my uncles in whom I sensed a communal woundedness, or with a friend, wandering in this grand emptiness allowed me to survive my blinding in reasonably good mental shape. I don't in the least mean the purely idyllic. In northern Michigan it is frequently cold in the summer, or too hot with clouds of mosquitoes, blackflies, horseflies, deerflies, wasps, and hornets. But it was wild, crisscrossed by old logging roads, and properly used to adolescent exhaustion the natural world can draw away your poisons to the point that your curiosity takes over and "you," the accumulation of wounds and concomitant despair, no longer exist. The immediate world for hours at a time becomes quite beyond self-consciousness. You are more purely the mammal beneath the clothing of the culture, the civilization. The reading will take place in the evening near the oil lamp on the roseate oilcloth covering the picnic table in the corner of the cabin. But now for the time being you are merely wandering with your five senses, which, without your usual self-absorptions, are uncannily alive. Decades later I wrote an odd poem about this state:

Walking

Walking back on a chill morning past Kilmer's Lake
into the first broad gully, down its trough
and over a ridge of poplar, scrub oak, and into
a larger gully, walking into the slow fresh warmth
of midmorning to Spider Lake where I drank
at a small spring remembered from ten years back;
walking northwest two miles where another gully
opened, seeing a stump on a knoll where my father
stood one deer season, and tiring of sleet and cold
burned a pine stump, the snow gathering fire-orange
on a dull day; walking past charred stumps blackened

by the '81 fire to a great hollow stump near a basswood
swale – I sat within it on a November morning
watching deer browse beyond my young range of shotgun
and slug, chest beating hard for killing –
into the edge of a swale waist-high with ferns,
seeing the quick movement of a blue racer,
and thick curl of the snake against a birch log,
a pale blue with nothing of the sky in it,
a fleshy blue, blue of knotted veins in an arm;
walking to Savage's Lake where I ate my bread
and cheese, drank cool lake water, and slept for a while,
dreaming of fire, snake and fish and women in white
linen walking, pinkish warm limbs beneath white linen;
then waking, walking homeward toward Well's Lake,
brain at boil now with heat, afternoon glistening
in yellow heat, dead dun-brown grass, windless,
with all distant things shimmering, grasshoppers, birds
dulled to quietness; walking a log road near a cedar swamp
looking cool with green darkness and whine of mosquitoes,
crow's caw overhead, Cooper's hawk floating singly
in mateless haze; walking dumbly, footsore, cutting
into evening through sumac and blackberry brambles,
onto the lake road, feet sliding in the gravel,
whippoorwills, night birds wakening, stumbling to lake
shore, shedding clothes on sweet moss; walking
into syrupy August moonless dark, water cold, pushing
lily pads aside, walking out into the lake with feet
springing on mucky bottom until the water flows overhead;
sinking again to walk on the bottom then buoyed up,
walking on the surface, moving through beds of reeds,
snakes and frogs moving, to the far edge of the lake
then walking upward over the basswood and alders, and field
of sharp stubble and hay bales, toward the woods,
floating over the bushy crests of hardwoods and tips
of pine, barely touching in miles of rolling heavy dark,

coming to the larger water, there walking along the troughs
of waves folding in upon themselves; walking to an island,
small, narrow, sandy, sparsely wooded, in the middle
of the island in a clump of cedars a small spring
which I enter, sliding far down into a deep cool
dark endless weight of water.

As pleasant and innocent as this life seemed at the time it created
enormous problems beginning at the age of twelve and these not
unique problems still very much confuse my life. You live in a small
town without claustrophobia because the town ends so suddenly, its
borders clearly defined. Most people in the town have known one
another for generations and there is no particular reason for anyone
there to move away, or anyone to move in for that matter. Most often you walk home from school for lunch, or walk to your father's
office in the county courthouse and ride home a few blocks with him.
Your mother is ironing, tending baby Judith, and singing along with
whoever is singing on Arthur Godfrey on the radio. On Saturday she
listens to the opera broadcast directly from New York City far to the
east. You are a bit out of hand ever since your accident a year or two
before. You're in the third grade and just learning to read. All you
really want to do is ride around with your dad and visit farmers. Once
he left in the evening to help a family when the farmer hanged himself in the barn. Another time you got to help pull a difficult calf from
a mother cow who was making an improbable amount of noise. Second grade was horrible and for some reason you were punished for
pissing on the cloakroom floor. Third grade was better with Audubon
cards to identify birds and the insufferable nonsense of words like
"when where what why who and whom" finally resolved themselves.
School had gotten better but you still didn't want to be there. You
simply wanted to be at the cabin safe from the confusions of who you
were, what you looked like, and the inevitable report cards that came
in every societal form and still do over fifty years later. You dammed
a creek with friends without knowing it would flood the neighbor-

hood. The deputy said you'd end up in reform school. You boarded a boxcar while the train was moving and an adult reported you. You rode your bike fifty miles and it got dark and you had to be retrieved. Three months at the cabin seemed to solve everything with days of fishing, swimming, and wandering. You were in love with this life as deeply as is possible and it imprinted itself in your brain and heart just as deeply, bone- and marrow-deep, permanently altering brain chemistry.

The trouble is that over fifty years later this life still lives within me and has presented unpleasant difficulties, including claustrophobia that is occasionally acute. It isn't the hokum Daniel Boone-Robert Frost, city-country, civilization-wilderness thing, which is far too simple for actual humans, though it occurs regularly in our mythology, especially the aspects of the "mythos" that arise in television and movies. And low-rent fiction. You know, the guy has a pooch, a pet bear, says "darn it" a lot and can't "abide womenfolk." I mean something closer to the Portuguese notion of *saudade*, a person or place or sense of life irretrievably lost; a shadow of your own making that follows you, and though often forgotten can at any moment give rise to heartache, an obtuse sentimentality, a sharp anger that you are not located where you wish to be, an irrational and childish melancholy that you have cheated yourself of being married to a life essence that you have never been able to quite gather to yourself.

On the simplest, most ordinary level I've seen this in the small village near my cabin in Michigan's Upper Peninsula, a location I found and moved to because it reminded me of the ambience of my childhood cabin. People who used to live in the village, were children there, come up for holidays, usually Memorial Day weekend, or the Fourth of July, from what is called "down below," the cities far to the south of the Mackinaw Bridge that connects Michigan's two sections and where they make their livelihoods. When they first arrive back home there is often jubilant drinking, then the next day fishing or hunting, and by the second evening a vague unrest often settles in. Things, of course, are not what they were in the old days and though these feelings are bearable the disappointment is always there.

GROWING UP

In the middle of my sophomore year in high school when my funda-
mentalist religion had begun to wane I began to think about getting
out of town. I yearned for the places I had read about in Richard
Halliburton but they were too unlikely and it hadn't occurred to me
that they had changed since Halliburton's travels just after the turn
of the century: Timbuktu, Kathmandu, the Pampas, the Forbidden
City, the latter doubtless possessing everything the Midwest lacked,
a thousand nude Susan Haywards demanding the head of John the
Baptist she had earned by acrobatic dancing, or Cyd Charisse kicking up her long legs in the torchlit tent of a sultan. These were places
I clearly belonged and the lovely limbs of my cheerleader friends fell
short of the top.

So I wrote letters to the West that held mountains I'd never seen.
Start with mountains, I thought, then move on to oceans, and cities
where I could act Byronic what with Byron having recently replaced
the New Testament. All the western resorts I wrote to replied that at
sixteen I was too young and had to wait until eighteen. The solution
was a non-Protestant fib about my age and I was finally accepted by
the Stanley Hotel in Estes Park, Colorado, as a future busboy. I had
been president of my class and student council and these dubious po-
sitions won the day though the age fib was probably significant.

My father thought it was a fine idea to "get out and around" and
my mother wondered why I couldn't stay home like "everybody else."
I took the Greyhound and while I was waiting to transfer in Chicago
a burly homosexual tracked me here and there. I didn't know what
he was at the time but memory told me a couple of years later. I arrived at the Stanley a full week early to the manager's momentary
dismay but he put me to work helping cooks and porters get the

kitchen ready, a lucky stroke as I got to eat their wondrous foreign food, a pleasant shock that made me feel truly away from home. The cooks all spoke French, and though they were probably from Montreal, I was quite overwhelmed by their gruff sophistication. The maître d's wife liked to tickle me and brush my hair after she finished her dessert and stinky cheese, an odor to which I quickly adapted after solving the mystery. The employee's concrete bunkhouse wasn't heated yet so I slept under many blankets, getting up at dawn to wander in the nearby mountains, the air warm but the snow not yet melted. I also helped and met some of the maintenance crew, three of whom were tough, older Jewish guys from the East. At the time I hadn't met a Jewish person except for seeing the fabulously beautiful Joanne Nedelman, an East Lansing high school girl, in a drugstore. My reading told me that Jews tended to become scientists and classical musicians but these boiler-room workers at the Stanley were muscular, used wonderfully foul language, and drank a lot, reminding me of my uncles.

It was a picaresque summer. I climbed a disused, rickety fire tower with a waitress from Ohio State who shed all her clothes save her panties. This was an age of heavy petting well before the sexual revolution. Eisenhower was the nearly invisible president, and the dining room staff, all college students, were decidedly nonpolitical. Many of the hotel's patrons were Jewish, from Chicago, St. Louis, and Kansas City, and were touchingly generous with our clumsy service. I soon had hundreds of dollars in change in my trunk, more money than I had ever seen. The patrons seemed to be truly enjoying their wealth (unlike the present) and were both kind and curious which stretched my fibbing capacity as I suddenly became a self-invented sophomore at Michigan State. Though I was the youngest of the dozen or so busboys, I became the "captain," which gave me the duty of collecting our share of the tips from the waiters and waitresses. This took a sharp tongue and some spying as they were always bent on cheating. My newly inflated sense of importance became generally troublesome as I threatened management with strikes over bad employee food, usually leftovers that gave us diarrhea. We won the right to have a cook for employees who prepared us fresh food.

I had become a general pain in the ass and was fired for throwing an egg in the kitchen which hit the cashier, and for ordering prime rib which I ate in the laundry room. I despondently packed my gear and hitchhiked to a cheap lodge where they needed a breakfast cook. I spent a sleepless night wondering how I was going to figure out how to cook and when dozens of folks entered the dining room I fled out the back door and down the mountain with my gear. I've often wondered what they all did about breakfast that morning, whether the manager said "the sensitive cook has fled."

Luckily for me the Stanley was hosting a convention of federal judges in a few days and I was able with humility and apologies to get my job back. With pride I was able to pour coffee for Supreme Court judges Earl Warren and Tom Clark. My unrest, however, returned, and as an admirer of Walter Reuther and John L. Lewis I "fomented," as they say, more labor unrest and was made uncomfortable enough to quit in mid-August. I was pretty flush, partly because on my days off and some midafternoons a bellhop friend, Ronnie, and I organized horse races with stable nags. Older patrons would watch and bet while Ronnie and I jockeyed these horses as fast as possible across a wide field. The tips got pretty large from happy bettors and I continued to money-order my earnings home.

On a whim I decided to hitchhike as I felt I was missing too much country by taking a bus that continued through the night. This decision also fueled my romantic notion of myself as a vagabond. I spent a couple of days getting through Nebraska which struck my fancy then and has continued to do so. I was awakened one dawn by a group of Hereford calves as I slept in a pasture on the banks of the Platte River. I felt at home and still do when I visit Nebraska.

When I reached Duluth, Minnesota, I made the mistake of buying a blackjack for a school friend, Roger Wilson, back home. A Duluth detective saw me put the blackjack in my boot outside the pawnshop on the street. I was taken to jail and interrogated about a robbery. I was pleased when the cops wouldn't believe I was sixteen. They finally took me down to the bus station and made me buy a ticket for home which was somewhat humiliating for a vagabond.

After all this it was more than a little banal to go back to high school as a junior. My unrest had become permanent, and the only consolation was the hormonal violence of football, the reading of fiction and poetry, doing poorly in my schoolwork. Byron was supplanted by Keats and Walt Whitman, Sherwood Anderson, Faulkner, and hopeless romantic biographies of artists like Romaine Rolland's *Jean-Christophe*.

Strangely, I've rarely been claustrophobic in New York City except on the plane getting there, and during occasional dinner parties when I've had to slip away. I think this is because early on New York City represented the figure of complete "openness" to me, and still can when I see an appealing photo of the city's skyline. This feeling started late in my junior year in high school when with a friend, Randy Scott, an escape to New York City was planned. Randy had been sharing my interest in romanticized novels such as Irving Stone's book on van Gogh who we were convinced suffered too much. We were more immediately taken with Pierre La Mure's *Moulin Rouge* about Toulouse-Lautrec who drank a lot but frequently bedded "sensual" whores. At the time we were very taken by the word "sensual" and used it whenever possible, a word far from the pallid and drudgery-ridden confines of our lives in the Midwest. Under the ruse of visiting Randy's cousins up north of Albany (we eventually did) we headed for New York City and its much dreamed-about bohemian quarter, which we pronounced "Green Witch Village." We carried along a couple of extra second gears for Randy's '49 Ford, a fragile part when you continually wound it up to sixty a second, but rather easy to install.

We drove straight through in twenty hours with a few flat tires and one new second gear on the Penn Turnpike. We checked into Hotel Marlton on Eighth Street and immediately asked an old bellhop if there was any "sex" available. He asked us, "What kind?" and we were swept away by the sophistication of the place. To guarantee our Toulouse-Lautrec motif we bought an expensive bottle of cognac, sipping the harsh liquid as we waited for love to arrive in our rather dismal room which we decided was quite artistic. She came in the form of a tall bulky redhead who thought we were a "hoot" but was kind enough to cooperate in our Lautrec charade, pouring herself a water glass of cognac before saying, "Let's get down to business." Randy went first and she was certainly a short-order cook. After my own turn was speedily finished I caught myself thinking I had spent two full days' pay working at digging footings for cement foundations at construction sites, but we were too exhilarated by accomplishing our mission for a letdown. Our virginities had been tossed away for a life of art.

The cognac, whore, and long drive put us to sleep until evening when we went out on the streets. Typically, my memory keys on food and I recall we bought Italian-sausage sandwiches with fried onions and peppers from a street vendor for thirty-five cents apiece. The sandwiches were indescribably delicious so we had a second each. Our luck continued with a chamber-music concert in Washington Square, a tearful pleasure on a summer evening in that we both loved classical music but had never heard it "live." I recall it was Telemann, Buxtehude, and Monteverdi.

This was the kind of grand trip to New York City that predicated the future. Sadly enough it seemed to also pave the way for certain mental problems, or at least accelerate them. It's hard to happily finish high school in the heart of the Midwest when in the East, in the true bohemia, people are painting paintings, writing poetry, drinking red wine, and eating meals with lots of garlic cooked by beautiful women wearing black turtlenecks and mascaraed eyes who were doubtless free with their sexual favors to deserving young men like myself.

In my junior and senior years of high school, in the years 1954–1956 and deep in the Eisenhower senescence, I had also begun reading a great deal of French novels and poetry which energized my unrest. Now there was Paris added to New York as a golden city. I had pretty much given up painting as I could use more in paints a day than I earned, an easy economic lesson, the kind I haven't learned well but one simplified by my perception that I wouldn't be another Modigliani, and the only thing I possibly shared with van Gogh was a propensity to depression. It was many years before I realized that a writer-artist can't go it alone and during my teens I had no one really to share my obsession with art and literature except my younger sister, Judith. I talked with my dad and my brother John about books but not from the viewpoint that I was ever going to end up making books. Judith and I would light a red candle upstairs and play Berlioz and Stravinsky on a small record player I had bought for twenty bucks all the while examining our small collections of Skira paperback art books. This isolation was to become a habit and possibly not a good one.

In my own nickel-plated Zen self-training I have often wondered whether when you search for your own "true character" you might come up with something less than admirable. It is easy to number physical shortcomings from my blind left eye to the time when I was in my mid-fifties and my mother said to me, "We were sorry when you were a child and we couldn't afford to have your leg fixed." This was a fine comic moment in that I had never noted anything wrong with my leg except that when I tracked myself in the woods my left foot turned inward. She died without telling me what was wrong with the leg and I remained without particular curiosity. My face got smashed playing football without a face guard but this merely resulted in the uncomfortable redrilling of sinuses. Teeth were eventually lost to various impacts. High blood pressure was caused by the garden-variety vices of drinking too much, eating too much, and smoking too much. All of these are perhaps less viable than a very wide stupid streak, a tendency for lackadaisical drifting with an edge of pouting over the long periods of my life that were sorry indeed.

These character deficiencies started early in life with a slowness to get up in the morning, a difficulty in dressing that still persists. O Christ the same bloody thing: underpants, socks, pants, shoes, trying to pull on socks over wet feet you forgot to dry after a shower. Falling back on the bed and reading something with the sock half on. The banality of belts and buttons. I was encouraged reading Graham Robb's biography that my early hero Rimbaud hated buttoning his clothes so much that in Ethiopia he designed buttonless clothing for himself. Tying shoes is still a difficult chore. Of course it's only the torpor of the ordinary that smart people adjust to. Last year in L.A. my longtime agent (over thirty years) and friend, Bob Dattila, showed me a methodical and easy way to dry after a shower but I quickly forgot the steps. It is impossible to see these problems in other but ludicrous light.

When you add to all of these deficiencies a certain dog-in-the-manger quality of sitting back, preferably in one of hundreds of thickets, and waiting impatiently for something wonderful, however undeserved, to happen, you get close to the core of this lugubrious masochism. I, along with my family, would have been quite adrift if it weren't for the essential Calvinism of background that made it unthinkable to be late for work, miss a plane, fail to finish an assignment, fail to pay a debt or be late for an appointment. I still remember painfully twenty-five years ago during a time of tunnel-vision depression that I failed to write a review of the poet David Wagoner for a magazine called *Parnassus*, also take my family to a picnic I had agreed to attend. We were driving through Sutton's Bay and I could see only the road and none of the buildings on either side of the street, but then I don't remember many other incidents other than the extreme pleasure of not doing assignments when I quit college for the fifth or sixth time.

This benighted Calvinism can also make you hard on others who don't have your devotion to the relentless clock. I asked my secretary to come at 9 A.M. and she's now three minutes late! Dinner isn't ready at six and I'm doing the cooking! If I consider myself as lazy as the ball of suet hanging from the bird feeder and have written twenty-some books, a hundred or so essays and reviews, many versions of twenty screenplays, then beware others and their excuses for doing even less. This is admittedly a bit crazy and there's a smiling, miniature, whispering gryphon back in my brain hissing, "Who gives a fuck, go fishing." The tombstone inscription "He Got His Work Done" is essentially sad and at the same time laughable.

Anyone who has lived a reasonably full life and is not an out-right fool must say, "It always could have been otherwise." This is a good cautionary note for the kind of arrogance that is a permanent resident in the artist's mind. For instance, my eye injury cost me my savings I had accumulated up through the middle of my senior year in high school. I had visited an eye surgeon who was as cold as a pump handle and he had assured me rather slickly that there was a good chance he could restore an appreciable amount of vision to my blind eye. Twenty years later I was told by a top surgeon in New York that this prognosis was absolute venal nonsense and that nothing was possible for this eye, which remained true until recently. Anyway, I spent the twelve hundred bucks I had accumulated at the rate of a dollar and a half an hour. I later appreciated the regret my parents felt over having no money to help out in that there were now five children in the small house what with Mary and David having come along.

The operation was the most miserable failure conceivable and I spent two weeks in the hospital, the first of them totally blinded to keep my eyes still. The idea was to design an early version of a contact lens but this proved thickish and painful to install and wear and more important I couldn't see a thing except a vague perception of the color green. I threw this plastic gizmo into the swamp out back of our house and quite naturally entered another depression, this one more dangerous as it had the tinge of the suicidal. I had spent the money that was going to get me to Paris via New York City where in a few weeks I would learn enough of the French language to get by at my final destination.

This is a rather Dickensian story and it has occurred to me a number of times that on a strictly biographical basis three-quarters of the world might be tempted by suicide. I'm a little nervous about the Heraclitus notion that "a man's character is his fate" which, though suitably wise, ignores the alternative of what fate does to people irrespective of their character. I have mentioned some disarm-ingly muddy aspects of my character but I scarcely wielded the bottle that gored out my eye, or designed the genes that determined my imperfect leg. In fancy Los Angeles hotel rooms there is always an uncomfortable number of mirrors that remind us why we are not movie stars. There is even the designed presumption that we are all narcissistic enough to wish to watch ourselves on the toilet as if this is as close as any of us will get to sitting on a throne. Every morning my beloved English setter, Rose, heads for the myrtle bed with its violet-colored flowers, and while she does her necessary function she gazes off to the songbirds fluttering in the young cottonwoods, the mesquite and hackberry trees.

I have no area of expertise outside of my imagination but that has to be enough because that's what I have. Once during a dark time my father and I were fishing for a mess of lowly but delicious bluegills. This was in the early summer a few months after my unsuccessful operation. We were up north to put in their first indoor toilet for my aged grandparents, and had taken a break from our work to catch fish for dinner, a favorite item for the old Swedes. My father was concerned about the time length of my melancholy state and while we fished I was asking him about the odors in the air from the flora along the shore where clouds of redwing blackbirds were noisily floating over the cattails. He had an uncanny ability to identify weeds, flowers, bushes by smell, and he suddenly said that curiosity will get you through hard times when nothing else will. Your curiosity had to be strong enough to lift you out of your self-sunken mudbath, the violent mixture of hormones, injuries, melancholy, and dreams of a future you not only couldn't touch but could scarcely see.

I hadn't specifically thought about curiosity in this manner but knew from experience what he said was true. A month or so after the operation when there seemed to be a hot nail in my eyeball I was sitting out on a log in a woodlot for several hours. It was a warm, late April afternoon heavy with the scent of dogwood buds. I was thinking about my first love who had recently abandoned me because I was unwilling to marry right after high school. Such girls wouldn't sleep with you in those days, being of a religious nature, but were certainly eager to be in a state where sex was permissible and that could only mean marriage. You would neck, paw, and grind until your dick was an abraded, skinless hot dog but the results were inconclusive.

After a long time sitting on a log, perhaps an hour, my mind emptied out into the landscape and my preoccupations with the girl and other problems leaked away. In the stillness garter snakes emerged to feed on flies that buzzed close to the ground among dead leaves and burgeoning greenery. Birds came very close because I had been so still in my sumpish reveries I had ceased to exist to the birds, and gradually to myself. I had become nature, and the brain that fueled my various torments had decided to take a rest by leaving my body and existing playfully in the landscape. The air became warmer and moister, so much so that it seemed densely palpable, swollen enough to touch. It did not so much begin to rain as the air quite suddenly became full of water. Given the circumstances the rain could not help but be a baptism. The natural world would always be there to save me from suffocating in my human problems.

When you've been involved in only the low- to mid-range arena of human suffering you become puzzled by what those at the top have developed in the sense of the compensatory in order to endure. In my own limited experience I have noted that physical pain is more endurable than mental. You retreat into your animal body when part of you hurts badly and this remnant of an ancient life seems to help you distance yourself a bit from the pain. When I was seven and the postoperative "discomfort" (a medical term) was severe I could swim, walk as far as possible in the woods, or simply lie down and curl up beneath fern level, or if it came at night, I could be swept away by the wind, or more especially the blessed sound of rain on the cabin roof only a few feet from my head because I slept in the loft.

I have clocked seven depressions in my life that might qualify as "clinical" beginning at the age of fourteen. There is the obvious conclusion that in each case I was behaving in a way I shouldn't preceding the depression, living an outward life my inward being couldn't accept, reaching a level of raw perception that my current life couldn't

accommodate. I'm certainly not saying that I understand this phenomenon in a larger sense, only in my own peculiar life. The most
consistent feeling is suffocation, lack of oxygen, an atrophication of
the strange breathing apparatus of the soul life. I quite realize that all
of this is ordinarily treated by drugs, chemicals, but then as a writer
my life depends on my perceptions and I've never felt that drugs were
an operable alternative. I tried Valium in my thirties but there was
the persistent visual image that I had become dead meat wrapped in
plastic in a supermarket. I couldn't write any language that retained
its music, raise a good memory, or truly admire anything I read.

I admit that I never had thought very deeply about the idea of family
until a recent Sunday morning, with the vague circadian remnants
of all of the early Sunday mornings of my life. Even with church no
longer in the prospect it is still somehow there, also the special Sun-
day-morning sweet rolls, well frosted, that my mother would bake and
then sometimes split and fry in butter. My father liked to make buck-
wheat pancakes and our house in Reed City had enough maple trees
to tap that we would make our own maple syrup. My father also liked
to fry up pans of salt pork and side pork but when we moved south
one hundred fifty miles from Reed City to near Haslett these items
began disappearing from our diet, as did the Saturday-night glories
of herring and beans.

But that Sunday morning I skipped work and thoughts of church
and we took our dogs south a dozen miles to the grand San Raphael
Valley that borders Mexico. Our small casita near Patagonia, Arizona, is in the mountains on a creek, surrounded by a huge dude ranch,
the Circle Z, on which we have walking privileges. There's no reason to go anyplace else except for reasons of curiosity and the rare
late fall rains, and intermittent winter rains, have germinated and
produced a bounty and variety of wildflowers we hadn't seen in our
dozen winters here.

The vast San Raphael Valley was utterly empty this Sunday
morning—we didn't see a single soul—and my English setter, Rose,

ran off to satisfy her own curiosity which is what she does when quail season is finished and I'm not carrying a shotgun. My wife strolled away with her English cocker, Mary, and I walked along looking at the ground and certain barely emerging minuscule flowers I had never seen before. I thought of my mother and her obsession with birds and wildflowers and then I looked upward and south across the pale green valley into Mexico, reflecting on the very apparent gift the Mexicans have for family life. I've been down there a fair amount and Patagonia itself is about half Chicano. Mexicans have a closeness and intensity of family life that seems to make us northerners cold fish indeed. It also occurred to me that nearly everything you hear about Mexicans in the great north is utterly untrue.

When they were available in the gully near our home in Reed City or at our cabin I always picked wildflowers for my mother when she was irritated with me which was frequently in the years immediately after my eye injury. Perhaps I had been a bit spoiled by the attention my eye injury had brought me but then this somewhat erratic behavior had continued under the truly questionable self-righteousness of the strongly willed.

We all got along fairly well and what is called "sibling rivalry" was nonexistent. The house in Haslett was smallish compared to that in Reed City but it was the size my parents could afford. I've often wondered if my parents wanted five children because that was the number in the families they grew up in. With seven people in a small house with one bathroom you have to maintain a specific etiquette. I'm foolish enough to have always had seven as a lucky number even though I know very well there are no magic numbers. Magic is in the whole life and is not detachable. If I repeat a prayer seven times on an airplane it's because I'm always a little surprised when I survive an airplane trip. At age ten I flew with my friend David Kilmer and his brother and father, a well-heeled doctor, from the airport in Big Rapids, which was twelve miles from Reed City, down to Meigs Field in Chicago because Dr. Kilmer wanted us to see a train exhibition and to visit the Field Museum. Dr. Kilmer flew a Stinson Voyager and was reputed to be a little impulsive, having wrecked a plane in

Canada the year before while moose hunting. We came into Meigs
Field, which is an island, broadside to a big wind and the plane started
wobbling severely. The Stinson didn't seem to have enough power
to pull us out of the wind gusts, and we touched down and began
turning cartwheels, which ripped off the wings of the plane. We then
skidded upside down to the water's edge of this island airport. We
were hanging upside down in our seat belts and I noticed that my
lace-up shoes had somehow come off. A fire truck came and covered
the Stinson with foam. The only injury was a slight cut to the doctor's
head and we managed to visit both the train exhibition and the Field
Museum. It was truly wonderful when we got our picture in the *Chicago Tribune*. The whole experience was exciting rather than trau-
matic to a ten-year-old.

Through the passage of time you pull well away and look at the
family almost anthropologically. The house becomes a den where
seven primates happened to live. There was no television until well
after I left home so the family played cards, games like Scrabble, or
read, both good literature and bad. My father liked the historical
novels of Hervey Allen and Walter Edmonds though I also remember
him reading Hamlin Garland, Theodore Dreiser, and Sherwood
Anderson. My mother loved Willa Cather but this did not prevent her
from stooping to Edna Ferber and Taylor Caldwell, then rising again
to John O'Hara. There's a great deal of nonsense now about how our
children can't read but then how could they in their terms of imitative
behavior if their parents don't read and there are no books in the house?
If books aren't treated as beloved objects like the sports page or the
television why would a child wish to read? You wonder how disgustingly
low-paid teachers must spend their lives trying to overcome parental
stupidity, but then in our money culture everything is considered merry
and bright if the parents show up for their often dismal jobs on time.

I suspect that nothing is idyllic except in retrospect. (The ugly
phrase "nuclear family" shows the paucity of imagination among
sociologists.) You are tardily thankful that you grew up in a close
and loving family only when it becomes apparent that so many
haven't had the same luck. All of us kissed each parent good night.

When I was sixteen and finally admitted to my father I intended to be a writer he promptly went out and bought me a twenty-buck used typewriter rather than giving the usual parental lecture on practicality and the doom and shame in the lives of artists. He wasn't particularly upset when I quit college for a while after my freshman year because he told me that he knew my heroes Sherwood Anderson and William Faulkner had backed away from college. To tease me he added Hemingway, knowing I didn't care for this author who seemed to me a kind of woodstove that didn't give off much heat. He told me about trout fishing with a relative of Hemingway's who was worried that cousin Ernest was off wasting his life in Europe. That statement made me more curious and sympathetic about Hemingway because I wanted to run off to Europe and waste my life, doubtless ending up in a garret with one of those long-necked Modigliani models as the thought of them tended to give me a hard-on even when I was out hoeing the garden or digging a new garbage pit. When I first lived in New York at nineteen I admit my eyes brimmed when I finally saw an original Modigliani in a museum.

An interest in genetics is complicated when you wonder how five children could differ so widely from one another in character: John as the eldest son was stuck with being responsible, reliable, a leader, an Eagle Scout, though possessed of a hot temper. Once in high school he was having a fight with a star athlete and I thought I might have to back him up. The other guy, Pinky by name, was using his fists but John slapped him silly with open hands. When John was a senior in high school and I was a sophomore we both started on first-team football though neither of us was very coordinated. We made up for it with what is euphemistically called "rough play" in the Midwest where one Big Ten announcer used to refer to it as "good ole smash-mouth football." It is this sodden and violent tradition that is falsely thought to build character. Later at Michigan State I saw bar fights between these football behemoths that would have sent Mike Tyson wisely running for cover. Football is war without guns.

About the time my brother became an Eagle Scout I was drummed out of the Boy Scout tribe for general mayhem. I didn't want to march or learn how to tie complicated knots or be yelled at by leaders for improperly folding the American flag. The Boy Scout crusade against gays is especially amusing. At one wretched camp three boys were sitting outside a tent waiting their turn for a blow job from a boy with a talent in that direction.

Judith was irascible, quarrelsome with our mother who insisted on braiding her hair before school, a Swedish tradition. Judy was very boyish and liked working in our huge garden with our father. When she got into her teens she was equally devoted to art, literature, and her somewhat private religion which didn't exactly put the brakes on her behavior. She wrote me a card from a camp in Wisconsin where she was a counselor announcing that she had won the contest for speed-drinking a six-pack of beer.

I had moved out before Mary and David entered their teens. Mary was by far the most graceful and gentle member of the family. She had an unobtrusive intelligence and sharpish sense of humor. David, like me, had problems learning how to skip, tie his shoes, or ride a bicycle. He learned to read in his third year and by kindergarten a test said he read on the level of a university graduate student. He was a little round boy of six or so when my parents gave him Ferguson's scholarly history of the Revolutionary War, which he hugged to his chest and said, "I've always wanted this book." By the time he was five he could beat everyone in the family at Scrabble and it was about this time that we gave him a nickel and he learned his multiplication tables from 1 to 25 in a half hour. Mary and David graduated from Kalamazoo College, and David went on to the Kennedy School of Government at Harvard for graduate school.

So much for family, the raising of young who left the nest in reasonably good mental condition except myself. Not quite a truly black sheep but close. When I think of early heroes such as Rimbaud, Richard Wright, Dostoyevsky, Walt Whitman, I am less surprised at

my behavior at the time. Books can be so utterly powerful to someone quite vulnerable in their teens, the eyes clouded with hormones,
and a wistful heart looking for an artistic Eden far from the shovel
and hoe, the locker room slugfests, the urge to find a girl other than
your sister who actually reads books. And on a mundane level there
was a small farmhouse on a hill between my grandparents' farmhouse
and the village of Barrytown where a woman lived who had published
a story in *Collier's* magazine, instilling in me so early the banal mystery that a person could write something that appeared before the
great world and, according to my parents, get paid enough to afford
a modest farmhouse on a hill.

There are some days when your consciousness isn't able to "access,"
to use a contemporary word, to any viable degree. At times the past
lives in a region where "whirl is king" as Aristophanes would have
it. And further, if you could write an entire memoir within a single
day, say every day for seven days without cheating, each day's work
might be quite different in nature. Visual memory arrives first, then
sounds, the smell, the fragility of touch and taste. And the brain is
perfectly capable of creating memories that didn't happen at all,
given certain suggestive prodding. In my early twenties as a manual
laborer on an experimental horticulture farm I used to alleviate
boredom by "mentally" listening to Stravinsky's *Petrouchka*, one of
my favorite pieces of music at the time, which went well with everything from picking apples to laying out irrigation pipe. I'm sure that
there's a scientific explanation for this though for a poet the science is doomed to be less interesting than the experience. Surprisingly, playing the music in my memory lasted about the same time
it did on record.

The burgeoning of early sexuality can be jarring in memory. Wet
bathing suits. Wet wood of dock, body and sun heat against dock. In
the warmish water Arlyce who is a head taller than me at age ten
wrestles me underwater. She says she's going to drown me with my
neck stuck between her legs. In the swirl underwater I see the crotch

of her bathing suit. I could get away but don't. We wrestle to the point of exhaustion, feet digging into sand and mud, then fall silent, swimming out into deeper water, our faces still burning.

It is a warm, grainy, nonspecific sexuality that you feel even in your elbows, your nose against the wet hair of her neck, the soles of your feet as if you were walking up warm, oily planks. The mole between her breasts is planetary, and the bathing suit pulled up into her bottom makes the brain lose any of its speech.

The next time you see her at the county fair she utterly ignores you though you are cutting a fine figure wearing a yellow shirt with a special diagonal zipper. She's walking with an older kid who already has a few hairs darkening his chin. They lean against his pen with a sow and piglets and she listens raptly to his pig talk. You sidle up until you're a few feet from her but she glances irritably over the top of your head. She has a mosquito bite on her left calf. Your heart drains away in the midway dust but then you help a red-haired girl brush down her heifer. You get a peek down the front of her blouse. There's not much there but enough. Outside the cow barn 4-H Club girls in shorts and halters are having a hose fight. Arlyce returns and aims the hose at you and you're too disturbed to even move. She noticed me!

That sort of thing. You vaguely know what it's all about but the general feelings are too strong to even think of closing the deal. At Percy Conrad's gas station an older boy, maybe thirteen, who rolled his own cigarettes and spit a lot claimed to have done it with a girl named Cheryl. A few of us sat on our bikes and listened to this braggart, Faron by name, who was spindly and no bigger than a ten-year-old was. Faron weighed less than a hundred pounds and Cheryl weighed at least twice that much so it was hard to imagine. A little boy dog tackling a big bitch we thought, the only basis of comparison because a little bull and a big cow was too far-fetched. Every girl in my class knew that when you dropped a pencil you were trying to see up her legs so the pickings were slim indeed. One kid had stolen from his uncle back from the war a nude photo of Barbara Stanwyck though you couldn't see her face clearly enough to make sure it was Barbara herself. I preferred Jeanne Crain and Diana Durbin, who were in *State Fair*, or Cyd Charisse dancing with many veils before a powerful, evil Arab sheikh. The final, tormenting sexual straw was Tarzan's Jane in her leather loincloth, diving in a jungle pond to frolic with Tarzan, played by the great swimmer Johnny Weissmuller.

It takes a long time, if ever, for this all to get less than confusing. The crudest lessons encouraged versatility. One summer our 4-H Club (Head, Heart, Health, and Hands; what this specifically means has escaped me other than it brought together farm kids separated by distances) arranged a trip on the *Milwaukee Clipper*, which made the trip across Lake Michigan from Ludington to Milwaukee and back, about six hours each way. When we left Reed City in the middle of the night in a group of cars I was lucky enough to be jammed next to Felicia, a new girl in the area, dark-complected like myself, and whose father was a new and impractical kind of farmer in that he owned a dozen quarter horses. We boarded the huge ship right after daylight and after I made my curious rounds and returned to my group—there were bunches of club members from all over northern Michigan—I discovered that Felicia was already involved in another boy who had brought her an early-morning bottle of Coca-Cola. Naturally I was miffed what with my left hand still feeling warm from holding hers. The ground beneath my feet became unstable, partly because we were on a ship in mildly rocking seas.

What did this mean? The usual lump in my throat arose, which was alleviated hours later at the sight of all the strange creatures in the Milwaukee Zoo with boys jumping up and down screaming and laughing as monkeys jerked off, plainly primates themselves, and girls indignantly slapped at them and huffed off. What's more, I was being pestered by a geeky kid who was somewhat ostracized because it was said he made love to his heifer standing on a milk stool. I had been following Felicia and her new boyfriend at a distance around the zoo, hoping for reconciliation but wallowing in romantic melancholy, and this bestial loony was disturbing my mood so I slugged him in his Adam's apple and fled. Sentimentality quickly becomes anger and I sat and stared at an orangutan who had buckteeth like my own, properly thinking that he might be a distant relative.

On the long trip back to Ludington and as early evening fell on the now placid lake some other disappointed lovers, whether male or female, played "You Can't Be True, Dear" repeatedly on the lounge jukebox and a couple of sappy lines inscribed themselves in my memory: "You can't be true, dear, there's nothing more to say, I trusted you, dear, hoping we'd find a way." The young quite literally seethe with palpable emotions until the emotions become an indulged habit and not one trace of the comic is allowed entry.

I was not one to question my own errant affections though I remember feeling apologetic toward Jean Peters when I fell for the more vivid and scary Ava Gardner who was then replaced, in a devout Christian period, by Deborah Kerr, who in *Quo Vadis* was tied to a stake to face an enraged bull (to a rural boy a bull is the ultimate in sexual danger) only to be saved by the gladiator Buddy Baer. My Christian sentiments were seriously addled by Deborah Kerr's diaphanous gown, which the breeze plastered to her forlorn, lovely body. While she prayed and Buddy struggled there was the question of what this beautiful woman looked like bare naked.

All of this was taking place in the mind of a boy who was very brown because he couldn't bear indoors compared to the outside, and had pronounced buckteeth, a foggy left eye focused outward, hair that stood up in the back in the shape of what was called a cowlick. There was also the idea that these beloved actresses were as unlikely to show up in northern Michigan as the German and Japanese bombers. So many preposterous illusions are bred by desire. The homeliest men who couldn't rationally look at themselves nude in the mirror feel free to comment critically on any woman. A man whose entire body is virtually a stretch mark will proclaim the dislike for stretch marks and a man whose ass wouldn't fit in a barrel says that big women don't "turn him on," all a logical consequence of the desire unconnected to reality that is sold in the culture. Our learning curve is wobbly indeed and our gift for wisdom quite inconsequential.

I know that our move from Reed City down to Haslett when I was twelve produced the religious upheaval late in my thirteenth year that continued until I was sixteen. When the large going-away party in the Grange Hall took place a few days before we left the north the fatality of the move finally impressed itself upon me. I was saying good-bye to all of my girlfriends, many of whom didn't know they were in this position. I was being uprooted, not to speak of the rest of the family. I knew it was a promotion for my father and the primary aim was to get us near a university but this didn't help. If you have five kids and make a small wage it is necessary to move near a college.

I was going to a place where there weren't any rivers, no trout, no cabin (which was being sold to my uncles), no loons or blue herons, no bobcats, no endless forests to wander in. There were doubtless lots of people who would regard my eye as the mark of Cain, and who wouldn't know I was a noble adopted Indian boy from Canada, at the time the large garden-variety figment of my imagination. I couldn't very well run through the forests when there were no forests, and my ambition to catch a five-pound brown trout had to be put aside forever. No solitary dawn swims to a reed bed in the middle of the lake, shallow enough to sit down, where if you were perfectly still a mother loon and her young might come gliding past.

It took only a decade or so to realize that all of this caterwauling was misplaced and the faux alternatives that tug each other in the past are quite without meaning. How can you become an Indian tracker when you're not even an Indian and there's anyway no demand for your services is a pertinent question the boy never asks. When at age seven my father had given me his *Two Little Savages* by Ernest Thompson Seton he would have had no idea the unrest that this would cause. The book was an instruction manual on how to live wildly in a coming age when the possibilities of such a life were faint. There was also the mild schizophrenia of deeply enjoying listening to the opera on the radio with my mother, and the fantasy of walking into my fifth-grade classroom singing like Richard Tucker, or the popular Mario Lanza.

Given my curiosity and wandering nature I would have been a poor bet at operating a Standard or Mobil gas station which seemed also like a good idea at the time. The move to Haslett put us in a six-mile range of a good bookstore in East Lansing, a fine library, also the university library which I could visit because my dad's work in soil conservation and the restoration of depleted watersheds meant an adjunct position at the university. Added to this was a theater that showed foreign films, and the university auditorium where I heard my first symphony orchestra, an experience that was a true skull popper.

Only much later in life did I come to understand that there was a bridge between my early life in the natural world and the arena of literature, music, and painting. It was the moral and aesthetic equivalent of the "suburbs" in between that goaded my intolerance.

When I got "saved" at a Baptist revival at fourteen it was an emotional rebellion against the tepidity of my life as a good student and a class literati. I needed ecstasy as it were and the sexual possibilities didn't exist in the middle-class deck being played. Religious conversion gave me actual emotions that were the equivalent of Beethoven's Ninth Symphony, which I already loved. The fact that no one else in the Baptist Church appeared to see this correlation is what finally drove me from the church. The glory of a God and Jesus that exclude Mozart seems grim indeed.

It was a good run for one addicted to emotional excesses. I had a number of visions though this experience became uncomfortable: the hem of Isaiah's robe stretching miles across a seascape, all the different creatures in the world drinking milk from an immense golden bowl, the perilous caves, and passageways inhabited by evil spirits that changed shapes, the dark path that ostensibly led directly to God though I definitely didn't get that far.

There's an urge to make light of frightening experiences if only to assure yourself that you're standing on the earth. Even mildly visionary experiences can give you an immediate lust for the ordinary, whether it's eating, walking, going to the tavern for a drink and immersing yourself in conversations with farmers, mechanics, construction workers, some of whom you've known for thirty years. Talking to your dogs can be especially helpful.

Every year or so in the late evening, usually right after I go to bed, my mind will enter a whirling fugal state where all the stops are pulled with the mind rushing all over the earth and well into space, to the depths of the ocean where the process slows and you can walk along the ocean's bottom. You're literally out of control though not at all violently, passing through the homes of friends, huts and kraals in Africa, the bottom of the Amazon's many rivers, inside the mouth of a lion, the short nap (a split second) in the heart of a whale. One of the most interesting came in the early seventies visiting galaxies that had the beautiful appearance of the later Hubble space photos, pale blue and roseate clouds of stars.

I'm no longer inclined to get upset with these experiences though occasionally there is a temporary loss of balance when you have the vivid illusion that you're actually seeing time herself in a clearing in the forest or, more often, on a riverbank while staring at the passing water. Another more frequent experience, say two or three times a summer, is the strong illusion of seeing holographically. You walk through a landscape and you see all sides of it at once. This is particularly hard to describe in that you're both within and outside the sensations of your body at the same time, a plainly impossible thing though the mind can arrange it. You also wonder at the mind's impulse to present you all sides of a tree at once or to move within the body of a bird. As I say, these experiences need not scare you and your sense of the comic enters to keep you on earth.

The only truly frightening occurrence came when I was already "in extremis." I was about fifty and still hadn't learned to behave well, to put it in mild terms. I had done fairly well financially, though it was episodic, and Hollywood like boxing seemed to promote the kind of behavior that quickly used up the purses won. My wife had quite seriously, if irrationally, become sure that if we died our daughters would become destitute. I felt very guilty and vulnerable at the time and quite suddenly quit drugs and drank far less, and began working myself so hard that I daily felt complete exhaustion, which, as many writers and others know, does not stop the work. For instance, when I finished writing *Dalva* and a couple of screenplays in the same period I went to the doctor and discovered that both of my eardrums were broken from an ignored infection. I had reached the end of my already frayed tether and went north to the cabin to convalesce, which I wanted to be an overnight procedure.

It was muggy and warm in the north and through the screened windows a loud whine of mosquitoes mixed with rumbling thunder far to the west. I was simply too distraught to open the whiskey bottle on the counter and had eaten less than a quarter of my dinner. I took a long walk in the twilight and was temporarily lost in the horseshoe bend of the river. I had been so cranky that even Sand, my yellow Labrador, was upset though a walk usually made her forgive everything. I went to bed naked covered with sweat unsure that the bed itself was stable. In the middle of the night I awoke and thought I saw car lights. My anger over someone coming to visit was so immediate I thought my skin was on fire. I seemed to burst through the air howling, striking my forehead against a metal chandelier adorned with deer horns, and cutting my head. I raced to the heavy wood door and tore it open without unlocking it, pretty much destroying the door. I ran outside howling but there was no one there. The flash of light was an approaching thunderstorm. I lay down in the damp cool grass feeling my normally hairless chest which seemed to be covered with hair, and my face abnormally large and hairy. I watched lightning directly over my head which helped me to return to "normal." I started the generator, leaving it on for the rest of the night for reasons of mental safety. I found my dog up under the bed in the loft but she wanted nothing to do with me. I checked the bathroom mirror and rinsed the blood off my face. I got out a hammer and tried to fix the door but without any luck. I wanted to read the Bible but there was none in the bookcase so I settled on a bird book. I poured a glass of whiskey and fried some eggs.

The next morning I very slowly coaxed my dog back to friendship with chunks of Wisconsin sharp cheddar cheese. I reflected that when my bird dogs have heard coyotes up at the cabin they barked out the window, but on the two occasions that they have heard wolves they have crawled quietly up the stairs to the loft and hid under the bed. In the aftermath, I as a writer of course had to research the matter and my conclusion was that I had had a simple attack of lycanthropy, fairly innocent in that I had hurt nothing except my head and my dog's feelings. I tried a little howl a day later and she wasn't amused. Years later I still occasionally look at my bed and then the chandelier, mentally measuring the distance, and wondering how a burly fellow could make the jump which would be demanding for a good athlete.

Curiously enough I have never had any interest in occult matters and have often thought it sad that someone with deep interest in such things could have appreciated the experience. In a fairly long lifetime I can recall having only two accurate intuitions, both of them a little comic. On my way back home from the West I had gotten up before dawn to minimize Chicago traffic problems, and passed in the early-morning light a munitions plant between Joliet and Chicago. I stepped on the gas when I had an odd feeling that there was going to be an explosion. I quickly found out on the radio that it was true and I had been lucky enough to get through before they closed the expressway. I don't think there were any serious injuries.

My second successful intuition was very specific. I was in New York City for the usual screenplay meeting and after work one day called my wife at home which was a daily habit. She was upset because there had been a blizzard back in northern Michigan and three of my neighbor's English-setter bird dogs were lost. They weren't accustomed to spending the night outdoors in subzero weather and my friend Nick, the owner, was worried because the dogs had never run off for more than an hour or so and now they had been gone all day. That night in New York City I had an especially vivid dream of the path the three dogs took, including crossing the grave of a friend of ours and Nick's, and then heading through a marsh and over a frozen creek down to a thick woods bordering Lake Michigan. The next morning when I left La Guardia I dismissed the dream as nonsense, the mind merely wishing it knew where the dogs had gone. I knew from an early-morning call that they hadn't reappeared which made my trip home dismal as I had hunted with these glorious creatures. Sometimes we would release my two setters plus four of Nick's into the field together and it was wonderful indeed to watch them work coverts each in its own way. Anyway, I got home in midafternoon, rechecked, and dressed warmly, then headed out to the cemetery about eight miles south of our farm. I was a little amazed to see three sets of tracks crossing the grave of our friend, Larry Price. I then drove directly for the dogs' destination in my dream, about two miles farther away on the lake road. There was nothing there and I beeped at which point the dogs popped up from behind a big snowbank where they had evidently buried themselves for warmth. They were pleased to see me but got in the car without comment.

These kinds of experiences are what scientists call "anecdotal," hence unreliable, perhaps specious, but then I have a leg up because I don't care if they are. I'm more inclined to believe the wonderful Acoma Pueblo poet Simon Ortiz, who said, "There are no truths, only stories." Far more interesting to me are perceptions that considerably enlarge my notions of natural and human behavior, thus I spend a great deal of time clumsily reading books related to brain structure, botany, anthropology. I am so poorly trained in the sciences that my comprehension of these books is minimal. I like to know that bacteria survive in deep undersea molten fissures that reach twelve hundred degrees but I can't really tell you why such information thrills me except that it enlarges my perception of reality. This could be true also of experiences termed "occult" but then this easily becomes an ornate succubus devouring otherwise sensible lives. Two accurate intuitions makes for one every thirty years, a truly unimpressive average.

I think that it was Wittgenstein who said that the real mystery is that the earth exists. This is easy to dismiss on a conscious level as being unreachable, but the puzzlement evidently reaches deep into our unconsciousness. One winter I was having a particularly severe slump due to exhaustion over a number of items in my life and at my lowest point I had a dream of God standing in space before time "was." He was hurling countless trillions of nearly invisible specks of material into the void. When I awoke instantly—this was the kind of dream that wakes you—I was fearful because I remembered from childhood the biblical admonition that if you see God you die. I got myself off the hook by thinking that the God in the dream was sort of a comic-book version: vastly globey, but with definite humanoid features.

A few days later I was sitting in the backyard of our casita, which borders a creek in the mountains down near the Mexican border, our winter residence the past twelve years after a half century of snow. There were uncommon rains in the area in late October and early November that continued on sporadically through the winter and spring where the year before we had gone through one hundred and fifty days without water. Now I walked through a normally barren mesquite thicket and found an evening primrose big as a bushel basket with thirty-three purple-and-cream-colored flowers. Even my bird dog took a curious sniff.

Anyway, I was sitting in the backyard thinking of the nature of this wild efflorescence in front of me, listening to the burble of the creek over rock and sand, counting the nineteen bird species around the feeder, and vainly trying to remember the details of an article on the human genome in the *New York Times* science pages. But sitting there I escaped my body and saw the genetic nature of all the plants, trees, shrubs, the birds, the two dogs, and the cat, the moving water itself, even the earth beneath my feet, which E. O. Wilson said has a billion bacteria in each spoonful. It was clearly impossible but this cellular life of the natural world was making itself visible so that the landscape shimmered and seethed with its infinitesimal life. I was plainly in a trance in which my rational consciousness had no gov-

ernance, though near the top of my skull there was a cold point of
animal fear that I was being sucked into a world I didn't want to visit.
Afterwards, while eating a sensible Hebrew National hot dog (with
sauerkraut and hot mustard), I poked fun at my poetic vision of what
any natural scientist finds available every day. But then I'm only a
writer and this engaging view of the minuscule building blocks of
existence lifted my sodden spirits. After all, we have carbon and iron
in our bodies because we are made in part out of the dust of stars.

Every few years I come across a particular quote from a Rilke
letter, the last time in Richard Flanagan's startling *Death of a River
Guide*: "That is at bottom the only courage that is demanded of us:
to have courage for the most strange, the most singular and the most
inexplicable that we may encounter. That mankind has in this sense
been cowardly has done life endless harm; the experiences that are
called 'visions,' the whole so-called 'spirit world,' death, all those
things that are so closely akin to us, have by daily parrying been so
crowded out by life that the senses with which we could have grasped
them are atrophied. To say nothing of God."

It is apparent to me now that the nature of the Rilke quote is
what fueled my curiosity and investigation of so many third-world
cultures from Africa to Brazil, Ecuador, Costa Rica, Mexico, and a
lifelong obsession with our own Native American cultures. It is simply
the fear of missing out. To really learn much about another culture is
a very long and slow process and you're not liable to receive anything
in a spiritual sense unless it's already in yourself waiting to be discovered. In the past two decades there's been a great deal of spiritual
shopping which, though understandable, carries with it and is disastrously married to our culture's collapsed sense of time, where speed
is, finally, of the essence. There is a fatal impatience to quickly count
spiritual "coup" and get on with it. This includes a great deal of the
eco- and ethno-travel "opportunities," and the comic aspects of faux
shamans selling three-hour "power visions" for a few hundred bucks.
That's just us, whether it's the Zen of tennis, or fishing, or shooting,
the Zen to make you a better businessman or help you write "sponta-

neously," or the "Apache" and "Redskin" football teams that abound, the warriors, the mightily white Mohawks, the secrets of Black Elk learned in an afternoon seminar after which Indian fry bread is served and then a buffalo ghost is ridden back to the suburbs. Of course there is no kind of absurdity we'll refuse to perform if the economics are tangible. If anyone is truly sick of "the fucking white culture," as I frequently hear, they better get ready for a long haul. An hour staring at a fifty-ton Olmec head will offer you a preposterous emptiness that all the sugar in the world can't sweeten.

Back to school. We failed each other. My love of books didn't include chemistry, biology, geometry, and algebra, and barely history, certainly not civics. The chemistry and biology classroom naturally stank and that was enough. I gazed at the chart of the elements in firm disbelief that they could be the components for the contents of the world. How could I study chemistry when I was enthralled by John Keats, and earlier, how could I get interested in our governmental structure when the book open on my desk was by Richard Halliburton, a record of his travels in India and Africa. At the time the school was called Haslett Rural Agricultural though the area was quickly becoming a suburb of Lansing and East Lansing. Many of the students were country people, some of the boys of loutish nature so that when Mr. Birdsall would say, "We have a reasonable idea of what the moon is made of," our all-star quarterback Ken Schaibly bellowed, "Bullshit." This is hard on a teacher.

But I had a couple of wonderful teachers. One, Berenice Smith, somewhat thwarted in her own life, would pass on to me her subscriptions to *The Nation, Harper's, Atlantic Monthly,* and so on, plus her enthusiasms for Willa Cather and Trollope, the English Romantics. Another, James McClure, a POW in Germany for years during World War II, gave me Thorstein Veblen, Vance Packard, Beard's histories, Crèvecoeur. McClure was obsessed with Thomas Jefferson and told us his own tales of eating bowls of fish heads in prison camps. An-

other of his idols who became mine was the great labor leader Walter
Reuther, also Eugene Debs and John L. Lewis.

In a somewhat predictable nature my religious obsessions con-
verted their energies toward literature. There was no middle ground
and the public ecstasy of fundamentalism and being a young preacher
transferred themselves into the private obsession with literature. This
borders on psychobabble, an addiction of our culture, but is probably
true. It is easier to see at a distance in Ireland where becoming lapsed
Catholics fueled the early careers of so many writers.

What is the nature of beloved objects that are wrapped so tightly with
our emotions they can't be separated in our brains until death? I see
a gray and black teddy bear, frayed and singed (having been tested
by me in the oven); a new oilcloth from Montgomery Ward, its roseate pattern becoming the first grand painting for the child, the wonderful smooth surface and oily, sweet odor; the packet of Audubon
cards given out to third-graders with each card a glorious bird that
you yourself might find locally, a scarlet tanager in a blooming peach
tree that still doesn't seem quite possible; the leather-bound King
James Bible (with complete concordance) earned with a 4-H project
where you grew a large plot of staked tomatoes and sold them for
seventy-five cents a bushel, the Old Testament poured into the mind
over and over until forty years later verses still pop unbidden into the
mouth. Doubtless people have felt religious ecstasy since the Pleistocene though now it is largely ridiculed, mostly because of the char-
latan behavior of the leaders. I certainly don't view fundamentalists
as more threatening than the somewhat fascist monoethic of our
surging, prosperous young middle class who were educated with the
usual politically correct fodder to the point that they seem to keep
totally to their own kind. Blacks, Latinos, and Native Americans are
well out of their purview. They live in a consensus world of day care,
Little League, stock portfolios, healing, closure, ergonomics, with
pablum concerns about air pollution and smoking (in their immediate areas). It is a version of life much closer to Huxley's prophecies

than those of George Orwell. Imagine a serious discussion of whether thirty-five hours a week is too much television for the little nitwits they are breeding.

Oh well. I've spent a lifetime with the accusatory question "What if everyone were like you?" I'd respond, "Poets are mostly the pulse of the wound that probes to the opposite side," as Lorca would have it. He was, of course, executed by the Falangistas, of which we have many in sheep's clothing in our own culture. But then there's the not so amusing idea that our writing adheres so closely to our culture's money ethic that only a small minority takes it seriously, and none regard it as dangerous. The PEN and Amnesty International statistics on murders of writers and journalists in other countries are startling. I suppose the idea that we thrive here is a testimony to both our democracy and our indifference.

Curiously and perhaps due to my religious youth, I have never felt that being an artist was in itself any excuse for wretched behavior. Toward another pole it is also quite obvious that we as Victorian Romans in a Silver Age frenzy are producing whatever is profitable in enormous quantity. Publishers as well as literary presses are as market-directed as our corporations. The real reason we have a profligate number of MFA programs is that, as with cocaine, Pampers, and Budweiser, the demand's there. When it was only the highly competitive programs at Stanford and Iowa it seemed sensible enough, a boon to some and harmless to others, but now the proliferation seems to be drowning the literary novel by force of numbers and peculiarly arch uniformity. In recent years I've received several hundred galleys and manuscripts a year and most would have benefited if the writer's experience were of a less concentrated academic variety. Seventeen years in a row in institutions presents a narrow spectrum. Gone are those cornball days when book jackets proclaimed the writer had worked as a truck driver, a proctologist, a stripper, a dishwasher, a furrier, a cowboy, an unlicensed plumber, a Peace Corps worker in five different countries. But then in the middle of the night it occurred to me that I didn't really know why it gets light when you turn on the light, and when you turn it off it gets dark again. What do I know?

What is going on in the air with light and dark is accessible information though I'll probably never give it enough time to truly understand it. What we don't understand is inevitably more interesting. Maybe all the MFA programs are training a super-race of readers who will understand all of the processes of the printed word. And this, after all, is the age of the triumph of the process, say a computer, over what actually might be stored within it, the contents.

I'm drawn again to Wittgenstein and the mystery being, simply enough, that the world exists, but within this world you have a five-year-old piss-pants heading on foot to kindergarten on a winter morning, a path to school that will be repeated in different forms for the next seventeen years. The memories of wet wool and cold feet are more pungent than anything learned, the cherry smell of flour glue, the way that the tops of the teacher's stockings cut into her plump thighs, a student vomiting breakfast on a radiator. Drifting back from his brother and friends he turns off before the school yard, cuts down the alleys behind houses until he reaches the lumberyard where he climbs to the top of the coal pile and watches the morning train pass by. Circling down by a creek he reaches the factory where they make railroad ties, then treat them with creosote, the heavy scent thick in the cold air. He's a little sad because his dog Penny has been punished for biting the creamy tops off milk bottles delivered to porches by the horse-drawn wagon. On zero-degree mornings the milk begins to freeze pushing several inches of yellow cream through the top and the dog bites off these frozen cylindrical chunks, eating them with pleasure.

It was very hard to go to school and easy to be dissuaded by impulse. Many years later in college your Italian-language professor walks by just as you are entering the movie theater and cutting his class. You accidentally punch a teacher who has shaken you awake, get kicked out for a term, hitchhike to New York City, which has become your threadbare nirvana. Seventeen years passing in a state of torpor except for classes that dealt with the beauty and meaning of language, the path to school always difficult, missing the morning classes to talk to a lovely diner waitress named Willie who was from Paducah, Kentucky, and her left leg was a few inches shorter than her right but she walked with a sexy wobble, her voice raspy with tales of marital woe. She'd play Faron Young and Hank Williams on the jukebox, we'd drink coffee and smoke cigarettes looking out the window at the mounds of dirty snow in the parking lot. I kissed her only once, back near the walk-in cooler when she was retrieving a box of hamburger patties. Willie prepared me better for my beloved course in the French Symbolist poets than anything else could. I loaned her a couple of Henry Miller books but she thought he had a "dirty mouth," then accused me with "certain men favor a woman with a bum leg." She blew smoke in my face and hobbled off to feed the jukebox. She was perfectly beautiful except for that bad leg which I could no doubt heal by rubbing it with my blind left eye.

I suspect that at its best your education's main motive is to fuel your curiosity and teach you how to find out things for yourself. This is adequately simpleminded to cover the situation. Nothing much is remembered without the emotion of curiosity. Even your dogs and cats are full of it. You are unlikely to feel emotion for material unless your teacher has it. The educationists seem to think in terms of methodical steps but a teacher brimming with passion for the subject is what actually works.

After the age of sixteen it seems I had no defense against the world and my own preposterous oafishness than language, my own written word and what I read, which I used as armor. At eighteen my heroes were Dostoyevsky, Faulkner, Dylan Thomas, Rimbaud, Henry Miller, and James Joyce. I read *Finnegans Wake* over and over as a college freshman trusting that its music was a substitute for wisdom. I was a peacock, an aesthete, an asshole, to be frank, and with my few friends I discovered that talking and drinking could construct in themselves an acceptable reality no matter that this reality had disappeared by the next morning and the process had to be repeated.

Meanwhile my studies suffered, as it were. I remember the day when I had the highest score in three sections, one hundred twenty students, in a humanities examination, only to score the lowest in the same number of students in an exam in natural science. The science professor thought I had chosen wrong answers on purpose as it seemed "statistically improbable" I could go that far astray. If there were a hundred samples of fifteen different types of rocks in a jumble how could I identify only three correctly?

I also couldn't tie a necktie. In the four times I quit college as an undergraduate my father would pre-tie me a dollar tie or two in case my trip to New York City offered up more than a menial job. There were two stays in New York, one in Boston, and one in San Francisco, all reached by hitchhiking with a cardboard box bound with rope inside of which were my typewriter, volumes of Faulkner, Dostoyevsky, Rimbaud, a few clothes, my mother's cookies, a tin of Argentine beef. I usually had at least fifty dollars split between my wallet and my sock to prevent theft, which caused a slight limp in order not to grind my grubstake into powder.

In New York I worked in Marboro Books, a discount house on Forty-second Street and at Brentano's up on Fifth Avenue near Rockefeller Center. I had a windowless room on Grove Street, and once for a few months a room and a half with a stove on MacDougal near Houston. My landlord and an Italian woman across the street taught me how to make marinara sauce with garlic and herbs. The woman across the street, perhaps in her mid-forties, would undress in front of the window and I'd return the favor, though when we met on the street we never mentioned our secret vice. I knew almost no one except other bookstore clerks, and a Jewish girl whom I met at a Washington Square concert. We loved each other but her mother wept lavishly when she met my shabby beatnik self. This girl was only eighteen but way ahead of me intellectually, headed for Barnard from Music and Arts High School. She read Apollinaire and Valéry to me in French, a boggling act to a midwesterner. We shared the refuge of the Museum of Modern Art and when the crowds were sparse we could neck right in front of Monet's *Water Lilies*, or Picasso's *Guernica*, our hormones overcoming the suffering in the latter painting, a wayward eye catching the howling bull.

Curiously at the time I was an ineffective left-winger, active in civil rights demonstrations, including picketing Woolworth's in East Lansing. I was speechlessly impressed when I heard Martin Luther King Jr. in person though much of my thrill seemed to dwell on his mastery of the rhythms of language. At the time my close friends would listen only to jazz and rhythm and blues, the latter available from a black radio station in Inkster which was part of Detroit. The Inkster station also played the marvelous sermons, half sung, of Reverend C. L. Franklin, who was the father of the great Aretha Franklin. And around this period when I was in New York I attended meetings of the Young Progressive Socialists (free donuts, radical ladies) where I attempted passionately to sign up to fight with Fidel and Che in Oriente Province. I was rejected as an obviously daft *poet*, which I gave as my occupation even though I assured them I was handy with a rifle and stalking from years of deer hunting. My feelings were hurt for several days though I definitely wasn't interested in dying for a cause, however noble, except for my calling of poetry. Perhaps the singular reason young poets are attracted to writing programs is out of loneliness, the need to be in the company of their own strange kind.

Unlike my mother, my father looked on my wanderings, with tolerance and a little envy. He was a bit to the left with a populist background himself, referring to the wealth of the Fords and Rockefellers as "unpaid wages." He, however, was quite aware that there was a fine line between looking for a source of meaning for one's life and becoming an utter fool, and hoped that I wouldn't "disappear up my own asshole," in his country idiom. He had made the leap from rural life to a profession, from bib overalls and hard labor to a suit and office, no matter that his profession was agriculture. There was a similarity here in my father and my best literature professors who had survived the Great Depression and were grateful and enthused to be teaching, the central passion of their lives. My college professor Herbert Weisinger had told me that his friend the anthropologist Loren Eiseley had been *on the bum* a number of years and I've thought that this fact extended the grand range of Eiseley's writing. Years later at a literary dinner I spoke with W. H. Auden about this matter and he was untypically effusive, being a fan of Eiseley's. He said that "scraping by" had always been good for his work.

I was lucky that John Wilson, the director of such matters at Michigan State, always gave me back my tuition scholarships when I returned from my trips. Wilson was curious to hear of my adventures and as a former Rhodes scholar he liked the idea that I intended to "make" literature. This was in the late fifties when literary hubris was in short supply in the Midwest. Wilson once mentioned that I was less gaunt after my Boston stay than in New York, but then in Boston I was a busboy at a Prince Spaghetti House and meals came with the job. The cooks were a little puzzled when I brought to work a book by the contemporary Italian poet Ungaretti. I was embarrassed by my presumption when it dawned on me that though the cooks spoke Italian to one another they were largely illiterate, though very kind to me, cooking me simple Neapolitan specialties and occasionally sending me home to my miserable cold room on St. Botolph's Street with meatball sandwiches. I had moved to Boston because I had read that it was the "St. Petersburg of the United States," and since I was an addict of Dostoyevsky that made Boston irresistible. This was well before urban renewal and St. Botolph's was suitably murky, squalid, and cold during the winter. In my rooming house there was a hare-lipped merchant sailor who kept telling me that "drinking doesn't pay dividends," an Irish bachelor named Frank whose room was walled with books and who would walk every day to his mother's house in Dorchester for a free lunch. Many years later I figured out with the novelist Tom McGuane that Frank was likely one of McGuane's cousins. Another roomer was a young writer aspirant named Pete Snyder with whom I later hitchhiked to New York (back to short rations). We were fortunate enough to spend two evenings at the Five Spot with Jack Kerouac whose *On the Road* had recently been published. Kerouac was celebrating in a way that would eventually kill him in his forties, but then drinking has always been the writer's black-lung disease as Tom McGuane said.

Later when I talked to Gary Snyder, John Clellon Holmes, and Allen Ginsberg, separately, about these years there was a sense of puzzlement about Kerouac's slow form of suicide by alcohol. For unclear reasons some of us draw up short and others can't. Having had a number of periods when I didn't care if I lived still doesn't explain it to me.

There is the Rilkean quandary of the exposed heart being richest in feeling and the point at which the exposed heart cannot recover. The idea that it is self-inflicted is neither here nor there. The half-dozen suicides I've known seemed to have nothing compensatory to balance the life of the mind. I mean writer suicides. With my good friend Richard Brautigan there was the chicken-and-the-egg question of whether he was a writer who became a suicide, or a suicide who became a writer. We actually discussed the matter while trout fishing in Montana and he said he would never commit suicide as long as he could still write and his lovely daughter Ianthe depended on him. The news was terrifying but somewhat expected.

Oddly, the grace note of my own early life was manual labor. Michigan State started as an agricultural college and the campus is still splendidly landscaped. Whenever I returned from my wanderings I could get my job back at the college horticultural farm where I did everything from prune grape plants, hoe, and dig trenches to set up large irrigation fields with forty-foot sections of pipe. One day I lost two fingernails in the pipe clamps which even then I knew was easier on the system than mental suffering. Of course the knack or skill at physical labor is an accident of birth as is the submersion in the natural world that comes so easily from early exposure. When broke and hungry in San Francisco I could always take the labor bus, sometimes an open flat rack truck out of Market Street, for a day or two of bean picking which would then afford me five days of reading, writing, and walking. Of course when you're nineteen or twenty what you eat and where you sleep are small items indeed compared to the pleasure of walking from North Beach all the way out and through Golden Gate Park to see the Pacific Ocean, which was my announced intention to my father when I left home. We were talking a lot that March while hand-digging a sloping hole twelve by fourteen feet for a basement extension below the new bedroom, a lot of digging but a fine way to decompress from the office and college. The fact was I needed to see the Pacific Ocean very badly and had impulsively thrown the textbooks I was carrying off a campus bridge into the Red Cedar River. My brother John, freshly home from the navy and back in college, reminded me that three of the five textbooks were his.

To a young rural flatlander cities like New York, Boston, and San Francisco are impenetrably immense, incomprehensible. You don't understand why they are there any more than why you're there except they are exciting, especially contrasted to manual labor and the torpor of college. And in these cities invisible novelists and poets were writing books so it was logical to go there and invisibly write a book. I had a journal I had filled with gists, piths, quotes, apothegms, quotes of brutally inclusive wisdom. (Whitman said poets must "move wild laughter in the throat of death." How?) There's nothing quite like reading great literature on a daily basis to freeze the writing hand. You had convinced yourself, your parents, and a few friends that you were a poet and now all that remained to do was write some poems. You had pumped up your ego, your hubris, to an unconscionable degree simply to mentally survive but the evidence of any real talent was lacking. Every single day and into the evening you drew in what Ginsberg called "incredible music of the streets." I even got Babe, the bartender at the Kettle of Fish, to read me Ungaretti and Gaspara Stampa aloud in Italian though he appeared to be somewhat embarrassed. Louis, a waiter from Positano, was very touched and I got a free serving of chicken cacciatore before closing. The discovery of garlic seemed an important aspect of my development as an artist, equal to that of figuring out that red wine was better for the imagination than beer. One afternoon Babe introduced me to the renowned politician Carmine DeSapio who asked me what I did and I said that I was a poet. He said, "Why not?" One night I was attacked by a burly guy in the toilet and managed to demolish him. I was utterly shocked when Babe told me that the guy liked to be beaten up. This was a subtlety of behavior I hadn't encountered in the Midwest.

New York and living in the Village made me think I was part of something larger even though I definitely wasn't. I wrote my mother letters when I spotted Marian Anderson and Richard Tucker in person as she was a fan of the voices of both. I followed Aldous Huxley for several blocks at a polite distance. He was guided by a lovely young woman because of his bad eyesight. I had read all of his novels and craved to trade elegant aperçus with his characters. I think my wages at both Marboro Books and Brentano's came to about forty bucks a week which made for short rations after paying for my room, subway fare, beer or wine. Sometimes hunger would get sharp and I'd spend my last money on the usual Italian sausage on a roll with onions and peppers, which meant I'd have to get up an hour earlier to walk fifty blocks or so lacking subway fare. In one three-month period I had only one full meal and that was when a bookstore clerk friend, Bruce Kellner, who later became a scholar of American literature, cooked me the first curry of my life, a delicious chicken curry with a whole chicken. Bruce wasn't a dim-witted Midwesterner and cued me toward inexpensive musical events and I saw both André Eglevsky and Erik Bruhn dance at Lewisohn Stadium, also sat near the piano when George Shearing played in Central Park. I had begun reading Hart Crane, Rilke, Lorca, and W. C. Williams, all of whom tugged at one another for my fidelity, though my journals became less strewn with faux Schopenhauer and Nietzsche musings and more full of physical images drawn from my life.

What did I have in mind? A scantily drawn self-portrait of that time brings on a little squirming, a shudder or two. In this rendition I wanted to avoid the sense of pumping out the basement because in our evolutionary curve we are most frequently "educated" by memorable experiences that involve pain. A dozen girls danced with you in Key West but you remember the one who hissed "no" in your face, right down to the Listerine on her breath, the wart on the palm of her hand. The great blue herons in the white pine, the loon circling a reed bed towing her young, a young bear peering down from a popple tree are lovely images drawn up from the past, but not quite so sharp in definition as the water snake that bit your ankle, the hornets you couldn't outrun, your only quarter lost at the county fair, Grandpa dying in the oxygen tent, thinking that down the stairwell you heard your parents say that you would be fed garbage. The dark basement pantry where the canned vegetables and preserves were kept can be flawlessly recaptured because you were sent there for behaving badly.

What did I have in mind setting myself aside that young? You try mightily to create a way of being that can't go wrong in your path to being a poet, a mode of survival not altogether unlike the manner in a primitive society in which a young man becomes a hunter and gatherer. Rather than elders you have books. Your father and teachers may have taught you the ways of the world but this giving over your life to the making of literature is a solitary effort. The religious sense of a calling tries to totally ignore the biblical puzzle of "Many are called but few are chosen," though this dictum settles itself in the back of the mind and is easily retrieved in the melancholy of self-doubt.

And the sense of the comic never totally dismisses itself. The room I rented on Grove Street was a real bargain because it was interior and the only opening was a window on an air vent at the bottom of which rats could be seen at work and play. Even the snazzier room on MacDougal had a rat hole in the corner over which I put a stove grate, and then with empathy I would drop in bits of bread for them to eat. On the wall I had taped a photo of Rimbaud from the Gallimard leather edition, also a drawn portrait of Dostoyevsky, two suitable heroes for a young peacock who was all display and no performance. The daily effort was to build a sustainable ego, an exhausting process that left little energy for writing anything. I was quite drunk with language and the playfulness of my own consciousness, and any wisdom I came across to help me order my language seemed beside the point. It was already apparent that you had to utterly give your life over to language with minimal chance of success though that was far from a deterrent at the time. The indomitable mixture of hormones and the daily budget of a quart of beer carried you along. The bartender at the White Horse Tavern who was said to have served Dylan Thomas his fatal nineteen double shots of whiskey advised me water was the best writing aid but the advice didn't take.

THE REAL WORLD

I had fallen in love with a girl back home, which brought me back from the San Francisco trip earlier than I had expected. Doubtless there are trillions of pages that have been written about love, and billions of people of all cultures who have experienced it, but the specifics of the feelings of love seem no clearer than they were in the times of Homer and Sappho. I'm sure at some point a brain physiologist will exactly locate the emotions but I have doubts that anyone will truly illuminate it. Perhaps the text that comes closest is Emily Brontë's *Wuthering Heights*, and perhaps throw in Knut Hamsun's magnificent *Victoria*. It takes a full resonance of poetry or fiction, or cinema in its highest forms, to come close to the sheer amplitude, the curious emotional weight of the experience.

Naturally I was still a lunatic when I hitched home though I had had the calming event of being stuck by a roadside in Nevada for a dozen hours when the temperature was over a hundred and my lips blackened. This served to make me more than ordinarily homesick, a set of emotions not unlike romantic love where the breast actually swells with longing, the throat constricts, and the brain whirls with visions of green fields and cool azure lakes. The homesickness was further propelled by a tussle, a euphemism, with a crazy bum beneath an underpass the evening before when I was trying to catch some sleep. He announced he was going to rob me and put a hand in his jacket pocket as if he held a weapon. All I had was a jackknife but then I didn't really want to hurt anyone, or be hurt myself, so I punched rather too hard, missing his chin but hitting his Adam's apple. He rolled around choking and I walked off quickly. A few hundred yards away in the twilight I looked back and he was still lying beside the road but then his hands fluttered upward so I guessed he'd live.

When I finally got a ride in the midafternoon heat the next day my throat was too dry to talk. The car was a junker driven by a couple in their seventies. They looked at me, shook their heads, handed me the best cold beer of my life before or since. I had spent the clear night drowned in stars but was glad to see day come, a delight that didn't last long.

Four months later in October I was married, a rather hurried affair as Linda was pregnant. I was nearly twenty-one and she was two days short of nineteen. Neither set of parents was particularly happy about the pregnancy but the worst of it was over by the time Linda had returned from Stephens College down in Missouri. When I told my parents my mother actually said, "James, we've always catered to your aberrations. Now it's time for responsibility." After that rather literary little speech my father asked if Linda's parents knew, and I said no, that she didn't have the craw to tell them over the phone. "It's up to you to go over and talk to them," he said, "but remember you didn't do it by yourself."

I was ignorant of it all at the time but not many years later I realized what an antique, old-world gesture it was for a young man to visit parents to tell them that their only child was pregnant out of wedlock. I had met them a number of times and it was accurate to say they didn't seem overfond of me, a euphemism in itself. If I had been her parents I wouldn't have been fond of me either.

My news didn't go over well. Linda's mother started wailing but William King, essentially a kind man whom I always thought of as "the last gentleman," said, "Frankly James, I think you're a bastard," then went immediately to the phone to call Linda at college and set her mind at rest.

When Linda returned home in two days I wasn't allowed to see her until a decision was made as to whether or not she might prefer to go visit an aunt for a year, but she wanted to marry me. We had first met when she was fourteen and I was sixteen and after she graduated from high school and we began seeing each other it became apparent, despite my problematical character, that we seemed destined for each other. "Destiny" is a cheeky word but an intimate part of the fretwork of romantic love. Luckily for all, including myself, at the time of our shotgun wedding I was immersed in the work of Rene Char and William Butler Yeats, rather benign influences compared to many of my other enthusiasms.

With marriage my world of freedom disappeared but at the time I was more than happy to give it up. It is said of Yeats that he never quite got off his stilts. How admirable. However, when a young poet like myself walks on one stilt, it is awkward and possible for only moments at a time. I was fifty years old before I realized that I got married in part because I doubted I would survive alone. I would guess there is something in us that unconsciously tries to ensure we will continue to live. I was simply unable to hold off the darkness offered by my perceptions by myself. Even then I was aware of the Jungian admonition of living "too high in the mind" but I could not help myself for any prolonged periods. Maybe I still can't. The idea has also arisen that growing up in a very close and loving family doesn't adequately prepare you for life outside that family. This is mildly heretical but strikes me as true. You grow accustomed to a densely warm creaturely love that you do not find when you step off your front porch. Admittedly I haven't probed too far in this direction but I have watched how very cold people seem to thrive in this cold world in the arenas of corporations and politics. In both you see the unconscionable and frivolous use of language that has suffered dissolution to the point you believe no human being could speak this way.

    In marriage I found something to tie me to earth. I was too naked to survive and I discovered clothing in this day-to-day etiquette of love. In weak periods I could at least imitate my parents' steadfastness when they sat on the porch, my father with his arm over my mother's shoulder with five children wandering around in stages of obsession and disarray.

Forty years later my wife, Linda, went to England and Ireland with our two adult daughters, Jamie and Anna. I faxed a letter every day even though it might not have been desired. Because of my professional life I'm often away weeks at a time but when away I often remember our courtship when we wrote to each other every day. For reasons emerging from her own family I believe Linda needs this closeness as much as I. I do know that darkness more easily overcomes me when I'm not in her presence.

A few years ago in late April I crossed the dunes abutting Lake Superior near Grand Marais in the Upper Peninsula of Michigan. When I reached the edge after an hour's walk I looked down the shoreline three hundred feet or so below me and there, partly shrouded by fog and icy mist, was a large iceberg maybe five stories high and a hundred feet in diameter. The iceberg was covered by several dozen ravens who were waddling around pecking at the ice with their strong beaks for anything to eat that might be in the frozen ice. I watched them with my monocular (being blind in one eye I don't have to carry cumbersome binoculars) as they shared a particularly large lake trout that had probably died of old age.

I came back on five successive days to watch the ravens, twice reaching the area before the birds and trying clumsily to hide from them in the scant shubbery at the dune's lip. After a few scolding squawks they ignored me except for a full-bearded old one who flew silently close to my hiding place so I could see an eyeball aimed at me. He seemed to be the raven who often hung out near my cabin and I was judged a safe observer. A warm spell had arrived after a particularly hard winter and by the fourth day the iceberg rocked a bit in the waves, having shed much weight into the water. At a certain depth of the iceberg the ravens had found a mother lode of frozen fish and were jabbering like people at a large, very good dinner party.

On the sixth day the iceberg was gone and so were the ravens. Shape-changing again, I thought, always ready to draw a metaphor through the reluctant teeth of reality. The week that had passed had been full of natural oddities, from walking through swirling, low-flying clouds to reach my ravens, to stupidly tracking a sow bear and two infant cubs across the sand dunes. It is best to leave this kind of mother to her own preoccupations. Most of all, though, I had been obsessed by the passage of time, and during one frightening half hour I had lain in a pocket, a bowl of sand, while a thunderstorm tormented the sky a few feet above my head. I had the feeling that I was seeing the actual face of lightning and its strokes, which must have passed in a split second, elongated themselves in time, which had stretched and distorted itself.

Soon after the storm sunlight appeared and I continued on toward my ravens, noting that the lightning had hit a promontory of dune turning a patch into a glassy substance. My ears were still ringing when I thought I saw my father, perhaps fifty yards away, leading a group of girls who were dancing along the edge facing Lake Superior. My sister was close behind and there were six other girls I had known, three of whom had committed suicide, and three who had died in accidents or from cancer. My body felt hollow and I attributed this vision to the effect of the close lightning strikes, the electricity in the air prodding an unused part of my brain. The group headed down the face of the dunes and disappeared into the water. At that moment I realized how often I was a vulnerable, fragile, and frightened man who wondered so deeply how he got from there to here, the questionable nature of the arc or trajectory that accumulates its energy when we are so young and then we are carried with it despite the presumed control over the character we have constructed moment by moment.

This was all quite exhausting and I flopped down in the sand in the manner of a very large baby thinking of the fleeting thrust of time through marriage, the creation of children and books, the ways I had made my living, the nature of the three places I lived. First came the farm in Leelanau County which started with just a few acres and a fine barn, and a granary that I turned into a studio, bought in 1968 for eighteen thousand dollars. The land expanded to a hundred acres, the house growing with remodeling, and Leelanau County itself, a peninsula jutting up into Lake Michigan changing radically in the thirty years from basically an agrarian culture toward one directed to tourism and wealthy summer residents, but always the "family home," still a consoling place however adumbrated by the many wealthy people (people who arrived in the past decade with their sure compass for lovely places), a kind of bourgeois paradise with the bottom half economically coming up missing.

What happened is that freshly married I managed to finish a B.A. in a year, then attempted graduate school. It was in this period that I had the first inkling of the primary dichotomy of my life, a nearly schizoid pulling at the soul. Simply put, it is inside and outside. In the late fall and winters I worked at the university library and covered the waterfront of Western literature. We lived in a modern though squalid compound called "married-student housing" with our infant daughter Jamie. In early spring, though, I'd be liberated back to the Horticulture Farm and my spirits would lift and our young marriage would improve. Perhaps it was only outside that I could digest my winter's reading: Rilke and Eliade are still synchronous with setting up irrigation fields, Valéry and Wordsworth's "The Prelude" with digging a root-cellar extension. The memory of the very long hours I worked, forty a week at minimum in addition to classes, are jumbled permanently with what I was reading. Rabelais is a well pit while my first immersion in Lorca is picking McIntosh apples from a championship tree that yielded sixty bushels before it died. Nabokov is digging fence-post holes.

This is all germane now, the driving force of claustrophobia, because other than the home farm there is a cabin in the far north where the room I work in is windowed on three sides with the sound of the river on my left. In the scruffy yard I see birds, rabbits, a sow bear and her two cubs, a Cooper's hawk snatching a red squirrel, three young ravens trying to figure out the bird feeder and giving up in boredom, and in the evening I hear owls, whippoorwills, bullbats, coyotes yipping, and on stormy nights Lake Superior roaring in the distance. And the ne plus ultra, on two occasions a wolf howling along the river to the west.

Our small winter casita borders a creek in the mountains outside of Patagonia, Arizona, a scant fifteen miles from Mexico. The spring before she died my mother counted seventy species of birds from our patio. There are also javelina, deer, bobcats, and the occasional mountain lion. At my studio at our friends the Bergiers' Hard Luck Ranch up the road I have Mexican ravens, roadrunners, quail, and seven cow dogs to keep me company. To some extent all dogs offer you the comfort of your first dog.

So by luck, accident, and design I have been able to make a compromise between outside and inside. On the morning I finished my novel *The Road Home* a female trogon appeared in the pyrocanthus tree only a few feet away from where I sat writing "The End." Such a rare bird returns you spontaneously to the first time you saw a certain bird as a child and you are overwhelmed by your good fortune in living in such places. Rilke wrote, "What is fate but the density of childhood?"

II

SEVEN OBSESSIONS

ALCOHOL

It all began early with stolen sips. More often than not we had no whiskey in our home because my family couldn't afford it except for the holiday season when a few bottles would arrive as gifts. Even beer was an occasional weekend matter but certainly not often, maybe once a month, though in the summer my uncles Walt and Arty, recently home from World War II and bent on sedation, would bring out to our cabin a bottle of Four Roses and a case of A&P beer, the latter costing about three dollars. The beer was usually drunk while catching enough fish for supper and the whiskey rationed out through a long evening of poker and a gambling board game called Tripoley.

My two ounces of beer in a juice glass tasted harsh and wheaty followed by an unpleasant burp. The untouchable whiskey had a hollow stink similar to sticking your head into a big pipe at an oil-equipment storage yard near our home. All the adults drank and smoked, talking randily, terribly glad to have come home from the war alive though scarcely in one piece. Spending the entirety of the war in the navy in the South Pacific is not fairly represented by books, even less so by movies. It shows itself best in the faces I remember from fifty years ago, stricken faces that were laboriously trying to resume life.

I suppose the point is that if you spend a day behind a shovel or in an office grinding your mental teeth, alcohol is the rite of passage to your time off, the rest of your life that takes place when not getting your living, the evenings and weekends spent in the constitutionally entitled pursuit of happiness.

"Happy" is the word though its dimensions are muddy indeed. The boy notes immediately that the sips make him feel a little dumb, though not unpleasantly so. The beer clearly doesn't taste as good as a Heath bar or fried meat so alcohol becomes a mysterious medicine that adults willingly take to become dumb and happy, a pleasure certainly not equal to playing with your weenie in the outhouse behind the cabin at the edge of the woods. Years later you think of this privy when you read the Yeats line "Love has pitched her palace in the place of excrement." Ironies abound though they are only slowly learned. If the adults drink too much and laugh too loudly late into the night they are quite miserable in the morning. Peeking down from the cabin loft you see your lovely bare-breasted aunt Barbara holding her head in her hands and saying, "Goddammit, I've got a hangover." The breasts divert you from the idea that beer and whiskey can cause pain.

On your mother's side of the family, the Swedes, there is no visible sign of the effects of alcohol except in Great-uncle Nelse, a wonderful smelly old bachelor who lives in the woods and curls up on the ground of the lilac grove after drinking too much. To say that Swedes are nondemonstrative is a euphemism. Salt and pepper are adequate condiments for a lifetime. The only discernible glitch in the drinking of Guckenheimer whiskey, the very cheapest brand, is that Grandpa has the tendency to cheat on the pinochle score if he drinks too much of it, and also might miss the spittoon with his chaw, though only by critical inches. Years later in a state of truly melancholy homesickness I tried to order a shooter of Guckenheimer at the posh Beverly Hills Hotel and the bartender thought it was the funniest thing possible.

My boyhood friend David Kilmer had ready access to whiskey because his father was prosperous in our little town and also owned a cabin down the shore of the lake from our own. We stole some for our camp in the woods but the scotch tasted like laundry day though it seemed to work as a mosquito repellent. It was also good for starting a campfire.

The first time I got drunk was at seven in the evening on a New Year's Eve. My mother made me get in a hot bathtub where I vomited out my thirteen-year-old heart. This experience drove me to religion and athleticism. As a high school sophomore I was second in the countywide half mile. I could chin myself a hundred times with one arm. I was profoundly mediocre at softball, baseball, basketball, and football. Losing an eye to a childhood injury does not help in these sports. I developed a size-nineteen neck by the relentless swiveling of my head to see what object or person was going to hit me next. I turned to art and literature, which everyone knows are paths conveniently lubricated by alcohol. As a senior in high school, buried in the glories of James Joyce, a friend of mine and I stole two cases of Haig & Haig Pinch scotch whiskey out of a rich man's garage. Over forty years later I still can't touch scotch unless nothing else is available. As William Faulkner, a noble boozer, said, "Between scotch and nothing, I'll take scotch." I hopefully sneaked some of this Haig & Haig into a girlfriend's pop at a party. "A dog pissed in my drink," she screeched. Her undies stayed on. A friend got drunk with a woman and split his dick. There was a lot of blood in the backseat of the car. He was a star and we lost the big game he missed. There was a lot of gossip but no one teased him because he was the toughest guy in school and could drink a six-pack in fifteen minutes, a habit that makes one careless in taking aim in sex.

This is all the etiology of something that apparently didn't quite become a disease in my case. The disease model for alcoholism is frequently in dispute. It is simply enough true for some and not for others. People lie mightily about sex, money, and drinking. It takes a real pro to see the fibs clearly. There is also the question of why shouldn't they lie? Despite the economic and social interests of the dominant culture it is possible to look at life as more than a self-improvement plan.

With money you say you make either more or less than you do depending on the situation. If you are in the company of less fortunate friends who might want yet another loan you infer you are not doing all that well. In conversations in which sex is featured there is the helpless incursion of everyone's fantasy life. Rarely, if ever, does anyone say, "I was sleeping with this famous model but I only had a half-master, the head of which turned back and said 'nope.'" Talking about alcohol is shot through with a rich lore of queasiness. Five martinis become three, and three bottles of wine become two in contrast to everyone's earlier years where our essential loutishness caused us to bray, "I drank a case of Schlitz," when midway through the third six-pack we fell asleep with a half piece of pizza sticking out of our mouths. By dawn eager flies had gathered.

The other day at a local bar while I was having a single Absolut on the rocks with a twist (some days I have two) a friend told me about his annual physical. This is a moderately expensive procedure for a man of sixty so he thought, "Why not be honest?" When the doctor pro forma asked about how many drinks he had a week my friend said, "About one hundred." This is not an acceptable answer, needless to say. "You know, some days just a few pops, but then a couple of days a week I do thirty or so, then taper off to fifteen." This is a remarkably sturdy fellow, aged sixty, of middle-European descent and a biggish body, no liver or kidney damage. I don't know about his brain though I did considerable study in brain physiology for a novel. In conversation he functions mentally at least as well as, maybe better than, our current president. He is the rarity who can drink an amount that would be slowly lethal to 99 percent of us. Many try, many die, as it were.

Everything I say about alcohol is deeply suspect but hopefully pungent. Suddenly life has become quite full of monoethic ninnies and nannies who address life solely as a problem to be solved. Just the other day on TV a man who lost a close relative to Tim McVeigh said after witnessing the execution that he didn't feel any "closure or healing" afterwards. If someone doesn't comprehend that this kind of language rape is brutally stupid there is nowhere to go with them. A life guided by inane psychologisms is scarcely a life, fresh evidence of the new Victorianism of the monoethic. Seeing this reminded me of several years ago in the depths of a particular Hollywood mudbath where late one evening I was watching part of a local late-night TV show wherein a rather attractive young woman wept tears of rage over the idea that people were smoking cigarettes. It developed that she was an aromatherapist and didn't go to bars, nor did the vast majority of Californians who eventually voted to ban smoking in bars. What are we to make of this? I think that it was Christopher Hitchens who pointed out that the cigarette hysteria began at the time of the decline of communism. If they drink at all the embouchures of these monoethic types are locked permanently into the word "chardonnay," though last November a lady who winced at my Sapphire martini and American Spirit cigarette managed to say "merlot" with muddy diction. Meanwhile, one must beware of the gaggle of amateur therapists who have of late come to life. Whether it's your alcohol, cigarettes, or food, they are going to try and piss in it.

Back to the personal drawing board, the brainpan herself, on whose delicate feminine tissue my memories are less than indelibly etched. Once after a very hard night up on Halibut Point in Massachusetts my young daughter told me that when I woke up flies were "dancing" in my mouth. I recalled a few lobsters with butter chased by cut-rate Old Thompson whiskey. Having lost several members of my family to drunk drivers and seen all around me the destruction caused to families by acute alcoholism in either parent I am quite aware of the dangers. Alcohol can be Bosnia or the Congo flaring with a million machetes while the proscribed marijuana is more on the order of the fabled Mary Poppins's harmless first period. I was never good at getting stoned because it made me drink to get over the feeling of being stoned. Marijuana also gave me a desire for cheeseburgers, a food item I don't normally touch more than once a year. Fatty foods and butter kill millions every year. It is clear why drunk driving, a crime I've never been convicted of, kills about twenty-five thousand people a year. It is less clear why sober drivers kill an equal number. Of course there are a great deal more of them but if the propaganda is correct they should be perfect.

Two decades ago in my drinking prime, a matter of volume, my pain threshold was such that I could endure hangovers and still function as a writer. This became less true in my early fifties and as time continued to pass, which it seems to do, I lost the ability totally. Evidently I was far more devoted to my art than alcohol and developed sensors to be able to check myself. Tom McGuane once said to me, "You can't quit anything until it gets in your way." Historically we miners of consciousness have had a decided propensity in this direction. Walker Percy, both writer and nonpracticing doctor, thought of it as a "reentry problem" wherein alcohol could ease you back from the imaginary world of your work to the supposed real world where you did your actual living. This is obviously true in small doses but becomes less and less true as the doses get larger. And at a certain specific point it becomes not true at all. It is not pleasant to watch people hit themselves hard in the temples with this ancient hammer.

Long ago I misplaced the list I used to keep of writers I knew who had to quit drinking to stay alive. I remember the number had reached nineteen and it must be nearly double that by now. Perhaps it begins with alcohol dispelling the essential loneliness of a solo art, and then for many the habit gets out of hand and swallows the life. I wish I had never seen a certain photo of Faulkner, taken after he had emerged from shock treatments in an asylum for his binge drinking. In the photo he looked like a bruised purple plum, or an old picture of a hanged man with a posse looking on telling jokes while their horses shuffled in the dust.

Ultimately writers aren't anecdotally all that interesting. The truly bad behavior is indulgence with a superstructure of shabby myth. For instance, Hemingway scholars haven't been quite up to the fact that his accident-proneness was a result of getting pie-eyed every day after his morning's work. In the time around the Liberation of Paris Hemingway liked to have a magnum of champagne for breakfast in his quarters at the Ritz. At nineteen I had to sit on the same bar stool at the White Horse Tavern on Hudson Street in the Village where Dylan Thomas drank his nineteen double shots and was from there taken to St. Vincent's where he could not be revived. Literary history is littered with the iconography of booze and coming to maturity as poets in the 1960s so many of us seemed to think it was obligatory to become willing victims of the disease model of the writer and alcohol. It was all a wonderfully sloppy comedy of stuporous poets and novelists writing as fast as possible before imminent death or decrepitude. The media and public at large seem overfond of these spectacles of disintegration, which confirms in them the wisdom of their own desuetude. An artist's gift of perhaps excessive consciousness includes a susceptibility to wanting to get rid of this overflow.

We are all specifically encapsulated in what the French think of as the *comédie humaine* in which our behavior might strive for the original but is destined for failure. When a country song says "There's a dark and troubled side of life" many of us actually see it right, left, back, and front, on the periphery of vision, but then tragedy classically requires people of high degree warring with enemies, fate, and destiny. Students of literature understand that tragedy doesn't include hangovers. No matter how acute, the pain of hangovers can't rise above farce.

I was sympathetic with a friend who was identified by the police by his room key when found sleeping in the desert in Las Vegas. Another friend found himself in the Los Angeles airport after having a few pops the day before in a West Side bar in New York City. Having never blacked out I find this phenomenon interesting. One of the primary joys of my life has been sleeping which has always stopped me well short of the blacking-out phenomenon. I'm a bit of a piker, as it were, or life's secret forces after a bottle of wine drive me toward my bed. The terror of blacking out should stop anyone in their damp tracks. The feathers on your chin mean that you ate the parakeet.

Doubtless Western culture would suffer great damage if it weren't for the corrective of hangovers. The origin of the riot-producing English Gin Tax centuries ago was simply that gin had been too cheap and people weren't showing up for work. It's no fun to be in the Westwood Marquis waking up to an early meeting at Columbia Studios (now Sony) and due to hangover foibles you are remembering all of the lyrics to Nancy Sinatra's "These Boots Are Made for Walking." In your mind's eye you can see Nancy herself prancing around the stage on *Ed Sullivan* in her little white boots. You're not remembering lines from Yeats, Lorca, or Whitman, only this fungoid song, as ugly as the carrot juice you ordered as a health nostrum for breakfast, a song as ugly as the toilet bowl where you poured the carrot juice rather than out the window so that someone far below could have said, "My God, carrot rain."

Hangovers have all the charm of a rattlesnake cracking its jaws as it swallows a toad. My last hangover was during a book tour in New York City when Mario Batali cooked us a nineteen-course meal. On the way to La Guardia at dawn I meditated on the amount of effort it took the magnums of wine to penetrate through the food but it got the job done. During a plane hangover you're always flying solo in an inward, self-referential trance full of the whimsicality of modest self-pity, modest because the wound is self-inflicted. Doubtless if the plane lands upside down you will be the only fatality. Both murder and hangovers are deeply sentimental, more so than Mother's Day or first love. The lost sock, the boiled-over oatmeal, the defective coffee-maker are taken personally. Self-pity must be the most injurious of the faux emotions. Mope and slump in your sludge, your brain chemistry a canned soup of insincere regret. The big boy on book tour conveniently forgets the decades when no publisher bothered asking him to tour.

Quite some time ago I turned an impressive corner with the emotion of wanting more consciousness. I wrote two pages called the Principles of Moderation, which had a wondrous, albeit slowly evolving, effect on my life.

Drinking causes drinking. Heavy drinking causes heavy drinking. Light drinking causes light drinking.

The ability to check yourself moment by moment has been discussed at length by wise folks from the old Ch'an masters of China all the way down to Ouspensky. This assumes a willingness to be conscious.

The reason to moderate is to avoid having to quit, thus losing a pleasure that's been with us forever.

We don't have much freedom in this life and it is self-cruelty to lose a piece of what we have because we are unable to control our craving.

Measurement is all. A 1½-ounce shot delivers all the benefits of a 3–5-ounce drink. A couple of the latter turns one into a spit dribbler. Spit dribblers frighten children and make everyone else nervous. On any sedative there is a specific, roomy gap between *smoothing out* and self-destruction. There is no self-destructiveness without the destruction of others. We are not alone.

Naturally there are special occasions. Generally one can't have more than one a week due to the first paragraph. When you get older like me it's once a month, if that.

It's hard to determine pathology in a society where everything is pathological. The main content of our prayers should be for simple consciousness. The most important thing we can do is to find out what ails us and fix it. Often we need outside counsel, for clarity and to speed up the process. (I've had over twenty years with my mind doctor.)

In drinking, as in everything else, the path is the way. What you get in life is what you organize for yourself every day. There is an ocean of available wisdom from Lao-tzu to Jung to Rilke. It's there in a preposterous quantity. If you drink way too much it will kill you and the souls of those around you. If you moderate you can have a nice life.

There is another rather manly approach that has been useful, an offshoot of *bushido* I have drawn from occasionally (in *The Man Who Gave Up His Name*, etc.). It can sound corny but has been quite relevant for most of the history of human life on earth. The main point is that life is trying to kill you in hundreds of ways. You have to be alert by the millisecond. If it's not wild animals, it's your human enemies, your habits and conditioning, your lazy senses.

A lot of overdrinking comes from feeling bad physically.
One overdrinks to feel better in physiological terms. This can be
avoided by vitamins, exercise, and reasonable diet. Again, it's a
cycle: overdrinking causes overdrinking because you feel bad.

Another source of the problem is the unreasonable expectations we get from others and ourselves. Unreasonable expectations can be removed by thinking it over. They can't be
"downt," pure and simple. Everyone can't get to the top or
even the middle.

The aim is to remove horrors. This really takes a specific
level of attention. Pigs love mud and there is a real streak of
muddiness in our psyches. It can be soothing to wallow. We prefer to be stunned rather than overwhelmed. Unfortunately the
variations of self-pity are the most injurious emotions we have.

Oddly enough our main weapons in controlling drinking are humor and lightness. The judgment of others and self-
judgment (stern) are both contraindicatory. When we fuck up
we mentally beat ourselves up. It doesn't work at all and has
to be expunged. The reason to slow down is to feel better and
it works real good.

You begin by cutting it all by a third. After a few weeks
you go down to a half. After that your soul will tell you when
you listen. It helps to avoid pointlessly cynical camaraderie.
Often it is actually a matter of *one drink* too many.

We need always to separate the problem of virtue from the
problem of lack of control. There are too many lies in circulation as always. Certain countries, France for example, drink
more alcohol but have fewer problems. This is partly due to the
predominance of wine which is less of a stun gun on behavior
but also that drinking isn't connected to virtue or nonvirtue. It
is a practical problem. Drinking has to be strictly self-controlled
the moment it negatively affects our character and behavior.

These are relatively mild pointers though the consequences of
ignoring them are as fatal as shooting yourself in the head in a curi-

ous time warp wherein the bullet takes many years to reach its inevitable target.

With wine we approach sheer pleasure with bended elbow but not an upturned nose. I could have become a wine snob but didn't. The escape was narrow but my salvation was several near bankruptcies, and then quitting the screenplay business drew me up short of the income required to maintain a good home wine cellar, the yearly purchases that ensure in ten years and more you will not be stopping on the way home from the office for a syrupy California "cab" so favored by nitwits. I admit I still have some Mount Eden magnums from the seventies, and superb Joseph Heitzs from the same period, but California wines are not my metier. Is this because California has become a state where you can't smoke a cigarette with a glass of wine in peace? A little bit. Is it partly due to the ridiculous wine-rating system of the *Wine Spectator*, which occasionally suggests major advertisers are getting a break? Is it because some flatulent venture capitalist has announced that his recently acquired Napa vineyard will compete with Lafite Rothschild?

Back to the realities, the day-to-day stuff. Money can distort the buying and drinking of wine just as it distorts art with respect to the gallery and auction businesses. The most frequent question is not if the wine or art is good but how much did it cost you and what is it worth now? Money easily demeans our taste in art and wine with that bull-market attitude of look at me, I can afford to turn a four-hundred-dollar bottle of La Tache into pee-pee when the whim comes over me.

I learned wine by failure and shameful waste. Back before the bull market and the yuppie salad days I earned a bunch of money, as much as "high in the six figures" one year in wages, certainly not speculation. There were a few early lessons buying English gambling stock and Australian oil stock, both of which became worth nothing at all like an empty whiskey bottle. I can't tell you where the money went as my brain lacks that orientation. I have the feeling that the money simply took a bus out of town. The fact that you can't even go into a bank and look at what savings you did manage to accumulate makes it less than interesting to my peasant genes. Again, I tend toward the comic view of these years. The pre-bedtime line of coke called out for a vintage Margaux. The fifty-case deal I made with a man selling his collection, over half of them Premiers Grands Crus, flew out of the basement. The seller preferred a private party to a restaurant, someone who would providently take care of the wonderful wines that he had taken years in the making.

Some of it was well used with friends who were aware of what they were drinking during massive feasts of woodcock, grouse, and venison. This matter stops me just short of a sense of my total loutishness in that period, and my oldest daughter had the sense to hide some old La Tours, Yquems, and Lafites for her future wedding, but all in all I was an untethered swine in a fertile truffle patch.

My total turnaround was rather slow in coming but finally accomplished, the signal event a few years ago when I sat in a La-Z-Boy chair my wife loathes and stared down a fifth of Canadian VO, a long-term favorite that had become a slowish death of sorts. I simply loved the flavor and a tear formed when I poured it out in the sink after gazing at it for several hours. It's hard to comprehend the difficulty of breaking a habit so easily acquired.

I turned to wine with a passion that I had offered it sporadically. Obsession can't be expunged, only replaced. I'm clearly a daffy sort and one summer tested thirty-four Côtes du Rhônes in search of a house wine I could afford. Since then some of my favorites, Gigondas, Vacqueyras, and Domaine Tempier Bandol from farther south, have risen in price but I've decided I deserve them.

Unlike booze, good wine resonates so broadly it draws in the world that surrounds us. The effects of it are slow enough so that you can check yourself, an absolutely vital talent if you drink. As a Zen dictum says, you must find yourself where you already are and the effects of booze make this unlikely. Good wine increases the best aspects of camaraderie and sweetens the tongue for conversation. It softens the world's sharp edges in contrast to the blunting power of booze. In short, you don't become dumb at a blinding pace, and your mood swings from gentle to gentler.

It has also occurred to me that I'm drawn to wine for the same reason that fishing and bird hunting have been lifelong obsessions. The pleasure is in the path, the search for something good, that finding a fine, reasonably priced wine is similar to catching a trout in an unlikely eddy of a river, or two grouse in the bag on a cold, rainy October morning. It is celebratory rather than sedating, a nod to the realities of existence rather than an erasure. When I come into an aspen glade in May and find several dozen morel mushrooms I begin concocting a meal, perhaps the chicken thighs sautéed with wild leeks and morels devised by Tom Colicchio of New York's Gramercy Tavern, also Craft. If I were making the same dish with elk I'd drink a big Tuscan vintage or my all-time favorite financially reachable wine, Domaine Tempier Bandol. Mild dangers lurk in that before we left our casita on the Mexican border this spring I drank an assortment of fine reds with sweetbreads, fresh abalone, doves, quail, and elk. You can pay two hundred bucks to a doctor to find out this combination might bring on gout but you already know that. For some of us the inner greedy child is at work right out there on our skins.

The few great vintages I have left I reserve for the fall during bird season. Otherwise, to put them back in reach I go to France on book business once a year and mope around prayerfully. The French are relentlessly up for a special occasion and when a book is doing well my French publisher, Christian Bourgois, tends to order Côtes Roties from the seventies, and if I visit Lulu Peyraud in Bandol, I get to drink the older Domaine Tempier that has somehow disappeared from my cellar through enthusiasm. As with spotting a rare bird I remember the entire ambience and surroundings of a great wine. The magnum of Mercurey Clos des Barraults (1990) at Gérard Oberlé's in Burgundy includes the morning trip to the market in Moulin, the roses in the yard, his Alsatian dog, Eliot, barking at the neighbor's Charolais, the cooking of two lobes of foie gras, Gérard's so-so singing of

Purcell's "Come All Ye Sons of Art" as he serves the meal. With booze the most memorable aspects were the hangovers.

Years ago I had a short correspondence with the fine American writer Ray Carver. I remember thanking him for a review he had given me at a particular low point in my life. When he wrote back he apologized because he couldn't remember writing the review or much of anything from those years. And this from a grand talent, perhaps genius, seems sad indeed. Life is so short you want to remember all of it, bad and good. It moves so quickly you easily forget that it is utterly unforgiving. You wouldn't willingly drive a car without brakes, would you?

STRIPPING

When you are eleven and looking at a girl in the fifth grade, a class-mate you're fond of, it is part of the biological imperative of our spe-cies to wonder what she looks like without the pretty clothes. This is a decidedly nonintellectual mystery, and quite literally twists and forms our prepubescent bodies and souls according to its verbless dic-tums. When your third-grade girlfriend steps out of the outhouse on her parents' farm, lifts her skirt and drops her panties, bends over and yells, "See my ass," you are stricken with a feeling that you are walk-ing up smooth hot planks in your bare feet. This is desire before it becomes desire. There is the faintest recollection from Sunday school and other sources of the Great No that hounds our lives that naugh-tiness is present but there, twenty feet away, is the very bare butt of the beloved. You don't know whether to do a somersault, shit your pants, or run for cover, so you do nothing but stand there and gaze with eyes that are apertures taking a permanent photo, a rendering that will last until your brain dies.

This desire before it becomes desire is a cloud that moves non-directionally, a truly fuzzy puzzle for the young mind who is mere grape juice that has not yet begun to be wine. With other boys he posi-tions himself in front of the swings to watch the skirts flutter up re-vealing bare limbs. With other boys he dog paddles under the ladder up to the diving board to watch the legs and crotches ascend. He can even develop a fetish of sorts for this act of looking upward. There is a somewhat comic category of soft-core porn called "raised-skirt pho-tos," doubtless harkening the viewer backward to the first lineaments of desire: the ungainly boy taking a peek here and there and anywhere possible. He takes many peeks but hasn't yet taken aim.

I recall quite clearly when I was nineteen and had run off to Boston to become a great writer, how a Greek waiter explained to me that young men generally don't begin to know what they are sexually until the age of sixteen. He took me to a club where we watched a belly dancer who performed with astounding grace. Partial nudity seemed well adapted to the dance, which didn't count the prancing hermaphrodite I'd paid a quarter to see at the Michigan State Fair at age twelve. That particular set of plumbing seemed confused indeed. Age nineteen, however, is a time in life when a ballet dancer on the stage a hundred or so feet away can give you a hard-on. The ballet, *Petrouchka*, is supposed to be an aesthetic experience and I remember struggling to be high-minded but underneath the aesthete a beast of prey lurks. This pink-limbed young woman whirled and jumped with surpassing grace so that the heart, soul, and pecker lifted in unison. It wouldn't have been the same thing if she had been dressed in a pantsuit or overalls.

The human genome is an often insufferable dictator. We are directed by what still can't be seen in a microscope that costs as much as a Ferrari. Our life juices are electric. If only sex were what we pretend it to be. Once I had drinks in Missouri with a racist, right-wing ex-con, happily married with three children, who spoke with boozy affection for his federal-prison lover, a black transvestite with the marvelous name Tawna. I asked him if he ever tried to get in touch with him and he corrected me with "her." He insisted she was "all woman" though of course she had a dick. When he returned to my question of getting in touch with Tawna in Kansas City he said, "It wouldn't be right," meaning ethical. This avowed Christian who once had been caught with several hundred thousand Percodans had passed easily from a sexual attitude of any port in the storm to the sacrament of marriage. Life is like that, we agreed. You may control your own sex life with a strong mental dog collar and leash but your brain will continue to spin its own stories for you to enact.

It is our societal and religious rage for order that tries to confine sexuality to marriage. The fact that it leaves out single people and gays is irksome indeed. If we don't behave ourselves maybe the economy will cease working. As I said, if only sex were what we pretend it to be there wouldn't be all of these problems. The statistics on marital infidelity are boggling when you go to a movie, concert, or ball game and the numbers acquire faces. Doubtless the fear of AIDS has done more in favor of marital fidelity than religion or societal opprobrium. What is permissible? is the question. Self-righteousness has become both a disease and an industry. Sexual content on TV is avidly discussed in Congress as if there were no sexual content in life, but then historically political corruption has always been singularly humorless. The most degraded feebs in recent history have all stood foursquare for "family values," whatever those are.

Still, in every reasonably sized city in America there are porn stores, and at least an attempt at a strip club. The opponents of their existence should understand that these are relatively safe environments for lust usually with not much more character than the steam valve on a pressure cooker, which is their actual function. Strip clubs show you an often delightful parody of what you're in for if you have the time and inclination to seduce someone, or be seduced. On rare occasions in specific locations the dancers have extraordinary talent. Sometimes they seem so strung out on downers they trip over the dollar bills placed on the stage by burly businessmen and younger men who, having finally resolved their skin problems, have freak hots for this public display of fleeting genitalia or, if strictly monitored, wriggly damp mice trying to emerge from the G-string mouse strap. And on the rarest, rarest, rarest occasions you become a witness of true beauty, a marriage of nudity and dance so compelling that your breath shortens, the heart heats its staccato tachycardia of actual lust, the kind that persistently fills the world with people, the summum bonum of desire that the best of the world's poets have been singing for five thousand years.

* * *

I've occasionally wondered if the raised platform, the runway or stage, in a strip club isn't inadvertently designed to pander to our first sexual feelings. The nudity, full or partial, harkens our *cojones* back to aunts and teachers and, God forbid, our moms. Zow, I saw some hair, say playmates to one another. The girls onstage or runway look bigger than life just like women did way back when, when we weighed not much more than one of our teacher's big pink legs. Big eaters are admired in the Midwest and this teacher always packed five sandwiches in her flower-decorated lunch bucket. Under the desk the view was as mysterious as the first view of the Carlsbad Caverns. She shaved her legs short of her kneecaps which wasn't quite adequate. Over the decades I've come to know a few of these strippers as a wise older stepuncle and they're rarely big on ground level. The stage is, in fact, a raised enlarged pedestal of lust, a grand altar to summon our desire in the form of the money we offer. When I was fourteen a preacher advised me that "a naked pretty girl can pull at your heartstrings." He was on the money, though I did not accept the intended warning in the statement. Built into both Calvinism and Catholicism is the implicit threat that anything truly wonderful should also make you feel guilty, especially the skin we were all born in. As Jack Nicholson once said about network television, you can shoot a girl in the tit but you're not allowed to see the tit.

Back to the early days. At twelve, despite being in a state of continual tumescence, things can go wrong. In the hot tent with the not altogether healthy-looking strippers at the Michigan State Fair, with the extra twenty-five cents still in the offing to view the genitalia of the hermaphrodite, there is the disturbing odor of manure that men have tracked in from the exhibition barns for the cattle, pigs, and sheep, not to speak of the cackling breeds. This is not exactly a sexy odor even to a farm boy. The scent of the manure in the overheated tent mixes with the stomach's unrest from cotton candy and corn dogs, the french fries that were an effective wick for the grease. The boy has wriggled his way to the front and is smart enough to know that it all looked better farther back. There are grayish splotches of talc except around the arm-pits and inner thighs of the women where the sweat has absorbed and banished the talc, which smells of the baby powder his mother applies to his younger sister and brother. One very large and sallow stripper has a bounty of pubic hair, truly a wig dropped in the lard crock. Before the hermaphrodite displays the double whammy, the corn dog has begun to argue with the cotton candy which shrinks in terror from the french-fry grease. After this a trip to the swine barn and seeing the ass of a friend's Duroc sow will be a specific relief. A five-hundred-pound pig makes total sense to a pork lover and I've held in my arms a piglet this sow, named Myrna, has delivered forth.

Unless you are afflicted with satyriasis (an actual disease), mood is everything in sexual matters from which a high degree of pleasure is expected even though the pleasure might be limited to the visual. Mood is utterly dictatorial and sometimes it's as hard to reestablish a good mood as it is to reconstruct a spiderweb. Improbable, in fact. Sometimes the situation shows how dumb some of us are. In an Ann Landers column a wife was turned off during foreplay when her husband mentioned how sexually attractive he found her younger sister. When he got home from work this guy must have shut his head in the car door. This particular mood problem will last for a while, say in contrast to trying to make love to a girl in the backseat of a car on a college campus the night before the big game. In the distance a group around a bonfire is singing the college fight song. You are an aesthete and your pecker wilts when confronted with the naked banality of this song. You drive a dozen miles into the countryside where through the open window you hear only crickets and the rasping whisper of cornstalks, the moon wishing its own slow arc of flight through the steamy window.

At my favorite strip club in America, the Night Before, in Lincoln, Nebraska, which I often visit with prominent academics from the local university who use me for this purpose as strip clubs are not an acceptable activity in modern universities, I was feeling distraught one evening and not able to emotionally relate to my then favorite stripper, Bonny, though her pubis in the clutches of a violet G-string was a scant two feet from my nose. My mood was sodden but my mind was clear and I could travel back in memory an entire two hours to when I had ordered an appetizer of deep-fried chicken gizzards to precede a two-pound porterhouse. I can't say gizzards are delicious, rather an acquired taste to give you something to fiddle with delicately before the steak arrives. These gizzards, however, were proving to be obnoxious ballast. I couldn't very well forsake my cronies and wrestle with the gizzards in the privacy of my quarters at the Cornhusker Hotel (actual name). My academic companions had had their faces buried in books awaiting my summer arrival and now their normally mildewed faces were glowing. In short, I had to hang in there despite the fact that the gizzards had come back to life in my tummy.

I was saved by an electric moment. The Night Before allows you to hoist yourself over the stage rail and proffer a dollar, or a five or ten, in your teeth while flat on your back, and the stripper plucks the bill away by clenching her buttocks. According to Kinsey this is a view savored by many of our male citizens. The electricity came from a sturdy but attractive ranch girl who took off her cowboy hat revealing a pale forehead above a face darkened by the sun, a sign of authenticity, and flipped onto the stage with a fiver in her teeth. She lay down with a pretty grin and a hundred male faces tightened. The stripper paused, shrugged, laughed, then went for it. There were suitably wild cheers, in themselves a nod to sex in our time. Despite a hundred thousand laws enacted mostly by dead-peckered suits, everyone gets to do it. This experience is as vital as a bean-soup lunch and an envelope of cash for a Washington lawmaker.

Meanwhile, my gizzard gristle dissolved only to be met by a full discussion of sexual taste. Books have been written on the subject, albeit clumsily, not taking into full account our twelve billion brain cells and thirty billion synapses that conduct this taste with greater speed and completeness than Bill Gates's gizmos. I don't feel drawn to tall women but once I saw a tall stripper who reminded me of my tall seventh-grade teacher, Jeannie Phillips, over whom I fantasized moment by moment when within visual range. Suddenly tall women became a possible source of rapture. A friend with you might exclaim over a girl that reminds you of *Planet of the Apes* without the pelts. Her eyes are too close together and her left heel is excessively calloused. Her voice has a trace of the clarinet and her grammar is bad. I'm not a marine, I'm a poet. Luckily for them only one woman out of a thousand reddens my ears with lust. The ratio goes way up in strip clubs because you're not going through weeks of quiet suffering before you see their butts, plain and simple.

In a year I probably don't spend more time in a strip club than I do reading the Bible, another childhood habit, and just any old strip club won't do. If they're too fancy as in New York City or on my one trip to Las Vegas I don't feel at home. I feel shabby and literary among natty men flashing their bull-market or gambling thatches of cash. The air is excessively sanitized, the decor as expensive as a Westin lobby. The bouncers are in tuxes and call you "sir." All the titties tend to be artificial, well-fleshed softballs. The girls are Olympic gymnasts with a little too much gym time showing, and possessing all the spontaneity of a beauty pageant. And sometimes the girls are simply too beautiful, too perfect in the manner of the ten thousand anonymous starlets drifting around Hollywood, Westwood, Beverly Hills, and Santa Monica. There's a tinge of the android, of a miraculous walking form of Madame Tussaud's genius. Maybe they don't even need toilets in their apartments! In public they seem to eat lettuce and raw vegetables and perhaps like Peter Rabbit's sisters they leave only discreet droppings in the shubbery.

During my single visit to Las Vegas, a matter of sixteen hours, my stomach muscles ached because I had been laughing nonstop at the actuality of the place, which deafened my senses, a place that had zero to do with the history of Western culture but had everything to do with its future. In a place called Club Paradise all of the girls resembled these L.A. starlets. Seated a few feet away I looked hard, pondered, and craved for a few flaws. During a twenty-buck table

dance my nose brushed dry skin that should have been moist. I
wouldn't have been surprised if I had heard an electronic hum inside
her butt, which wiggle-waggled close to my nose and looked like it
had been used only in outer space. I admit my worm turned and my
heart beat faster but the girls were simply as unimaginable as Christmas every day, or God actually saying to you in basso profundo, "Take
heart, kiddo."

An intimate part of "what we wish sex to be but it isn't" is false male
gusto, an uncritical and affected enthusiasm for all things sexual. You
see a lot of boozy camaraderie in strip clubs that has more to do with
cronies on a night out than anything onstage. Even the most care-
worn business dweeb, the most devout techno-lackeys, like to feel a
little "naughty" though that word is slipping from usage. Once again,
how can you have pathology when everything has become pathological? Naughty presumes adventure and only failures have time for
it. Unbridled lust is a rare commodity that isn't liberally dosed out
for all eight girls in the rotation. Sometimes you have to wait a whole
hour again to see the girl you liked best and the other seven seem to
diminish with your impatience. You become as sullen as the twelve-
year-old you actually are at a strip club. During the downtime you
gaze around and note that all of these men are trying to look more
attractive than they are. A man in an unmodish business suit strides
to the men's room in the manner of a top-of-the-line street fighter.
Whenever men stand up they are filled with the effort of sucking in
their guts or modestly flexing their muscles. They cast smoky smiles
just short of drooling. However old they are, they have become
younger. With the help of naked women they are back at the fantasy
stage of "women want me but they don't seem able to express it." But
all in all it's not the least bit pathetic. And it's not voyeurism, which
assumes that the objects don't know they're being viewed. It's been
going on a long time and it seems apparent that it's not going to stop.
Men say to themselves, "At least this is real life, not fantasy." Of
course strip clubs bear the same relationship to reality as the musi-

cals of Andrew Lloyd Webber. If our man Herbert believes that this highly structured ritual is reality the management should be congratulated. This public display of beauty instigates desire, where in our "real" reality it is desire that instigates beauty. This is an important point. We have all read recently of the rampant sexual misbehavior in a western senior-citizens' community. A jaunty geezer feels a nut twinge and goes for broke, and equally often it is a granny that makes the first move. None of the residents by our culture's definition are attractive. There is a somewhat wretched country song that goes, "The girls all get prettier at closing time." In a bar a lady your own size, say about two hundred pounds, flutters at you with a witty "My body belongs to Marvin but he's a Navy SEAL stationed in the Philippines." No one wants to be attacked by a vicious SEAL, real or military. You feel smarmy desire. Certainly she is as attractive as a pork roast and you love pork roast. She leaves three lit Kools in the ashtray as she gets up, saying wittily, "I gotta take a piss." You have become part dog and you either hang in there or don't. She's been drinking maybe a dozen Kahluas mixed with orange pop, according to the bartender. What if she pukes in the family Subaru? This is another clear case of sex as it is wherein desire turns a pumpkin into Cinderella, a sow into a bulky Cameron Diaz.

In a desperate July recently I stared at thirty-seven galleys and manuscripts on my cabin desk, plus a pile of half-written poems and two partially written books, and precisely fifty-three unanswered letters. It was very hot and both male and female bugs—mostly blackflies and deerflies—were finding me attractive. My solace was rowing a little brown-and-blue boat counterclockwise around a big lake, which required four hours, lovely but somewhat autistic behavior. On a steamy morning I recalled that the great Zen master Yuan-Wu said, "Abandoning things is superior" and I planned a road trip, settling on the most exciting state in the union, Nebraska. I have several dear friends in Nebraska and the Niobrara River Valley in the Sandhills is my favorite beautiful spot on earth. The capitol building in Lincoln is clearly the niftiest state capitol building in the United States, but perhaps more important, Lincoln is the site of my beloved strip club the Night Before. My mom and dad always advised soul search-ing before making a big decision so I meditated a full second. My mom and dad preferred the straight and narrow where I, for nongenetic reasons, have favored the wide and crooked.

As I drove west I began to wonder if my own taste might be far from or near to the norm. Men, above all, are excitable boys, but that doesn't mean that my own aesthetic principles are readily expunged by any thigh on the block. For instance, I once spent an evening at the Crazy Horse in Paris, including at least two hours backstage with the owner and friends drinking vintage wines. Let's just say this ex-perience brought me very close to the heart of the matter. I felt a reverence that maybe Steven Spielberg owns after he creates one of those dawn-of-creation scenes. I tried to affect a mood of Parisian blasé about the girls who brushed my left elbow on their way to the locker room. It means a great deal more to be a writer in Paris than in New York and the girls wanted a group picture with me. Sophie Bernardin, the present owner, told me that her father who began the club would audition a thousand girls for every one he selected. It's a hundred bucks to enter the front door. Standing there with my arms around the moist bevy I simply trembled. I've addressed several thousand people in a theater with far less agitation. This was a clear case of too much, the moral equivalent of drinking a magnum of '49 Lafite Rothschild in thirty minutes. I felt the aftershocks, the tremors, for days, the experience similar to when a friend called during an L.A. earthquake and said, "The fucking tectonics are grinding the shit out of each other." In a perfect world the girls would have followed the lumbering Pied Piper out of the club to a remote manor in Burgundy where a gross of Viagra would have been depleted. Two years later I can still scent the lilac in the air, hear the laughing, dulcet French syllables, feel the weight of my thumping heart.

*   *   *

On this Nebraska trip I had only three evenings at the Night Before. People talk about discretionary time on their cellulars when they should throw them under a garbage truck and do what they want. Three nights was probably enough for a man who needed to get back to the Cornhusker Hotel and read Wittgenstein and a pile of civics textbooks. I was accompanied by an eminent folklorist and a well-known mental-health authority. Both wish to remain anonymous, having recently seen on CNN a man arrested for sticking out his tongue at women in a traffic jam. These are perilous times when the Supreme Court would turn the great Henry Miller into chum were he still alive. Don't stick out your tongue even if there's a dung beetle biting it. Nowadays, you'll be safe only when you're dead.

I'd say that out of at least thirty evenings my current three-day cycle was high medium. When the local University of Nebraska is in session a portion of the girls are from modern dance classes which adds a certain bourgeois zeal. On my last night a fetching lass picked up the slack by wearing a sorority-type pleated skirt. I had also seen this tactic in a Tucson club but in Lincoln the girl had the advantage of looking like a young Deborah Norville. Years ago just before the cameras rolled on the *Today* show I had made Deborah blush by dropping a pencil and pretending to look up her dress. This archaic midwestern sorority look has greater appeal onstage than it does in a motel where you learn they haven't even read Søren Kierkegaard.

I spoke with Ken Semler, who has owned the Night Before for nineteen years, about certain political pressures from the Lincoln city council. The direction of the criticism was concentrated on two other Lincoln clubs that had a somewhat more permissive policy but were too loud for me to bear what with my ears having been undimmed by rock music. Not oddly Semler reminded me of the manager of a first-rate restaurant. The man is obviously shrewd with a sharp eye for clean quarters, good air, and manageable behavior in his patrons. I mentioned my own notion that authorities are often threatened by a reality that doesn't exist. The arena of sexual confusion is wide indeed and the media insists on a state of lust we can feel only in isolated moments. Men and a fair number of women come into this

club, have a few drinks, chat, and watch nearly naked women dance
an often-comic parody of lust. As a freeborn American I am obsti-
nate in thinking a nude woman does not jeopardize civic health and
that if anything she encourages it.

Ironies abound. A hyperenergized greed has been the core of our
society for the past decade and it is evident in strip clubs. In the Night
Before the closest allowed contact with the stripper is putting money
in your mouth and having it taken by clenched buttocks or breasts.
This is an improbable metaphor of fascism at play that we cooperate
with because it is far, far better than nothing. By all evidence the
majority of interested men confine this activity to magazines and
computers. I've noted for a long time that I am flesh and I want to be
there in the flesh. The nakedness of women by all standards is the
glory of God. Men, too, for some. Why settle for virtual reality when
you can be there?

On my last evening, between the dinner slab of Nebraska prime
beef and our arrival at the Night Before, we stopped to look at a university agricultural display of Native grasses and wildflowers. I was swept
away by this beauty in the middle of the city. In the late twilight the
cicadas were deafening, as you would be if you had been buried for seventeen years and had just emerged for sex. Even Shakespeare said, "We
are nature, too."

Meanwhile, it's hard to figure out in public entertainment what
is thriving and what is waning, though I suspect strip clubs are in the
latter category for reasons greater than sniveling politicians. The
world of Aldous Huxley, or of George Orwell in 1984, is much closer
than we think, in fact their peculiar tendrils are wrapped thoroughly
around our lives. Both Orwell and Huxley would be amused at the
"safe sex" represented in computer porn sites, not to speak of the
dominance of politically correct behavior. And gradually the idea of
a job, which once was not much more than a livelihood, has come
to be equated to a life. Discretionary time to "booze and cruise" is
rapidly fading into the past.

Once men in large numbers traveled to the tenderloins of cities
to "let off steam," as the euphemism goes, and this still happens in

convention cities where high-end strip clubs are popular. Historically, the waxing and waning can be seen most clearly in the Northwest, where Seattle strip clubs were once a vast draw for loggers, commercial fishermen, cowboys, and farmers from the outlying areas. With the business gentrification of everything the torch has passed to Vancouver, British Columbia, a city closer to the true outback, and where in a dozen fine clubs no rules are noticeable.

I suspect, then, that it is the twilight of stripping rather than the high noon, but then twilight has always been my favorite time of day. When you're far from home and having a fine dinner with cronies and you are all tired of talking about how the lower fifty percent in our society are becoming social mutants (luckily I don't have friends who talk much about the stock market), you certainly aren't going to go to a movie where you can't have a drink, or to a simple bar where you will continue talking about politics until your collective pores bleed. Instead, you go to a strip club, abandon politics, have a few drinks, and dwell on what you've always thought was the most beautiful thing on earth, the body of a woman.

HUNTING, FISHING
(AND DOGS)

Recently in a poem I thought, "I was born a baby. What has been added?" What are these hundreds of layers of living clothes I've mostly unwittingly layered onto myself like the laminae of an interminable onion? What are the peculiar landscapes of mind that fueled the decisions behind how I lived my life, and what were the largely unconscious impulses? When you map your life in retrospect there's a bit of a blind cartographer at work. It's not pleasurable but you have to see the structure of the way you spend your hours as a palimpsest of time overlaying the whole brutish structure, a four-dimensional topographical map with the fourth dimension being time. Simply enough, what did I do with my time?

"Huh," the soul howls. I mean life outside the dominating force of your work, your livelihood, the jobs that offered only in the oldest terms "room and board." An omniscient time and study analysis would figure in the immensity of loitering, brooding, dawdling, reading, sleeping, meals, the banality of hygiene, the grooming we share with chimps and house cats.

The big items within discretionary time are our sports and amusements. In an infantile view of the afterlife the white-bearded gatekeeper will quiz us about what we did on earth under the assumption that when we enter the afterlife we are "off" earth, normally an expensive procedure when you look at NASA. "I spent an immense amount of time fishing and hunting," you answer, adding hopefully, "You know, enjoying God's handiwork."

This all presumes that you had spare time in the first place. One of the most frequent comments I hear everywhere, right up there with "What's for dinner" and "I want to be somebody" is "I don't have time to read," which is essentially telling you, a lifelong writer, that your profession is below that of communal spritzers and flossing, and frequent social ass scratching. Everyone has to learn over and over that at best time is seized and then you flee. If you're locked in one place people will always try to get you to do something they don't want to do themselves, or as a post-Calvinist nitwit, you actually believe you can clear your desk, answer all calls, all faxes and e-mails, have a few drinks, make a going-away dinner for twelve, and at dawn you will drive or fly in a state of total serenity to a fishing or hunting destination. Myself, I've found it easier to live next door to where I can fish and hunt, though I feel lucky in my profession as I know this contiguity is rarely possible for most.

After six decades I've only recently understood the degree to which I'm my father's son. You can rather easily go back further through several thousand generations, and according to the most recent DNA archaeological studies, we all began on a savannah in Africa hunting. It's seventy thousand years ago and the Neanderthals are disappearing. There's just us and we're rather black. When we move to the north for twenty thousand years or so we'll lighten up. We'll paint lovely pictures of our hunting and fishing expeditions on cave walls. Further on in time but well before Christ we'll even get more careful about our hunting. According to Herodotus the ancient Egyptians declared a death penalty for anyone who killed a hawk or ibis.

Back down to Dad and me, the keeper of the name Jim, a free item, who became a bit overeducated by dint of a radical curiosity. A casual interest in the news reveals, despite being in the gifted territory north of the equator, certain tribalistic difficulties in Ireland and Israel, specific Arab groups and us, not to dismiss what was formerly known as Yugoslavia, over which we have layered the thin lid of civilization on a Ball jar full of pissed-off hornets. The tentatively governable world is enough to drive you to the woods, let alone live deep within an empire with all of the preposterous greed and malfeasance of the Roman.

But maybe we should be aware that heading away from what we think of as civilization to fish and hunt is always more than that. It's amazing how many things are sold in terms of "escape." The other day while gassing my car on the way to fishing a yokel asked me if they were going to start draining the Great Lakes to water Texas and for no reason I said, "Absolutely," then noting his stricken appearance I added, "Only if we let them," and then he said, "We'll shoot the fuckers when they show up." That attitude was better for his own life, the one he had to live. He passed on a "secret" fishing place that I already knew about but the intention was good. Now I wasn't escaping the draining of the Great Lakes or any of another thousand raw sources of enervation but was simply going fishing, but then you have to carry your brain along with you so you can't escape anything, you can only make the world tolerable by offering yourself compensatory pleasure. In the arena of outdoor writing it is never admitted that sometimes the pleasure doesn't work. I recall when I was about ten years old, a few years after World War II, I was fishing a big bend in a river in northern Michigan with my father who was well upstream. I could see through the trees across the river, and across a broad green field there was a single railroad car on a siding. Unfortunately for the fishing expedition my mother had saved all *Life* magazines from the war years and I remembered a photo of an open railroad car near a death camp that was full of shoes, including a great number of children's and baby shoes. Even as a ten-year-old I had a fair sense of geography and knew the railroad car across the field couldn't be the same one but the woods behind me were dark and deep and a ship might very well have brought the railroad car to America from Germany and dark forces were hiding it in northern Michigan. I wasn't smart enough about history to draw any conclusions about death camps, except that particular history that evening resembled a ghost story and despite catching several fine brown trout the world was right there with me.

My long-dead father was a modest man and would not wish to be referred to in noble terms. He had an improbable work ethic which was handy indeed for a man who was the sole support of a family of five children. In addition to his work as a county agricultural agent, and later as a soil scientist and designer of watershed recoveries, it was his habit to have a huge vegetable garden for the after-work hours. Any other spare time before we had to move to southern Michigan when I was twelve was spent fishing. I was barely in school before I became similarly addicted, and when my left eye became blinded at age seven and my retreat from civilization increased in speed and volume, fishing filled the vacuum. I was too young to hunt but I think I was about ten when I was allowed to tag along to deer camp. I never did develop a passion for deer hunting that approached fishing but early on envied a boy down the lake who had a .410 with which he hunted grouse. Watching him and following along to try to help flush birds I could see that this sport would enter my life in a large way.

In the past few years when life seems to have become more of a single piece I have noticed that I tend to feel quite contemporary when driving to a fishing or hunting destination, but when I arrive a number of centuries drift away. There's no conscious sense of the atavistic, only that everything you've learned in school, university, your business life is of no use to you now. This is especially true if you're hunting and you watch your dog's hyperalert attentiveness when you let her out of the car. Her nose wrinkles and she sucks air in through her wattles as she looks at the territory, trying to pick up scent and see if she's familiar with the hunting ground. When you put on her beeper or bell collar you feel her trembling and you aim her in the direction you wish to start. When you move away from the car you quickly and consciously become a dog yourself as much as is possible. You are following her nose, certainly not your unsophisticated own. You might hope she heads for the right habitat, the particular mixture of flora that tends to harbor grouse and woodcock, but at the same time you know that her years of experience have taught her this. As my dogs have aged and slowed down I've been amazed at how much they've conserved their energy by moving directly from covert to covert without the aimless bursts of speed that typified their younger behavior. Hopefully your concentration on what you are doing is close to that of the dog and after a couple of hours, when you both are quite tired, you find that you have been so immersed in this creaturely behavior that you haven't had a worrisome or contemporary thought since you got out of the car. You have plenty of time for those when you reach home though the act of cooking dinner can further delay their arrival. If you hunt or fish a couple of weeks in a row without reading newspapers or watching television news a certain not altogether deserved grace can reenter your life. Newsworthy events and people, as always, have gotten along in the usual ways without your mental company.

"Inside" is for making a living, "outside" is for pleasure. That's how you first begin to structure the world when you grow up in the country. The pain of learning that the world is round and everything bleeds into everything else is gradual. One day under the guidance of my dog Rose I shot four grouse in an hour and was soon back at the cabin eating lunch and reading ancient Chinese poetry, the latter a specific nostrum against the inanity of the world. In T'ang Dynasty poetry you are taught over and over that nearly all public life and effort is basically inane, that you should spend as much time as conceivable in the natural world. I then took a nap and awoke rather startled with the fact that I was broke. I heated coffee and drank it hurriedly because it was nearly four P.M., the time I must, during hunting season, open a good bottle of French wine if I'm not doing an afternoon hunt. Four birds in a day are enough at the beginning of a long season. Two or three is actually better. In the past being a piggy about hunting has given me bad dreams.

If you're not careful being broke can make you feel broke which as most of the world knows is not a good feeling. I sat there absorbing the sunlight of Provence, a gift of the glass of Domaine Tempier Bandol I was drinking, and noticed that it had begun to rain outside in the Upper Peninsula of Michigan. The beckoning steps were ob-

vious. Broke people try to get money. I recalled a few years back during three weeks of fly-fishing for brown trout in Montana I received
one of those urgent calls from Hollywood demanding my immediate
presence to keep a project alive. The fishing was splendid and the
phone call gave me an actual heartache, the kind that you think might
precede your trip to the incinerator. I flew out in the evening and
had my meeting in the morning though the process through which
they fired me lasted several hours. During the final portion of the
meeting when their silly ax fell I positioned myself in the office so
that I could see out the window where my car and driver sat ready for
the airport. The frivolously vicious meeting ended and I shook many
hands that had never touched a brown trout, or spent cold, rainy
autumn days bird hunting. On the way to the car I passed masses of
Mercedeses, Jaguar sedans, and BMWs, none of them any good for
floating a river or getting out of a mudhole in the backcountry.

There is the discomforting idea that if I spent all the time I give over
to hunting and fishing making money I'd never go broke but then as
a writer I'm a very poor portrait of a faucet that can easily be turned
on and off. To function at all I have to maintain a state of being
concomitant with my vaguely childish idea of what life should be. I
begin the day with taking my dog Rose for a walk in the fields, woods,
or canyons, depending on which of our three modest properties I'm
spending my time. This is no big deal and settles the mind for the
day's work. A dog can escort you away from our current empire and
into a more private world where literature is allowed to thrive. Before Rose came Tess, Sand, and Missy, all hunting breeds, also Hud,
Jessie, Kate, and Mary, all farm dogs but no less beloved.

   When walking without a rod and gun you are mindful about how
deeply fishing and hunting have entered your consciousness and how
large the store of perceptions must be in your unconscious. They quite
literally have become a way of framing reality. Walking a stretch of
river with your dog from far up on the bank's edge you locate the holes
and the flow that concentrate the fish, and you also study the nature

of every thicket, the sugar plum, thornapple, chokecherry, and aspen, that may hold grouse and woodcock. It is impossible that there
isn't a holdover in the way you study the details of cities with their
human animals. In the French or Mexican countryside you are liable
to wonder what kind of birds, game or otherwise, favor what thickets, and what kind of fish favor the riffles or eddies of the Loire, Rhône,
or Yaquí rivers. Not to push it too far but there's certainly an element of stalking in a New York or Los Angeles meeting, and when
you enter a saloon you are prone to study which of the couple of dozen
human animals there might present a problem.

There's no particular virtue in hunting and fishing. The most irksome qualities about them are the sorry bumpkin mythologies surrounding the sports, and especially promoted by the industries that
supply the hunters and fishermen with equipment. When asked while
giving a lecture in Portland, Oregon why I still hunt I merely joked,
"Because I'm less evolved than most." A more honest answer would
be "Because that's the way I grew up." The most skilled hunters and
fishermen that I've known have almost invariably been the most modest and never to my mind identified their sports with our culture's
banal notions of manhood, which is a matter of costumery rather than
substance. There is nothing quite so fatuous as a man self-consciously
trying to act manly with our media's cues. (With women there is a
direct equivalent in the smirkish pouts of pinups that none of us have
actually seen in real life.)
     The fact of the matter is that if you're going to be any good at
fishing and hunting you're far better off leaving what you think of as
your "self" back home or at the office, or if you take a "self" along it
should be an earlier version, say back when you could be delighted
as a dog looking at a fresh place to hunt. If you wish to feel manly a
demolition derby or Big Time Wrestling is more appropriate. Funny
how true returning heroes of war more closely resemble Gary Cooper in *High Noon* than the braying John Wayne, as devout a draft
dodger as so many of our political leaders.

On the other side of the smudgy coin the forces of antihunting seem to be increasing, but then this effort is fueled largely by the idea that there is a sacred monoethic by which we all might live. If I readily admit that fully half of all hunters are swinish and regularly betray all notions of fair chase I haven't come up with anything that isn't typical of the norms of human behavior. People can have nearly terrifying limitations in terms of the life actually lived in our wide country. I once spoke with a well-informed antihunter in the questionable atmosphere of Washington, D.C., where everyone likes to forget where they're from. I described a South Dakota farm-ranch family that works improbably hard eleven months and three weeks a year, taking a single week off in the late fall for pheasant hunting. Why would you want to deny them this? He seemed to try hard to imagine this family but it wasn't possible. He couldn't mentally describe their world. Educated circles are shot through with a fungoid self-righteousness about matters with which they haven't had a filament of experience. At a party recently I was describing the improbable skills of a very large mixed-blood (Ojibway) hunter and fisherman I know who at times will drink a full bottle of whiskey with his dinner which is admittedly a bit much. A bright young woman, a sociologist out of the University of Michigan, said my friend was in "denial." Without apparent success I tried to point out that the word "denial" didn't exist in his world so it couldn't be a problem, and that a great number of people haven't been exposed to such concepts so why bother painting them with an etiolated academic brush? And why try to stop a UAW assembly line worker at a Buick plant from deer hunting as he's done for the past thirty Novembers? What would you put in his life rather than his late-autumn hunt?

Back to the beginning. Sometimes my father would take an iron skillet, a baby-food jar of bacon fat, salt and pepper, and a loaf of my mother's salt-rising bread along to the river so we could fry some trout for lunch. This was simple enough, far better than a sandwich, and an integral part of what you were doing. Catching fish, then eating them, goes back a long way. Years later while deer hunting we usually ate the liver and the heart right after the first kill. In my trips to Zihuatanejo the past two years we usually kept a few fish from the morning catch, which would be cooked for us on a tiny island shaded with palm fronds at noon.

In our personal mythologies ("mythology" in the old sense of the stories that are the main fuel of our beliefs) the separate pieces with age can come together and form a not totally familiar whole. Perhaps much of your life is too close to be comprehensible, just as if you wore seventy-seven layers of clothes and had become unsure if your body was beneath them. This can go on and on. A man can wear a corporate "mask" until he's fifty-five, retire early, then he finds that either he can't take off the mask or, if he does, there's no face under it. We can all become suffocated by daily career assumptions so that there's nothing left to distinguish us but our career assumptions. We leave out of our life the learning of skills that give us pleasure except those tied to our livelihood.

Our true daylight comes when we take some time off and are doing something else radically different enough to get a clear view backwards. Frankly, this isn't always pleasant, and when I'm involved in long bouts of fishing and hunting I know in my heart that despite the niceties of having my fiction published in twenty-three languages I'm basically a "working stiff" like anyone else, and that when I'm fishing and hunting with the right attitude I reenter the woods and rivers with a moment-by-moment sense of the glories of creation, of the natural world as living fabric of existence, so that I'm both young again but also seventy thousand years old.

It is interesting when you think of religion how evidently easy it is to defile our most sacred impulses. You need only read the daily newspaper to see that in our political life, religion is a way that all the money is cleansed, though greed has long since been abolished as one of the seven deadly sins. Over the years I've been told a hundred times by a hundred hapless idiots that money is the only way we keep score.

It's fun to tell them that what they say is doubtless the culture's motif but if universally followed we would be without a single thing to make life worth living, no art or literature or music, or any natural areas left that have not been trashed. You can even reduce the principle of defilement to the sacrament of marriage where you witness the joining of lovely, intelligent young people who are pasted to each other like decals, and a few years later they are in court with lawyers, filing their teeth and trying to spit on each other.

The most effective way of ruining hunting and fishing is to make them into the rigid forms of routine that doubtless and of necessity pervade the rest of your life. I must have seen dozens of businessmen treating their bird dogs like flunky employees and then becoming angry at the lack of response in the dog. A dog must become your platonic lover, as close as a friend gets. My longtime hunting crony Nick Reens will hunt four big running English setters for two hours and never utter a word except something kind for a good point or retrieve. Dogs are alarmed and confused by shouting. If properly trained they should feel absolutely free to find you birds with their miraculous noses with as little interference as possible. You are basically the "shooter" and the dog is your mentor as hunter. Of course I've seen grown men, including myself, break into tears over an irascible dog. My current English setter, Rose, has little concept of time and if she's thirsty and we're within a mile of a river she'll regularly run off for a drink and brief swim. She's not apologetic when she returns. Since you have no choice you say like a father with a wayward daughter, "It's okay as long as I know where you are."

The routine problem a fisherman can easily enter is the rather comic one of equipment: you simply think you can buy your way out of your ineptitude with the right expensive gear. Given, there's no question that quality rods, reels, flies, waders, and clothes are better than those of poor quality, but then I keep recalling an old friend, a true yokel, returning to the car with a creel full of plump trout and his battered eight-dollar fly rod and delaminating Japanese flies. Admittedly the fish were feeding well that evening but above all this miserable caster could "read" a river from long experience. If you can't perceive the nature of the five percent of the river in which the fish actually live, that two-thousand-dollar outfit doesn't mean anything. Knowledge of habitat, of habits of the prey, the simple fact that both game birds and fish like to hang out in their little natural restaurants mean everything. You have to have acquired the skill to cast or shoot but they both come with time.

The potential enemies greed and impatience are always there. One day it was lightly raining and getting colder moment by moment so that my pant cuffs were frozen and crackling and my fingers were numb. My dog at the time was a fat Lab named Sand who as she became older also became quite critical of my missed shots, which on that day had amounted to five in the hour I had been hunting. Three of the shots were difficult but two were easy and I knew it was my impatience, my rising anger at the weather and the idea that I had to leave my remote cabin the next morning for the responsibility of home. We were almost back to the car and there was a childish lump in my throat because I had planned on having a roasted grouse for dinner when Sand put up a bird far to my left on my blind side. I whirled and merely shot at the pine grove where the flying bird had disappeared, a thousand-to-one shot but, as they say, why save twenty cents? My critical dog retrieved the bird from the far side of the grove but, though it pleased me, it didn't quite leaven my shame over my shitty attitude. These were the days when any man can become ten years old, if not a monster killing machine or a game hog, an accurate reflection of our culture. I'm often reminded of what Big Soldier, an Osage chief, said: "I see and admire your manner of living . . . You can do almost what you choose. You whites possess the power of subduing almost every animal to your use. You are surrounded by slaves. Everything about you is in chains, and you are slaves yourselves. I fear that if I should exchange my pursuits for yours, I, too, should become a slave."

Years ago with my old friend Guy de la Valdéne, whose mother was a friend of the crooner, I visited Bing Crosby's home south of San Francisco. We were showing him a fly-fishing tarpon movie Guy had made starring a scruffy bunch of hippies, including Richard Brautigan, Jimmy Buffett, Tom McGuane, and myself, all successfully misbehaving in Key West though we did fish every single day. These were Bing's last days and he seemed to look askance at us as most of his fishing had been done with the sport's fashion plates. I was overwhelmed by his collection of fly rods and English shotguns, every single one exceeding my net worth at the time. Oddly, this beautiful equipment over the years begins to appear in a morose light since it tends to be bought as the time available to use it disappears. The equipment becomes mementos for a longed-for life.

The Wall Street mogul sorts through a thousand dry flies on a wintry evening in New York, glancing at the glass cabinets of fly rods and shotguns. I'm a poet acquaintance of his wife and have escaped her party to talk to this man who is happy to do so, describing his planned fishing in the coming summer that will include four days in Montana and an equal amount of time in Iceland for Atlantic salmon. It was nearly impolite but I admitted I had fished brown trout ninety days in a row the previous summer. I didn't say I had accumulated fifteen hundred dollars, which was enough at the time to support my wife and daughter for the summer months, offering me the freedom to fish and write poems. Mentioning small sums makes rich men nervous. He was looking out the window at the snow with ineffable melancholy, lost in the struggle between money and the heart's pleasure. Unfortunately, many years later while on a prolonged screenplay binge fueled by greed I was a similar man looking out a black window and wondering what if I make a bunch of money and die before I can spend it to buy the free time to fish and hunt?

I'm sitting on a hillock up in the woods listening to Rose's beeper in the distance. She's on point about a quarter mile away on the far side of a wild raspberry thicket. We're near the home farm and this covey of young grouse is doubtless tired of Rose who has been pointing them for months. The grouse often land in the mulberry tree at the far end of the garden and Rose points them from the yard, immobile and drooling behind the fence several hundred feet from the unmindful birds.

I can't walk up on Rose and break the point because I twisted my ankle yesterday. Luckily it's three weeks until the season opener and tomorrow we're heading for Montana where I'll fish out of a river drift boat for fourteen days. I like drifting because I never was an expert wader having been swept away a couple of times. The slippery rock bottom of the Yellowstone River doesn't allow the kind of dreaminess I can fall into while fishing, or hunting for that matter, where the quality has gotten me lost more than once, twice, three times. On the Yellowstone a half-dozen years ago I was thinking about all of the otter I had seen in my life and how much I like their curious voices and the way they can porpoise through the water. At the very moment the images of otter were passing I thought I saw a large one going for my floating dry fly and I jerked it away. Only it wasn't an otter. It was the largest brown trout I've ever seen rising to a fly in nearly fifty years of fishing. My guide and friend Danny Lahren looked at me strangely but said nothing. It was one of those days it didn't pay to be a poet.

Sitting there on the hillside waiting for Rose to break her point I remembered two years ago in Arizona when she was up a slope too steep for anyone but a goat or mountaineer to follow and I had to sit under a mesquite and doze while she pointed two quail coveys in succession that finally broke. This was one of the long silences in sport that Tom McGuane has written so eloquently about. In a fishing trance at my desk the other day I wrote this:

> I'm sixty-three and can drop dead
> at any moment. Thinking this in August
> I kissed the river's cold moving lips.

Last fall we were in Montana for my September trout fishing, a visit repeated nearly every year since 1968, a time when Michigan brown trout fishing began to disintegrate due to canoe traffic. (We have some nice rivers if you like night and dawn fishing, or care to hit the beaver ponds for brook trout, a pleasant if somewhat limited form of angling.)

On the Yellowstone River the first five days were a mixture of nasty weather, bleak fishing, and the equally nasty business of finding property on which to build a home. The fishing turned good on September 11, a date everyone knows. I was fairly gasping when I fled the house for the river, the brain whirling with tears and shed blood. In the ensuing days I gradually ignored television, opting for National Public Radio where thought is offered to the language. Television presents the questionable presumption that talking is thinking, that unpremeditated logorrhea offers something of value to the public, along with the ceaseless replaying of the visual of planes hitting the buildings, as if the controls of this media were manned by child psychotics. A thousand pundits seemed to rehearse the wisdom they offered us during the Y2K problem.

Meanwhile, on the river I saw rafts of ducks, hundreds of snipe, bald and golden eagles, the majesty of the river herself and the trout she held and nurtured. On two of the days I caught a half-dozen brown trout of around three pounds each and lost two grand fish whose power I could feel in my rib cage and spine. All anglers seem to have their species preferences but with each brown trout (banal name!) I remember the first one I held in my hand on the banks of the Pine River, the red and gold iridescent spots which held a fascination to a seven-year-old that would be equaled only far later by his first naked lady.

The last week of fishing was grand indeed except for the thousands of moments of consciousness when the world intruded its bloody fist, and at the end of the day when you stepped off the Mackenzie drift boat onto the shore and the consciousness of what had happened blossomed with the charm of the mushroom cloud we had all memorized as children. I was helplessly drawn back to my brooding over my uncles in the South Pacific at age twelve while I caught a brown trout in northern Michigan.

* * *

Back to my cabin and the early weeks of bird season with the wind off Lake Superior at over forty knots during a three-day blow, an autumnal torment that usually doesn't happen until mid-October. Though my dog Rose is nearly eight years old she doesn't recognize the meaning of bad weather. She watched me pack my hunting clothes and shotguns and after the five-hour drive to the cabin the rain that was sweeping horizontally across the cabin clearing meant nothing to her. I refused her pleas, drank a bottle of wine while making dinner, went to bed listening to the cabin shudder. Twice in the night Rose got off her couch, presumably to check if I was alive and would take her hunting in the morning. Desire and intensity mean a lot in bird dogs and with them come no recognizable limits. In the morning we hunted in a gale and I couldn't have become more wet if I had drowned but Rose was very happy with a completeness I deeply envied.

PRIVATE RELIGION

The first prayer went:

Now I lay me
down to sleep.
I pray the Lord
my soul to keep.
If I should die
before I wake
I pray the Lord
my soul to take.

Naturally when it was uttered every evening the prayer occasionally became rote or gibberish. During World War II I recall, "Bless all the children throughout the world especially those who are cold, sick, and hungry" was added. As kids we prayed for ourselves and for other kids, our own kind as it were, and these prayers became as familiar to us as those childhood paths by which we found our way around our neighborhoods whether rural or urban. If we had a dog we could still see its butt wagging before us through the thicket to an alley behind Mrs. Carlson's, her daughter tortured by paralysis, past Bozell's, Goodrich's, the woodlot behind the hospital where I lost an eye, across the street and through the Kilmers' hedge to their back door where their son David beat on a porch railing with a ball bat.

These paths located us in our young world. Much later prayer became asking the inconceivable from the improbable, whether clawing the rug in L.A. while drunk or drugged and trying to remember the Lord's Prayer, or reciting it on an airliner with a burning portside engine above the Sahara Desert. And the web of beloved paths began to stretch around the world, Cheyney Walk in London, counter-clockwise around the Luxembourg Gardens in Paris, beside the Yellowstone River in Montana, South American port cities, between your agent's apartment and your mind doctor or Elaine's in New York City, mountain paths near the Mexican border, the paths near the cabin and farm so familiar that you don't notice them.

I have supposed that the quality of wonder, or awe, as such, is curiosity magnified and exalted. Childhood, and perhaps adult prayers for some, allay fear, a word path to become less lost. Wonder gives direction to prayer. A child gradually is curious about who made the trees, sun, or moon. It certainly wasn't his parents. Humility is al-ready there because he can't be much smaller than he already is. The question day by day is how to navigate the incomprehensible world he has been thrust into. He has been taught prayer and has learned his own first paths with tips from brothers, sisters, and friends. Paths and prayers don't so much become confused with each other but are interwoven, arising as they do at the apex of our youthful vulnerabil-ity. Later on paths are followed for years without more than nominal attention to prayer except in dire emergency, or the deaths of any of those we love, or when uncontrollable fears boil over in addiction or divorce, other pathetic events soaked in invisible blood.

I never found myself in a dark woods in the middle of life's journey. I've been there all along for professional reasons. For a novelist and poet it is the "negative capability" that is to be valued, the willing-ness to hold before the mind the thousands of questions flesh is heir to without forcing an answer more questionable than the question. This position for a writer can easily become a posture so that rather than a lifelong dance with the multifoliate questions, one is a geezer who continues to mutter a sequence of no's that in themselves have become quite fashionable. The negatives are easily as mildewed as a museum cloakroom on a rainy day. Whitman thought that poets should "move wild laughter in the throat of death." And Yeats questioned, "What portion of the world can the artist have who has awakened from the common dream but dissipation and despair?"

Of course no one appears to have the definitive clue as to what happens to us after we die, the singular dominant answer the religions of the world deal with in terms that aren't altogether reassuring. I had old Northridge in my novel *Dalva* say, "If nothing happens we won't know it," which in itself is a fatalistic shaggy-dog joke. Few chins are held high when thinking of death within the very indefinite reprieve we are given.

Deaths we witness at remove can seem starkly individual. Not since the Civil and Indian wars have we collectively witnessed thousands ground into red library paste instanter than we saw in the World Trade Center. The only conceivable response was a howl as long as the breath could hold it, then to begin again and lapse into prayer.

We may live together but we usually die alone. I have tried to imagine the way Mozart rose up in his bed that evening trying to sing the alto part while others in the room rehearsed his *Requiem*. He died in the morning at age thirty-five but leaving us his immeasurable gift, his profound and antic spirit testing the limits of the beauty the ear could perceive. So few attended his thunderstorm burial we cannot be certain where in the earth his body rests. The Zennists say that "ashes don't return to wood," a lucid slap for everyone's vain face.

Curiously, our intelligentsia (of which I hesitantly number myself) tends to treat religion as if it were trying to keep the canned cat food off its hands. Not the least of the causes of this aversion is the profoundly bad behavior of the world's religions in historical terms, especially when they tie themselves to notions of ethnic virtue. This is no newer than the oldest shoe in the world, about 14,000 years old to be exact. Sheer repulsion in the ranks of the intelligent but literalminded is a simple enough antimagnet. I have noticed, however, with

certain surprise that within the history of the quasi-Modernist movement from 1870 onward that many of the grandest intellects, from
Kierkegaard to Einstein, have had no problem evincing a certain faith.
Of course a hundred of the largest minds on earth discussing God,
chaos, and the cosmos are still utter heathens in the minds of fundamentalists who somehow believe that the gays and feminists contributed to the demise of the World Trade Center. This kind of imbecility
is essentially comic and reminds me of the kind of southern preachers created by novelists Flannery O'Connor, Harry Crews, and Barry
Hannah. I must add that northern preachers aren't immune to these
rabid postures.

When I was around fourteen and became a Bible-thumping fun-
damentalist for a year or so it was my curiosity that stole my faith. A
Baptist minister told me that I shouldn't be reading Kant's *Critique
of Pure Reason* and that Beethoven and Mozart were the devil's music. I imagined that this included the Berlioz and Grieg that my sister and I loved to listen to on my twenty-five-dollar record player. I
must have read the New Testament a dozen times and found it quite
devoid of my minister's attitudes toward culture. Nearly fifty years
later I was further consoled reading Stephen Mitchell's splendid *The
Gospel According to Jesus* where the actual proven words of Jesus, about
a dozen pages in total, are as crisp and encompassing as a moonlit
winter night and as directly intimate as our breath.

Recently one night in the southwest I dreamt of a man who went
into the nearby mountains and saw a dancing god. While still half
asleep at daylight I imagined the end of the story. The man comes
back from the mountains and tells a disbelieving friend whom he takes
back up the mountain to see the dancing god. Now the word gets
out and the man needs to replace his normal livelihood and begins
charging people for their dancing-god tour. Fearing loss of power the
man strenuously preaches the lesson that the dancing god can't be
seen without his intercession. A temple is built at the gateway canyon to the mountain. And so on. There is no vision so holy that it
escapes its susceptibility to defilement. The earth is soaked with the
blood of religious entropy. A few years ago a friend visited a rather

threadbare sheikh in Saudi Arabia who was still quite irritated about the Crusades so many centuries before. Part of the impulse of the Methodist missionaries in getting the Lakota to wear trousers was that the Lakota would then work to get money to put in their trouser pockets, replacing their love of hunting, dancing, lovemaking, and fighting.

Nonetheless, how I prayed as a young Christian for the salvation of the world, with only the slightest filament of doubt that the prayers failed to penetrate the ceiling of my little attic room. My parents who were polite Congregationalists endured and indulged my silly *pronuncimientos* on the nature of sin though my dad teased that his own father had been saved at a Billy Sunday revival but the cleansing had lasted only "a couple of days." There were a lot of books and classical music in our home and that spelled doom for my earnest intolerance. I didn't stop listening to the opera on the radio on Saturday afternoons with my mother. I didn't stop reading Steinbeck, Cather, the naughty Erskine Caldwell, and William Faulkner. I could not stop the way that visuals of women's naked bodies would errantly pass before me while I prayed, or the way the intensity with which I tried to dismiss these visions made them even more lurid. I'd be praying for the salvation of my parents, brothers, and sisters, and there would suddenly appear an image of a red-haired girl from Bible club pulling down her white panties. The grief and confusion would disappear only when I was lost in a good book, say Gibbon's *Decline and Fall of the Roman Empire* where everyone seemed to drink too much wine and carry on, or better yet, Caldwell's *God's Little Acre* where women acted out my unwilling fantasies. (Many years later as an arrogant, neophyte Zen student I had no more luck with controlling my mind, and where once during prolonged sitting mediation a partially clothed Lauren Hutton emerged from a nail head in a pine board across the room.) It became apparent, though, by the time I was sixteen that I was not called to a holy profession as I had previously thought. "Many are called but few are chosen," the Bible says. I experienced a minor resurgence of devotion as a senior in high school when I discovered Dostoyevsky, who swallowed me whole. If I couldn't become a regular Christian I could at least fol-

low the lunatic versions of the Great Russian, not the best path for
mental health I learned. There can't be an author in the history of
Western literature who more thoroughly abrades the nerve ends, bursts
the neurons, than Dostoyevsky.

The intellectual or "learned man" can feel trapped by his doubt, his
cynicism not only about angelic spheres but about the very notion
of a religion itself. It would be especially difficult for an anthropologist to whom the primitive skeletal structures can be seen in most of
our cultural manifestations. To whom may a brainy anthropologist
turn in dire straits? He can repeat a hundred names for God from a
hundred cultures, utter dozens of liturgical glyphs, picture the ancient
friezes, tablets, scrolls with which the cultures try to frame reality in
an acceptable manner. At this point it might not be helpful for our
anthropologist to turn to our own historically peculiar culture in
which the most public manifestation of devotion appears to be money.
On our long way back from Montana to Michigan after the September 11 tragedy we saw many motel marquees that read "In God We
Trust," a message that is also on our money. We would have preferred
something on the order of "We pray that this doesn't happen again."

I daily wonder if the bedrock of my own private religion is fear and
incomprehension. Some degree of courage is in order if you wish to
fully admit your life. You have to take a draught of ego poison to
accept the full dimensions of your banality, your sheer corniness and
ordinariness, the monstrous silliness of private ambitions and sexual
fantasies, your loutish peacockery, your spates of sloth, all of which
is to say that you were specifically not destined for the spiritual big
time. The coup de grâce, the grand trump card in this little exercise
in self-knowledge, is when you comprehend the extent and full nature of your secret, your private religion.

    Here we may talk of contents: in my Dopp kit I have a tiny pink
pig my younger daughter gave me at least twenty years ago because I

traveled frequently and the pig would keep my plane from crashing. It's worked wonderfully so far. In my left trouser pocket I carry a small tubular stone that was extracted from a cave in New Mexico and polished. The stone reveals hundreds of slender layers composing millions of years of geological history. It is called a "jish" and is carried to remind you of mortality and that the earth is all that lasts. A jish is usually contained in a small bag made of doe leather but my bird dog Rose ate my bag with its pinch of corn pollen. It is consoling to give the jish a squeeze when life becomes especially difficult. I could mention the contents of my granary where I write but the dozens of objects I think of as somewhat "sacred" mostly reveal only my Pleistocene pack-rat nature. I've been accumulating and often discarding such objects since childhood, from "magic" marbles and ball bearings, to a sperm-whale tooth, to a brass body tag ("corpse no." blank) from our Indian Wars, to a clutch of bird feathers.

Why? I'm unsure. Crows, ravens, and bears mean a great deal to me and they are part of my life for much of the year. My obsession with wolves faded away because my heart was getting too aggressive. I think that all these objects of devotion tend to be from the natural rather than the man-made world for the somewhat accidental reason that I grew up in northern Michigan in contiguity with the natural world. In most respects I'm emotionally not far from the brokenhearted little old lady fingering her rosary beads, though my liturgical words are those of a rarer bird.

As I've said we must add awe to our fear and incomprehension. A bear tooth or raven feather in my hand enlarges my consciousness on an immediate level, sometimes in the manner of a slight electric shock. The imagination flies to deep in the woods and to fields where particular thickets are my functioning churches in several locations throughout the country, and one in Burgundy in France where I stay with a friend. I tend not to pray in these thickets but to let my mind alone until it empties out and I'm simply a human animal sitting in a thicket. When I say my morning prayers in my studio or car, I try to avoid making any sort of special case for myself. I admit I have prayed because droughts, the lack of rain, drive me batty what with having come from farm families way back when, and owning a farm at present, an ancient prayer to be sure. I generally circle around through family and friends, especially those who are mentally and physically ill. Here I am always startled by the sheer numbers with breast and prostate cancer. Sometimes, but more rarely as I grow older, I revert to the plaintive little boy and offer up something from a meager wish list. "I wish I could figure out how to make a living without commuting to Hollywood." That one was offered up years ago and was successful though I should add that my relationship with the showbiz community had been working toward mutual fatigue.

I've long supposed that this idea of making a special case for yourself is the biggest moral failing in prayer, and this is especially hard for a poet and novelist who has spent a lifetime making a special case for his vision of the world. We're getting close to two centuries of living with the artist whether sculptor, poet, writer, painter, composer (maybe the performer) as an isolate, Romantic hero, an outlyer and often outcast, a shaman without portfolio, a person who has with considerable wind, valid or not, blown up the ego to dirigible size in order to buffer himself against the blows of his fellow citizens, real or imagined. This is not the kind of person to admit that we are all "like sheep who have gone astray." He sees himself with often indisputable evidence as unique, but so is everyone else to an individually specific degree. We will ignore the Ichabod Crane–Don Quixote aspects of the artist because ridicule and irony are no help to us at this peculiar juncture of the twenty-first century.

And neither is the kind of religion that presupposes a virtue to wealth helpful at this time. Among a certain group religion is used to effectively cleanse money and the Gospels' admonition to take care of the poor is misinterpreted as "a few of the poor." How many times have we heard that five million children go to bed hungry every night? Not certainly as many times as we've read and seen pieces on the laudatory aspects of great wealth. The top two or three percent of our population has had a decade-long field day that never trickled down to the bottom fifty percent. In my own lifetime I've seen the apotheosis of greed as a virtue, and brutal insensitivity become enlightened self-interest. We may do as well as all but a few countries but that scarcely makes us a Christian nation except to those who bathe in patriotic gore out of habit and stupidity. Neither the emperor and consorts nor the citizenry is wearing the sacramental clothing it chooses to think it is wearing. A simple, private reading of the Gospels would tell them so.

There are comic aspects to reading religious texts, especially to a writer addicted to the sensuosities of language. Ostensibly sacred texts are almost invariably stilted to the degree that they resemble legal language. You wonder if this is so because the priestly and administrative classes in organized religion wish us to trip and fall without their help. Lucidity is undervalued and one is reminded of sentimental sex scenes where the orgasmic woman falls back on great waves of nothingness. If the great message is there, why is the language purposefully inept? Why the hushed, funereal tones to announce joy? I recall those sodden semimartial hymns of my childhood, so lugubrious your ass deadened against the pew in minutes. It was utterly startling to parishioners when a black choir was invited to my mother's church. This was a "joyful noise unto the Lord." Buddhist texts are often equal snoozers with notable exceptions of contemporary translators like Thomas Cleary, the roshi Nelson Foster, or Burton Watson. The diction of Zen students is sometimes quite silly, speaking as they do in the pidgin manner of a Japanese trying to learn English. All of which is to say the seeker must sweat blood, not necessarily for the answers but for the questions. Is there a God? What will happen to me when I die? Of course in the next few pages these questions will be answered.

In the past few years I've experienced the resurgence of the small after a lifetime of pursing the Big, including big novels, big fish, big animals, big country, big trips, big money, in short a big life. I can't specify the time and experiences that turned me to the small and indeed it was a gradual process, helped by reading E. O. Wilson, Harold Edleman's *Neural Darwinism*, the works of science writers David Quammen, Timothy Ferris, Gary Nabhan, and other texts, mostly clumsily digested, on botany, the human genome, and agriculture. I appear not to have the brain size I had assumed because this material was hard to understand, comically so as I would master details one day and mastery would vaporize by the next. In any event I began to write small poems, the genre of poetry having led me by the nose through my lifetime and opening the door to the novel, the essay, the screenplay.

A lot of bluster went out of my life during a mental crackup a recent winter over the death of Ana Claudia Villa Herrera, age nineteen and a hapless migrant who died of thirst after crossing the border of Mexico into Arizona. Her death was the nexus of an investigation I did into our border problems, well enough if it had stopped there but it didn't. The arc of my life, past and present, developed wobbles and curlicues. I had not only pulled the rug out from under myself, I had also removed the floor and basement. I could walk but I couldn't hunt for quail in the mountains along the border. If it weren't for my dog Rose demanding a daily run I would have become immobile. The radical difference between this depression and a number of others scattered through my life is that this one came from the outside rather than the inside. Mentally I was back at eighteen after radical eye surgery reading Dostoyevsky who, after all, had said in *Notes from the Underground*, "I maintain that to be too acutely conscious is to be diseased." Added to this was the fact that Ana Claudia was the same age my beloved sister Judith had been when she died at nineteen along with my father in a car wreck caused by a drunk driver, hence especially needless deaths. Ana Claudia and Judith began to wear the same face and though I didn't know Ana Claudia I began to give her many of Judith's characteristics. I also began to imagine myself in a dark basement and though the floor was cement it quaked in rhythm with my thoughts. In a curious, almost amusing manner I recognized this nadir as a nadir. I watched a French movie about the gypsies called *Latcho Drom* and found myself weeping copiously with the unselfconscious compassion a child feels for his very sick dog. My personality with its reassuring pretensions had fled and I wasn't interested in looking for it.

It's amazing how ineffective a mind can be when studying itself. The mind keeps trying to tell itself a linear children's story to cover the life it has watched the body live. The mind keeps trying to be an observer, a spectator, rather than the director. R. D. Laing said that "the mind of which we are unaware is aware of us." This suggests an extra dimension largely unavailable to us but doubtless vital. When you trek toward this mind country the borders you sense seem impenetrable but nonetheless visible. You see clearly that the linear is a hoax and the last thing the tectonics of consciousness follow is our world of letters and numbers. The bursting of your neurons follows paths that make the grandest computers look like McGuffey's Readers. This doesn't make me pessimistic about the usefulness of computers only that they don't create works equivalent to Shakespeare or Mozart nor are they meant to. Curiously humans have always been more interested in process than subject. A laptop at base is a stick used by a chimpanzee to get the delicious ants out of a hole in a log. Meanwhile the mind soars and plummets for a grace note to heal its inconsolable state. In my own case all of the clues to my plummet had floated around for years. The solace was everywhere, often infinitely small.

I think that I was nineteen when Rimbaud's "Everything we are taught is false" became my modus operandi partly because Rimbaud's defiance of society was vaguely criminal and at nineteen you try to determine what you are by what you are against. I was on the run among New York, Boston, San Francisco, and Michigan by thumb, or Greyhound bus if I was flush. My baggage was of enormous consequence, a change of clothes but mostly anthologies of Russian and Chinese poetry, volumes of Rimbaud and Apollinaire, William Blake, copies of poems of John Clare and Christopher Smart, and a few Dostoyevsky novels. Only recently have I realized the degree to which these books were my religious texts and their unavowed intent was to teach me the secrets of reality, in short to explain the meaning of life. In honor of the hesitant admission that there might be a world outside my head I'd unsuccessfully take courses in economics, anthropology, and forestry when I'd return to college after forays east and west. But it is poetry that has stuck with me as a solution to the impulse. Poetry is free from the predominance of profit and the best of it offers up no lies.

"Ruin has taught me thus to ruminate," Shakespeare wrote in a sonnet. Years ago I was surprised at the mail I got after saying in a food column that it was easier for me to believe in the Resurrection than in the existence of the Republican Party. You might remember that earlier I mentioned I would explain the existence of God and what happens after we die. Perhaps I should have asked first for each of you to send me a nickel in soft money to aid in my search. After all, I'm giving you an indication of a private religion. If a forsaken Native American can say, "Take courage, the earth is all that lasts," we must all come up with something better than the "In God We Trust" on that nickel I've decided not to ask you to send.

My own answers might not do you any more good than spending a night in your basement freezer. I've been very lucky in writing poems for nearly fifty years as this practice does not discount visionary experiences. When a voice in a dream told me simply to be thankful that I had a chance to exist this gave me the freedom not to make a special case for myself. That my answers might appear intellectually embarrassing is utterly irrelevant.

Last spring while struggling to emerge from my logical depression over Ana Claudia I sat on our patio overlooking a creek dense with surrounding underbrush. I saw the cellular life of everything around me seething with activity and inside the cells the DNA that indicated the nature of their existences. It was during the upcoming night that I had the dream of the figure of God before time started hurling trillions and billions of handfuls of specks into the void that would eventually determine the nature of the universe and its inhabitants.

It is consoling indeed to wake up from this dream. I had returned to the small and was again the boy who prayed leaning against a huge stump far out in the woods, praying for all whom I loved but also errantly wondering what the grand tree had looked like. Down on the border we don't have much ambient light so the stars can become dense and almost milky. I have thought while looking at them of Gandhi's notion that it's pleasant that there will be no religions in heaven. I'm certainly not going to allow my blank wall of incomprehension to temper my reverence for nature and the universe. Lately astronomers have upped the number of galaxies from 12 billion to 90 billion. That makes fifteen apiece for everyone on earth. You're free to name your own. I have this belief that we'll continue to exist in one of those invisible but infinitely large specks that make up our being. I said once in a poem that we will see God but not with our eyes. That's fine by me. Naturally I could go on forever but I won't. I'm shining the tiniest, nearly invisible penlight on the matter just as I did on the death by thirst of Ana Claudia, or my sister so long ago.

A SHORT TOUR DE FRANCE

There were certain countries that I visited that I thought I loved but to which I never returned—Russia, Kenya and Tanzania, and Brazil, among others, despite thinking on my visits that I'd like to live awhile in these places. In Russia it was purely St. Petersburg, the presence of which was added to immeasurably by all the Russian literature I had read so that the streets, especially Nevsky Prospect, were utterly fabled. Hotel Europa was wonderful and I drank tea out of a glass, absurdly enough, like my heroes Dostoyevsky and Yesenin. However, this was in 1972 and I couldn't get used to the machine guns thousands of uniformed men were wearing as fashionable accoutrements. The illusion of Russia was fully popped when I finally landed at Bourget in sunny Paris in late October and actually knelt and kissed the ground. These were the same machine guns I later saw in Ecuador and Ethiopia, Kenya and Tanzania. Even though I've never been in the military machine guns, as opposed to sporting weaponry, are there for the sole reason of making bloody holes in the bodies of malcontents, a group of which I've always been a member.

You don't see all that many machine guns in Mexico, which is a scant fifteen miles from our winter home and which makes it not far enough away for the "otherness" I seek unless I go as deeply as Veracruz in the east or the Seri Indian country in the west. For some reason I seem to need the somewhat unsettling experience of flying across the ocean seven miles up in the air during which there are the remote thoughts of how well I swim, though I know it's the dive in the plane that matters most.

Of course it is easy enough to say that Mexico, or France for that matter, is "just" another country, but this idea is the nexus of the

xenophobic trance that most of us live and die within, our "geopiety."
We all know there are distinct similarities in countries, the moon and
sun glow down, people eat, drink, and die, their separate stock markets
are invariably up or down. Most have trees that become visible at
ground level and are joined by flowers and shrubs. Some people farm
and some "buy cheap and sell dear," an ancient definition of business,
but inside the relatively new academic discipline of human geography
our sameness is diminished by our differentness. Beyond our field of
vision, and the vision of all the separate media on earth, which in
themselves form illusionary "melting pots" because of laziness, greed,
and stupidity, constructing us all as like-minded members of the family
of man, there is a world of amazing difference that must be mildly
sought out. In the lobby at my hotel in Paris while waiting for someone I read in a puffy and slick magazine with a truly extraordinary
photo of a young woman's tummy that "lingerie is the theater of our
intimacy."

I'm simply not aware of anyone in the United States, and I must
have met and read hundreds of our writers, who would say such a
thing. It is, as we used to say, a "far cry" from making love to a woman
bent over a front fender of a Chevy pickup on a warm summer night.
You might later take a dip in a lake and even afterwards you don't
recall if any underpants were involved. She wore Levis and a T-shirt,
as a matter of fact. A bit of beach sand was involved in the second
go-around and also a pint of cheap, odorous whiskey and warmish
beer. The stars and a fingernail clipping of a new moon seemed much
closer to earth than usual. That night lingerie was definitely not the
theater of our intimacy but later in life there was less a tendency
to discount it. After all, there was a memorable childhood rhyme
chanted in the school yard:

> I see London
> I see France
> I see somebody's
> underpants.

*   *   *

Back in Paris on a rainy October night, I'm willing to admit I don't have a true affinity for this country but I like it here. In a dozen or more trips, and despite having taken college French, I can't handle the language. Maybe being attuned to American English enough to write exhausted the language region of my brain. I'm astounded now when I meet the child of Americans living here for a scant six months and the little round boy is already fluent. I have this idea that even in private moments local dogs speak French in a pleasant world from which I am excluded. Maybe the birds in the garden next to the hotel also. I create and memorize French sentences that seem to make the listener immediately melancholy. They look like they wish they were spelunking in the Pyrenees. I feel as foreign as Geronimo at the New York World's Fair at the turn of the century. I get by because of the kindness of strangers. In restaurants the staff seem pleased when I eat two servings of *têtes de veau* (a mélange made of a calf's head) and drink a full bottle of wine or so, my meal a pick-me-up as soon as possible after I land here, though gout has slowed this habit but not to a stop. If you're tired of hamburger go to France and eat what our hot dogs are doubtless made of which is everything after the good cuts are extracted from a carcass. My dad, who judged cattle at county fairs, told me when I was a child that hot dogs are made of "tits, tails, and assholes" of cows and pigs. When I return to America after a trip to France, landing in the grand city of Chicago, I do not hesitate to eat a hot dog or two at O'Hare Airport. My midwestern roots plunge as deep as the barnyard and slaughterhouse. "Vache folle," mad cow disease, doesn't seem to be a poignant threat these days. I feel as ex-empted as a girl in a French television movie I watched parts of one evening. She was a lion tamer at the circus and strutted around a cage chock-full of recalcitrant lions. Appropriately enough, she wore an outfit as scanty as a bikini, and at the conclusion of her performance she stretched out on a low dais with her parts no doubt pulsing in the humid air of the tent. A male lion with his tawny jaws dropped a red rose on her barely concealed pubis. The crowd was delighted. So was I, though there was the tremor of the movie critic hidden in my soul. This was France and I must suspend my disbelief over such emotional hyperbole. After all, life seems mysterious because it is.

In the Massif Central the weather is quite warm for late October, a reprieve from coming winter. This is fairly high country, nearly five thousand feet, and midwinter often brings blizzards, the photos of which remind me of northern Michigan, where I recall high drifts stacked against our barn in the years before we had sense enough to buy the small casita on the Mexican border for the winter months. The Massif Central barns are made of thick-walled stone and the roofs are thick slabs of stone. To some the area might appear bleak but I immediately love it. From the window of my small hotel with three rooms, appropriately called Les Monts, there is not a single visible light at night except a three-quarter moon. At dawn the fog begins to slowly lift from the deep gorge of the Tarn River. This gorge is an actual gorge of thousands of feet and my heart thumps when we go for a drive. My host senses that I'm vertiginous and offers to call Paris for his helicopter to take me to Arles in Provence in the morning. I weigh my childish fears, helicopters among them, and decide I'd rather walk, an impractical solution.

Americans are completely unready for the Massif Central. We certainly don't include France when we think of remote solitude. Our own relatively wild areas exist only with government protection or because they simply aren't economically viable. Areas such as the Great Plains and especially dismal swamps in both the North and South retain their wild and beautiful character because they resist the possibility of profit. My own home area in Michigan's Upper Peninsula, once it sacrificed its first-, second-, and third-growth trees to successive waves of the timber industry, and all but a remnant of copper and iron were drawn from the ground, was left alone to entertain hunters and tourists of usually modest means. The same sort of thing seems to be true of the Massif Central, where the highly valued cows are released from their barns in May wearing ritual garlands of roses. The grazing appears as sparse as that in Montana and Wyoming.

Hopefully the cows aren't as vertiginous as I am because much of the country is as rough and precipitous as the border country near Patagonia, Arizona, perhaps more so. Walking out on a peninsula between two gorges with my friend Maxime, who was inspecting a hunting property he wished to buy, I had an urge to sit down so I wouldn't fall off the earth. Despite the near verticality these canyon walls are fertile with grass and shrubs and support the wild Barbary sheep. I saw a large *sanglier* (wild pig) near the road and wondered how hard he had to work at eating to become that large. He was without the trough I had been using in restaurants but had attained a daring similarity to myself.

Why would I rather be in one place instead of another? I admit I accept some of my travel impulses without questioning, recalling that for much of my life I was frozen in one area for economic reasons. This is true of most people and now despite relative economic freedom I'm too obsessed with my work to be the kind of traveler who is habitually called "inveterate." The other day in Arles, down in Provence, I had lunch with a man I had met socially who admitted that all he did was travel. When lunch was nearly finished I inscribed a French translation of one of my novels for the bistro owner. I certainly don't carry these around but the proprietor pulled one from his capacious apron. He hoped I wouldn't be insulted if the dedication was made to his dog? Of course not, I said, and he fetched a very large chocolate Labrador who had obviously been on the same life-long diet as myself. Before greeting me the dog, appropriately named Lanvin, checked out the empty tables in the bistro for a stray snack, then came over and looked at me hopefully. A crust of anything would be better than a novel. The moment I didn't deliver, Lanvin slumped to the floor and slept. If you can't eat, sleep, doubtless is a more functional philosophy than most.

We haven't transcended the creature world to the point that we can avoid being painfully homesick for our dogs. Unlike the scrawny street dogs of Mexico, French dogs are offered up for petting once it is determined you are worthy. This is a happy consolation and when as a houseguest I said "*couche-toi, mon petit*" to an immense Alsatian guard dog he flopped to the floor. Victory in our time! He understood me.

Now it is November 1 and in the middle of the night a violent wind arrived with gusts, I later learned, of seventy m.p.h. The shutters slammed like rifle shots and I was naked on the balcony of the Nord Pinus in Arles trying to figure out how to secure them when a scenario hit me. What if an errant gust caught these huge shutters and locked me out? Someone might respond to my bellows and call the police and I'd be caught in a spotlight. Luckily this is France and it's far less likely that machine guns would be raised toward my round brown figure. Just pondering all this made me think of my diet, not that I wanted to be all that attractive to the police. Metaphoric food leaps came to mind. This chilly wind is the first mistral of the autumn season. Below me in Arles's Place du Forum is the statue of Gabriel Mistral, a poet of note. His frozen glance is aimed vaguely at the Rue des Arenes, the location of La Charcuterie, a *bouchon* (bistro) Lyonnais, a rare place indeed down in Provence, the home of France's healthiest cuisine, the fish and fresh vegetables that might be making me less substantial. Surely the cool wind might call out for the sliced beef snout and sausages I had yesterday when the wind was warm but my artistic curiosity got the best of me. We're always praying for good health, a mental activity that can't overcome the biological imperative a bear feels when cool weather hits and he prefers to eat a fawn rather than berries.

Of course in a foreign country it is as easy to be brought up short by melancholy as it is at home. The question "What am I doing here?" is pretty complicated. I admit that the path between Michigan and Arles began abruptly. Back home the media, the Industry of Alarm, was moment by moment vomiting forth its distortions, and from

Washington our blimpy suits were addressing the American People
with a totally dishonest air of familiarity, then fleeing anthrax germs
in the reverse of any conceivable profile in courage under the misas-
sumption that they were more vital to our well-being than postal
workers. Our country drifted in a state of free-floating anxiety with
the single bonus that we no longer heard of Gary Condit.

What better to do than to make a trip to France and fight
terrorism with red wine and garlic? In the arena of such violence a
novelist and poet with his fragile armament of language reminds one
of the kitsch nineteenth-century painting called *Orphan in a Storm*.
Hundreds of writers were quite willing to say a piece but the New
York firemen were invariably more to the point. Current events were
never the literary writer's metier. It takes awhile to forge in the smithy
of your soul the uncreated conscious of your race, as Joyce would have
it. I admit it's pleasant when you can best serve your country by
shutting up and going to France and wandering around Provence and
Bourgogne, empty of tourists, eating and drinking and thinking not
very deep thoughts.

Perhaps there's a bit of xenophobia in the hearts of all of us. Years
ago two men I knew made their first trip to New York City, got separated at Grand Central Station, and never found each other again
until returning home. This is funny and stupid enough to be disarming. When I'm alone in a foreign country and get lost in a city or the
woods I admit I mostly enjoy the sensation. I also enjoy listening to
a language I don't understand because you're thrown back on the
fragility of the human race and comprehend again that languages are
only sequences of agreed-upon sounds.

In the seventies on my first trip to France I was coming back
from a journalistic trip to Russia. I was dead broke but managed to
wangle some money out of the Paris office of a magazine I occasionally
wrote for in the States. Some money is a palliative when you're unsure
if the meal you're eating is going to cost you a few bucks or a fortune
despite your arduous figuring of the menu prices. You've heard a lot

of fearful gossip about swindles and all sorts of thievery. You're actually quite sick from a Russian parasite but existing quite well on red wine, Lomotil, and the energy of your curiosity. In a bistro a lovely woman is wearing a transparent blouse and her nipples are perky. This must be a fine country, you think. The street running past the bistro was a hangout of two of your heroes, Apollinaire and Henry Miller. You're thirty years old and regret again that all the money you had saved for a trip to France at age eighteen was spent on an unsuccessful eye operation.

For me in the early seventies the cityscape of Paris was totally literary. It seems a little daffy now but at the time the idea that I was walking in the same places as Rilke and Rimbaud had walked was akin to a priest or nun visiting the Mount of Olives or Bethlehem.

Save for bread and wine everything I ate seemed new and exotic, and of course the bread and wine themselves were better than my sandwiches and graduate-student Gallo back home. I had eaten a little French food in Montreal at a lunch given our convention of poets by Pierre Trudeau where he quoted at length and by memory Valéry and Rilke in French and German, not the sort of thing Lyndon Johnson was doing at the time. I had also eaten twice in New York's Brittany du Soir, a budget place favored by Francophile writers. I'm never quite sure how I became food obsessive though I can exclude early training. Ultimately food is only a part of the fabric and life. It is mistaken to try to extrapolate the precise content of a society from it as many writers do with France. After a ten-day binge and eating aioli (cod and vegetables with a pungent garlic mayonnaise) for lunch now I'm aiming for a bowl of soup this evening in Arles, my curiosity about food momentarily assuaged.

If you add another key element to understanding a country, such as television, the view expands though still falls well short of a whole picture. Transpose your thinking to the United States and imagine the deranged portrait of us by a foreigner limiting his study to what we eat and what we watch on television. Our cultural differences, however, are indicatory on television. In Arles I had watched parts of three nature documentaries out of Paris, shown during the daytime hours when children are watching, that have caught polar bears, black bears, and immense ocean turtles coupling with gusto. The turtles themselves are lovely creatures but the filming was transcendent, showing the lovers on the ocean bottom then rising up in embrace to the surface for air. Any toddlers or children watching such programs might presume that lovemaking is a normal activity, perhaps an attractive possibility in the future, just as it isn't a criminal waste of time to make an effort to prepare a meal. Conversely, French television is in the Stone Age in their special effects for movies that are supposed to frighten you. At first I thought one of these programs to be a comedy effort but learned otherwise. The monster was unworthy of a cheapish Halloween costume in a Missouri suburb. This isn't a grand failing and the ladies in the lotion commercials leave you sucking hot wind. Now we're back in a world where lingerie is seen as a theater of intimacy. This is undercloth- ing that offers absolutely no protection from the elements and is not imaginable in Kansas or Wyoming. And the price of the ticket to this theater of intimacy is expensive indeed. Through the shop- window in Paris I deduce that a single article is worth a substantial meal and a very good wine.

Now, the night before I leave Arles, I phone down for a wake-up call and the desk girl quickly delivers some unwanted fresh fax paper to my room. I recall that when I was in Paris with a friend he called re- ception for two foam pillows what with having an allergy to feath- ers. He received a nice omelet and was pissed off in that he's quite proud of his language abilities. I drink and eat everything in France and it's never made me ill, which is more than I can say for Florida, but then I have to eat everything unless I specifically point at the menu. My memorized lines have offered remarkable new items in my culinary experience. It can't be totally my fault. Years ago when we were in Paris together and Jack Nicholson had just come up from Nice he said that once you've played golf with a group of Frenchmen you're quite surprised that the country is so well run. Despite the caveats

and our own technological genius France is still well ahead in the
not so simple matter of how to live life from day to day.

Where do I actually belong, if anyplace, in this country that has meant
so much to me as an escape, a balm, an immense reservoir of food,
art, and literature? Years ago I contributed an essay to an issue of the
Psychoanalytic Review that concentrated on the idea of "dislocation."
How, where, and why do we feel at home mentally if not physically?
Where can we isolate our seemingly genetic geopiety?

Answers easily evade us as they become too obvious, too close
to the nose to be noticed, just as we are blind to our own peculiarities, the idiosyncrasies that we have lived with so long that we are
surprised when others think them odd. And perhaps the dominant
advantage of travel for a writer is to pull oneself out of the nest
in whose comfort the vision can become self-serving, truncated, the
nest itself losing oxygen with time so that the life lived becomes
drowsy.

It's comic to look back and see how much you've missed by
immediately making a habit out of your location. In Paris in the early-
morning hours I like to walk from my hotel near the Invalides to the
Luxembourg Gardens, and if I have time after circling these gardens
I continue on to the Jardin des Plantes and then back. I've done it so
often that on some occasions the walk becomes somnambulistic and
I'd be far better off taking out my map and trying something new.
But now this morning, in foggy Burgundy, it occurred to me that my
patterns reflect the country mouse needing some reminders of home.
The gardens give me the flora I depend on for minimal balance, and
I stick to the Hotel de Suede on Rue Vaneau partly because it's near
both my publisher's office and his apartment but mostly because of
all the birds I see in the garden of the Matignon. I've even sat in the
bathtub with my monocular and a dampish French bird book in order
not to miss anything out the window. I also admit that on my present
walk I can't resist reading all the menus behind their little glass windows, or following an attractive bottom for a block though French

girls tend to walk much faster than I do. On the way back I stop for a glass of Brouilly at the Select, a café on Montparnasse, and might read a newspaper though in my later years my tolerance for them is short. At the Select the cat Micky greets me at my table as he does other regular patrons.

If I go back to my first trip in the seventies when I stayed with a friend at his mother's intimidating Normandy château, I had the reassurance of a forest, gardens, horses, birds, the Dreux River, part of which had been diverted to feed the moat around the château so that you could lean on a wall and look down at large pike circulating in the clear water.

Later on at St. Malo in Brittany where I attended a literary festival each spring for several years the main attraction was, simply enough, the Atlantic Ocean and studying the captured pools at low tide, watching elderly ladies pluck crustaceans from the rocks, the delicious oysters and fish available, the sound of the incoming tide through the window at night, the ocean herself an incredible weapon against the claustrophobia that has marred and often controlled my life. All my mortal valves open up fully when I walk the long beach at St. Malo.

With the Saumur area it is the presence of the Loire. I suspect river sounds have a genetic component for us. I heard that in ancient India the insane were often tied to trees beside rivers for this soothing aural embrace. There's also this feeling that if you see people fishing you are in a good place, though hours pass without them catching anything out of the Loire.

Arles is easy. The Rhône which frequently smells sick-unto-death is a few blocks from my hotel, the Nord Pinus, which has rooms large enough to write in. The city with its overwhelming antiquity is containable so that you can walk its borders. The market is a polyglot splendor, less bourgeois than the markets of Avignon or Aix-en-Provence. If your tummy is slow to recover and you're worried about your ability to eat lunch, drink a midmorning pastis and visit the market in Arles, the vividness of which will crank up your primal appetites. As I've said so many times before, "Eat or die." The Camargue is also close by and when you drive out for dinner at Chez Bob's (great name) you see grand salt marshes and clouds of birds.

Marseilles is a scant hour's drive or train ride from Arles and is nearly always an essential of my French visits partly because my translator and friend Brice Matthieussent lives there, and partly because it's a city in a lovely location and lacks the sometimes irritating show-place aspects of Paris or Marseilles's American counterpart, San Francisco. I was also drawn to the city by early French warnings of "Watch out for the Arabs and Corsicans," which are akin to our own "Don't go to Harlem, New Orleans, the south side of Chicago, or Detroit," the ubiquitous "Don't drink the water in Mexico, or Arizona for that matter, where alkaline water is sure to attack your entrails." Warnings have goaded me onward all of my life.

It is in Marseilles that I not only walk fearlessly in my Lone Gee-zer costume, and splurge by staying in Le Petite Nice built on a rock peninsula jutting into the Mediterranean (the hotel is also the home of the splendid Passadat restaurant), but I travel over the granitic and cactus-covered mountain past Cassis to Bandol to Lulu Peyraud's Domaine Tempier where I am fed a grand lunch and meet her chil-dren, grandchildren, and great-grandchildren and drink her splen-did wines.

My last stop of several days is in western Burgundy in the Morvan area where I stay at the home of Gérard Oberlé, a writer and book dealer, and his business partner Gilles Brezol. They live in a manoir with 30,000 books and a dog named Eliot who capably guards the collection and guides me to his favorite places on the property, ani-mal holes, an old shed containing a fox skeleton, a place along a fence line where he barks at neighboring Charolais cattle whether they are there or not. Over the years I have sadly watched him leap ahead of me in age as dogs do.

This area of the Morvan is densely forested in places and I never quite get used to the idea that Julius Caesar was one of the first promi-nent local residents because the land is so decidedly rural and half wild with a reassuring density of green that would make Ireland fans happy. There is a tendency to eat too much here at the Manoir de Pron, an amount, in fact, that can't be walked off by an older man and an old dog. Once I stayed here a few days after a long French book tour and when I finally reached Paris I spent twenty-four hours drinking water without even touching bread. Yesterday morning a gentleman took me fly-fishing for trout on a small pond but there was a stiff, cool northern breeze and the brown trout glided by as elegant and as unreachable as my unattainable French sentences.

Way back whenever Lewis Thomas said in his profound *The Lives of a Cell: Notes of a Biology Watcher* that at heart we humans wish to be useful. This feeling of usefulness can be difficult for a writer to manage in the places I live, whether the small farm in northern Michigan, the cabin near the Canadian border, the casita near the border of Arizona and Mexico. The love of literature is not widespread in these areas, a monstrous euphemism. I don't need a pat on the back all that often but once or twice a year it's nice to reenter the larger human community as a stray dog, whether on occasional trips to Chicago, or to New York, and especially to France where the worth of my lifelong efforts are presumed to be useful if not admired.

A number of years ago during a state of exhaustion caused by my greed in working too hard in Hollywood (why blame them?) I was invited to give a lecture at a literary festival in Aix-en-Provence. I nearly didn't have the sense to go and when I reached the destination I still had black butterflies whirling in my head, a French idiom for the blues, which seems more striking than our "lump in the throat." In addition I had garden-variety jet lag so got up in the predawn dark at the Hôtel Le Pigonnet and walked downtown, passing through the cathedral where mass was being said. Outside I sat down in the baptistry steps in the first light and watched dozens of men and women set up their market stalls of fish, vegetables, meats, and cheeses. Meanwhile, I had seen a striking young woman enter the church, tripping up the steps beside me. Naturally I followed and what with mass being over I thought she might light a candle and pray for a future boy-friend who might be a sodden American. Instead, she climbed up to the organ loft and began playing Bach at a volume that jellied my bone structure and overexamined mind. Back outside the music seemed to hum through the stone steps into my backside. People at some of the market stalls listened raptly. I admit that tears formed and continued throughout her rehearsal. I can't say my spirit began to soar but it at least levitated so that on the walk back home even my peripheries of vision widened and the world at large regained lyric possibilities.

At lunch that day with twenty writers at the Café de Deux Garçons I was nearly asleep in my chair when a waiter asked me to sign the guest book. Everyone seemed to be watching as I leafed through the pages, not getting the point. I noted signatures like Balzac and Camus and the sweat of midwestern embarrassment popped out on my forehead. I signed without a flourish wishing to hide under the chicken thighs (with lemon and garlic) and drank a glass of wine in a single long gulp, staring at the ceiling and wondering about future messages from the French gods, a country where living well is the only revenge.

THE ROAD

Valentine, Nebraska; Duluth, Minnesota; LaCrosse, Wisconsin; Rodeo, New Mexico; Ajo, Arizona; the Seri Coast of Mexico; Jordan and Ekalaka in Montana; Bluff in Utah; Oxford, Mississippi; and the Florida Panhandle, not forgetting Dalhart, Texas: all exercise a strong pull on me so that before sleep, or within the enervation of insomnia, I can re-create what I have noted in the nature of their human populations, also the flora and fauna of the area, the geology, the geography of their landscapes. These places are in the top ten, but I often have to hold back the flood of Grove Street or MacDougal Street in New York City in 1957; North Beach in San Francisco in 1958; or even Estes Park in Colorado in 1954 and Key West in 1970.

In nowhere but favored locations are the peculiarities of human taste more captious and evident. There's a fairly recent word in the academic discipline of human geography, "geopiety," to help account for our profound xenophobia, or my often remarked fact that I've been in a hundred places in the United States the locals call "God's country." These people jump up and down, dance, organize parades in annual celebrations of their beloved locales, calling the fetes names like "Daze of Yore," "Frontier Days" (or Daze), "Old-Fashioned Days," or "Mountain Dreams," but then these celebrations appear to the outsider as brief respites in the torpor of daily lives, the ordinariness of survival preoccupations that afflict even New Yorkers.

When you stay at home years at a time the ceilings definitely lower themselves. If you're a young man, say eighteen or whatever, jumping from job to job, from changing and mounting tires to being a shovel man on construction sites to rudimentary farm labor, the workdays are full of daydreaming of elsewhere, some based on fact from hitchhiking home from Colorado at sixteen, the impulse for going there to see your first mountains, to driving to New York City to be a bohemian for two days and taking the subway after inquiries to Far Rockaway to see an ocean for the first time. Your own '47 Plymouth bought for fifty bucks barely takes you to work on time. On hot days of manual labor the fantasies of escape intensify: perhaps on a warm night in a bar parking lot in Joplin, Missouri, you may meet a barefoot ballerina. She recognizes your intrinsic worth. You splurge on a motel so she can shower. (In fantasies errant details must be dealt with.) She has a car and you drive to San Francisco where you swim under the Golden Gate Bridge holding hands after a hard day writing immortal poetry.

Soon enough you save nearly a hundred dollars and hitchhike to California on Route 66, ending up in Bakersfield because that's where the last ride took you. It's the middle of a hot night and there are no evident parking-lot ballerinas. After a few hours of empty thumbing you board a bus for San Francisco where you get to heavy-pet with a young woman in transparent high-heeled shoes who has a flask of whiskey and chain-smokes. You mutually and noisily conclude and a nearby geezer wakes and hisses, "Animals."

A year later you're married and there's not much freedom for two decades except the driving that's related to the miserable road between the married housing apartments and the university, the holiday drives homeward to visit parents and in-laws, the pathetically short vacation fishing trips, and a few longer drives to Key West and Montana to fish. A poet technically is supposed to be a "thief of fire" but as easily as anyone else he becomes a working stiff who drinks too much on late Friday afternoons. You begin to overcherish the memories of the freedom of earlier trips. You settle for bar pool and spectator sports. You begin to remind yourself of all of the men you know who speak of their golden days in the armed services, the singular exciting time of their lives. Clinical depressions become more frequent. I made far less money than it took to support my family, which required about twelve grand a year. I did seemingly countless poetry readings in public schools at a hundred bucks a crack for the

National Endowment for the Arts, an experience that made me permanently loathe public appearances. I tried journalism which got me to Russia, Africa, South America, and France but the assignments paid for only the time it took to write the articles, leaving me little freedom to write what I wished, and the most obvious economic lesson of all became obvious: survival work requires your entire life. I tried university teaching for two years but the closest metaphor was life in a zoo. I had two years of grants, a release from the zoo but a little problematic. When you first release wild animals from cages they are unwilling to leave a known environment for a speculative future outside the cage. A man quite easily suppresses his longing for freedom until this supposed longing becomes a cliché without energy. It appears that man is the only creature capable of tying and lying himself into interminable knots. I had met Jack Kerouac a couple of times and it mystified me that his recent success with *On the Road* meant only that he had freedom to become hopelessly drunk. Of course I was just nineteen at the time and there's no one as abrasively judgmental as a nineteen-year-old.

With the immodest success that came after the publication of *Legends of the Fall* in 1978 my life quickly evolved a kind of hysteria that I attempted to pacify with alcohol and cocaine. Success wasn't "indigenous" to my family with generations of what southern writers call "dirt farmers" behind me and what we in the North merely called "farmers." I was utterly unprepared because I had been told by my agent that no one ever heard of novellas and my publisher had said it was an "archaic form." The book wasn't an overwhelming publishing success but suddenly David Lean wanted to film the title story and John Huston the novella called *Revenge*. Even more heady in terms of experience was the flood of money. If you have averaged twelve grand a year for a decade and then have a year when you make well over a million bucks in contemporary terms you are utterly unseated from your slow-moving horse. Maybe it was actually a donkey I had been riding.

My singular wise choice at the time was to buy a Subaru 4WD, at age forty the only brand-new car I had ever bought. Those around me ridiculed the humility of this purchase for a new millionaire but I had something else in mind other than Thorstein Veblen's "conspicuous consumption." Escape, pure and simple. Since childhood when my left eye had been blinded my favorite locations had been thickets and now I intended to search for new and better and bigger thickets. Gradually my definition of thickets came to include distant, anonymous motels in remote towns and cities. In actual thickets there is ideally a stump to sit on and enough brambles so that you may frame the surrounding landscape in the apertures formed by branches. If you sit there long enough the natural world that surrounds you resumes its activities, either forgetting that you are there or accepting the idea that you are harmless because you are behaving harmlessly. Best of all you can see out and no one else can see in.

When you use up your thickets it occurs to you that the country is full of thickets and you can air out the claustrophobia that success has brought into your life by searching for them, the set of impulses that brought me to road trips. When I bought a cabin in Michigan's Upper Peninsula during the first wave of money, the five-hour drive from our farm seemed an immediate and repeatable act of liberation. In fact when I bought the cabin itself, settled as it was on a riverbank in the middle of fifty acres and a couple of miles from the nearest neighbors, I signed the purchase agreement without going inside of it.

Of course any harried dog or cat knows how to take a powder. A not often discussed problem with sudden success is that it immediately overfills the life. Where there were one or two outside calls a week, suddenly there were a dozen or so a day. And if there is an influx of money you quickly learn it takes time to spend money. A child given one or two fine gifts for Christmas becomes happily preoccupied with playing with the toys, but dump a carload on him and he becomes petulant. An unstable man of forty feels guilty because his friends are still broke. He flushes his money away as if it were used toilet paper.

This is not whining but a record of fear and confusion. Any fool knows that success is better than failure and when it's preceded by two decades of struggle and near poverty there is a specific exhilaration in a big check. You might eat steak three days in a row and the half gallons of Gallo are pushed aside for French wine. At bars you move from the bottom shelf, where you dwelt so long to save fifty cents a shot, to the top shelf where you order doubles. The fear settled in when you perceived that the serenity of privacy, of isolation, that had left your life had taken with it the ability to write well. I also knew enough of literary history to mentally rehearse the way so many writers had allowed the costume of public approbation to freeze to their bodies and when they finally tried to take the costume off there was little identifiable body left underneath. It had become bruised and splotched, depleted of life.

But there sat the Subaru in the yard on a winter morning, not exactly gleaming because I never wash cars. The abuse of scrubbing them for quarters as a boy taught me to invent reasons not to wash cars. It hurts their skin by rubbing off protective oils. They feel more comfortable in dirty old clothes. The dirt contains many pleasant memories that I don't want to deny the car. That sort of thing. Maybe I should drive in a circle around much of the U.S., I thought. And so I did.

Many of us remember the pleasure of getting our driver's license when we were sixteen, or even the learner's permit at fourteen. At forty you reabsorb and relive the electricity of that thrill when it occurs to you that all along you have been treating your vehicles as mere utilitarian conveniences to get from here to there for specific purposes instead of understanding that the vehicle can be an instrument of freedom, of liberation from whatever might ail you. Our main problem, and one that we share with all other earthly creatures, is what to do next. Drive with no particular destination. Go on roads you've never gone on before. See different landscapes and villages and cities. Talk to people you've never met, especially those who are totally unaware of your motives and identity. Pretend you're a spy for the country of your own mind.

Over twenty years later I'm still doing it when I feel oppressed by the life I've so methodically constructed and which occasionally begins to suffocate me as if I had crawled under thirty-three wet blankets. It's even amazingly cheap when you avoid our major cities. Fifty bucks is about tops for a motel, and another fifty covers your meals given the stunning mediocrity of road food. Add two tanks of gas a day and I can live on the road a week for what a single day habitually costs me in New York or Paris.

A few months ago we were driving through the Texas Panhandle, the only route through that state I can bear. We were on our way from our farm in northern Michigan to our little winter casita near the Mexican border. This was not a trip, therefore, that lacked a destination, but we vary this twice-yearly sojourn by changing the route once we escape the heartland. This time we had spent a pleasant five hours zigzagging through Oklahoma where there are relatively unknown areas of astounding beauty, especially the country surrounding Bartlesville and Ponca City with great vistas and hills densely wooded with blackjack oak.

Here we reach an important point. Before I visited this part of Oklahoma I had read the work of Joseph Mitchell, a Native American who had built a house in this area and had withdrawn from the world for a stretch of nine years. I had also read the considerable novels of Native American authors Linda Hogan and Louis Owens. The beauty of a landscape needs help to endure in your mind. You must mentally people the landscape with human history and, more important, the sense of the quality of human life you can get only from first-rate literature. For instance, when I drive around and camp in the Southwest with my friend the grizzly-bear expert Doug Peacock, we have it covered because he intimately knows the geology, the flora and fauna, and the Native history of the area. A mere landscape can wear out for you like the photos of beautiful women you collected as a young man. Their power wore thin because you didn't know them, their voices, the smell and touch, the qualities of their minds.

I have often examined the unpleasant feelings I have about Texas when I drive through the state. These are on the surface level and exclude the splendors to be found in such writers as J. Frank Dobie, John Graves, Larry McMurtry, Jim Crumley, or Max Crawford, to name a few. I don't mean that my ire is defined by the predatory nonsense in the movie *Giant,* the notion of the Alamo, or the obvious phoniness of the Gadsden Purchase, though these might form a part of it.

Last week I had the perception near Amarillo of the laminated mythologies of Texas resembling a vastly compressed stack of waffles. Or maybe a cowplot in a moist halo of oil. Or Texas as the Johnny Wadd (John Holmes) of our States, the word "big" repeated until it was a nonsense syllable. As an example, on Route 40, the interstate through the Panhandle, there's not a single rest stop though they are currently building one, albeit tardily. When you pass the construction site it occurs to you that the Texans are building the largest rest stop in the world. Presumably the toilet bowls will be as big as hot tubs, imperiling children and the very old.

In the past a quick pass through Midland, Texas, and you immediately comprehended why the current George Bush yawns and snoozes when the environment is brought up. Midland doesn't have an environment other than the stifling sense of big money contrasting with the squalor at the bottom. Midland is simply a sun-blasted junk heap, the living dump of the oil culture. No one living there for any extended time would have a concept that there might be land worth preserving, land that exists outside the immediate purpose of making money. Unlike George Bush, though, I'd rather live in Midland than in Washington, D.C. In Midland you can always drive over west to the marvelous Guadeloupe Mountains and hide in a thicket.

By contrast there is splendid landscape in the Hill Country near Austin, the vast grazing areas around Dalhart, the mountainous country south of Marfa. It's easy to go into a semi-convulsive fit about western cities on aesthetic grounds. They're nearly all "outskirts" in a curious way, and the remnants of the late nineteenth and early twentieth centuries in the cores of the downtowns remind us how our garden-variety greed has aesthetically stunted us.

* * *

Nothing refreshes quite like a tinge of insecurity if it has a viable purpose. The idea of dying on a business plane trip to L.A. where money is the carrot at the end of a stick is a flawless example of questionable purpose. By contrast, the insecurity of a blizzard on a smallish state highway in North Dakota, say between Arnegard and Rawson, purges the soul because it was altruistic curiosity that got you in the mess in the first place. When I was able to follow a snowplow into Williston I had a number of what they euphemistically call "beverages" back home. The fact is I had seen this grand landscape in the summer and I needed to see it in the winter for the same reason I need to see an elegant trogon, a snowy owl, a permanently pissed-off goshawk every once in a while. I need to eat a mediocre chicken-fried steak out of pure hunger and drink the usual rotgut far from my own overloaded refrigerator and wine cellar. I need to hear a waitress tell me about her problems with her 1985 Plymouth. I need to see a girl in a green dress pumping her own gas on a hot afternoon in Nebraska. I need to visit remote strip clubs where the women are nearly as homely as I am. I need the insecurity of the snowstorm or an overheated car when it's a hundred and three in the shade in Kansas, the insecurity of stretching heart and mind far from the familiar. It is too easy to be sure of yourself, too easy to know what you are doing moment by moment, too easy to walk the same path until it is a rut that finally becomes a trench and you can't see over the edge.

You might begin as a "child crazed with maps," as Rimbaud early described what predestined his own life as an inconsolable wanderer. A period of restless hitchhiking is a tip-off, and the ready notion that the grass *is* often greener on the other side of the fence. The easily perceivable motive is more life rather than less, and the simple historical fact that we lost a certain exuberance when we began to squat rather than wander. We arm ourselves early with quasi-wisdom to support our heart's urgings. I remember my dad's consternation when I quoted William Blake, "Still water breeds pestilence," though he was indeed sympathetic to my "seeing the world" before I got married and settled down. It pained him that what with five children he couldn't help support my wanderings. This eventually proved good as the notion that if the lack of money couldn't stop me from hitchhiking to New York and California, the future lack of money couldn't stop me from writing. Heating a can of soup in the sink of your five-buck-a-week rented room could be seen as heroic because the motives came from John Keats and Walt Whitman and a dozen other great ones.

But then is then and now is now, in case you've failed to notice. You can build a conceivably perfect life and then one day notice that it's suffocating you and your marriage. As they say in Nebraska, you've "screwed the lid on too tight." You've no intention of abandoning your love for your wife but you wish to get rid of the remnants of this love that have died from overexposure. Locked in a house small differences gracelessly grow larger. Marriages can witlessly evolve into daily psychodramas that feed on tainted fuel, the often wretched effects of no longer present in-laws and parents, the traumas of childhood that can burst back to life in the practice of gruesome habit. In my own life I have occasionally been pushed toward the door. A writer around the house can be as satisfactory as a realtor, teacher, editor, or butcher, but a writer can easily turn into a rabid wombat, somewhat in the manner of an actor or director with three flops in a row. A writer can be as emotionally captious as a prom queen wired on meth.

When you leave, you can leave a lot behind. Simple as that. And when you return the bad stuff has all disappeared in your absence because you were keeping it alive. You've brooded and moped until your unnatural mental weight might very well plummet you through the floor, or the crust of earth on your walk from the granary studio back to the farmhouse. Your emotional theme song has become turgid "Volga Boatmen" rather than playful Mozart. You look at your snow- or dust-covered car in the driveway and think tardily that it might be time to drive away and collect some fresh memories. You're a predator of your own memories and you've eaten up all of those you managed to summon into consciousness.

*   *   *

So off you go, avoiding the interstates as much as possible because they are mostly efficient traffic funnels following the geographic path of least resistance for carrying a maximal flow. On interstates you understand our grotesque error in favoring trucking over our once grand railroad system. As our population continues to increase this error has an overwhelming presence. Once I had to wave a shotgun (empty) out the window at a trucker a few feet from my back bumper. This method worked though I don't recommend it. I also don't recommend driving through Chicago on Route 80 on a weekday as you can easily get encapsulated by four trucks and never be seen again. There's been a definite slippage in truck-driver training that merges with the growing fascism of our time, sort of "If I'm big I have an inalienable right to mistreat you." Truckers, however, don't present the dangers of the twin felons of the road, the very young and the very old drivers.

The inherent insecurity of simply taking off gives you the specific advantage of being more attentive than usual. A disproportionate number of accidents happen around home when as a somnolent squatter you are lulled into carelessness. In East Africa I watched where I sat down because I had an aversion to green mambas and suchlike. At home I sat down where there was usually a chair and knocked myself silly. There's a delicious freedom in being called upon to be attentive. Moment by moment you are extending time rather than diminishing it through your housebroken narcissism. You have abandoned the support system that mostly allows you to work rather than play. The insecurity allows more oxygen and you recall for the seventy-fifth time D. H. Lawrence's fabled notion that the only aristocracy is consciousness.

Back to my peculiar sampling of places. They mean a great deal to me because of their peculiarities, and in part because I came to certain decisions in these places that added greatly to the vitality of my life as a writer. There were dozens of possibilities but I chose impulsively, discounting trips with specific destinations like New York City where I once drove when irked at airlines and the parking garage at the Carlyle Hotel cost more per day than many of the trips into the hinterlands.

Valentine, Nebraska: set in the northern portion of the Sandhills along the magnificent Niobrara River Valley. Approach it from the east on Route 12 where you may not see another car for an hour. Dozens of pretty girls and women live hereabouts. Eat beef at the Peppermill where the steak is the best you'll get west of Peter Luger's or Manny Wolf's in New York City, or Gibson's in Chicago. Continue west on Route 20 toward Chadron in this fabled, mythological landscape after swimming in the Niobrara. Detour north to see Wounded Knee. Kneel on the ground of the massacre and do penance for the bloodthirsty greedy creeps that were your ancestors.

Duluth, Minnesota: approach from the west on Route 2 after crossing the country from Montana. You'll come over a very high hill and see Lake Superior and Duluth's harbor far below. Ocean freighters line up for midwestern grain, and thousand-foot ore boats pass on the horizon loaded with taconite pellets headed far south through the Great Lakes to make steel. Duluth is an improbable city built on a steep hillside. If you catch it right in spring or fall you can see thousands of migrating hawks.

LaCrosse, Wisconsin: the Mississippi makes a deep cut through here where it is still a mighty river rather than a polluted sluice captured by levees, as it becomes farther south. In LaCrosse you get a firm sense of the river it used to be. High on a hill in the east of town in the early- and mid-nineteenth century, young missionaries would gaze to the west and pray before making their ill-advised trips to save the souls of Native Americans, the reverse of what it should have been. LaCrosse is an amenable city for food and drink and historical interest, also athletic young women from the local state university.

Rodeo, New Mexico: not much here except a bar, post office, gas station, but a stunning valley about eighty miles, and along up the road to the east a couple of miles is Portal, Arizona, where Vladimir Nabokov of *Lolita* fame used to chase actual butterflies and where several dozen times a year I travel to look for the eared trogon, which has been seen a couple of times since the seventies. This hope-less search on foot is wonderfully healthy. I stay in the only motel and eat in a little restaurant attached to the grocery store, a tonic for my gourmand obsessions. The landscape was a suitable hideout for Cochise and Geronimo and continues to be for us ordinary mortals. There are superb thickets up Cave Creek.

Ajo, Arizona: an ex-mining town that is a fine stepping-off place for Organ Pipe National Monument, but more so for the Cabeza Prieta Wildlife Refuge, a vast desert area where I've wandered as much as three days without seeing a single other human. The Cabeza is a claustrophobe's dream and you must pay attention to preserve your own life. Take in plenty of water, and don't step on rattlesnakes or make love to a nest of scorpions, as they are natural feminists.

The Seri Coast of Mexico: make your way slowly from El Desemboque to Bahia Kino, both on the Sea of Cortez, otherwise known as the Gulf of California. There are only a few hundred Seri left when there used to be thousands, accounted for by the usual murderous reasons. Camp on empty beaches or in the desert. Climb a mountain and stare at the Isla Tiburon. Before going read about the ethnobotany of the area, also John Steinbeck's *Sea of Cortez*. The Seri Coast will give you a dose of "otherness" that will make your own hometown seem strange by contrast on your return.

Jordan and Ekalaka in Montana: Jordan is in the center of an area that is referred to as "The Big Empty," which serves as an ad-equate description. Jordan makes me realize I would have failed as a westward pioneer. If you, like me, occasionally get oppressed by popu-lation pressures make your way to Jordan and find solace. After a few days head south into the Powder River country to Ekalaka where until recently the town was the sole county seat left in America approach-able only by gravel road. Spend a day in the dinosaur museum exam-ining the bones picked up by locals. You, after all, have some related genes.

Oxford, Mississippi: this place is the pleasantest university town in America and it is not drowned in the usual student frivolities. There is a high density of actual readers, rather than people gossiping about books that they've almost read. Oxford was the home of William Faulkner who is right up there with Herman Melville. It's a good walking and eating and music town. Mississippi appears to have the richest literary heritage of any state when to Faulkner you add Eudora Welty, Walker Percy, Willie Morris, and currently Shelby Foote, Barry Hannah, Larry Brown, and others. You can spend a whole week in Oxford without growing tired of it. Buy a book at Square Books, then walk across the square to the Ajax Diner and eat too much soul food while you read.

Florida Panhandle: I like to drive here for the melancholy reason that this is virtually the only area of Florida that holds remnants of what Florida once was. When I pass through Destin I stop and eat a whole bunch of fresh fish at Charles Morgan's Harbor Docks in order to get me through until morning or whatever. It's fun to see a little wild piglet eat a big rattlesnake, then waddle off into a swamp for a nap.

Bluff, Utah: there is a splendid, dramatic emptiness in this area. Read about Navajo and Hopi cultures, also read the mystery novels of Tony Hillerman. Get out of your car and walk in one direction until you are afraid, then try to make your way back to your car before dark. Drive from Bluff to Kayenta and visit Canyon de Chelly at dawn.

Dalhart, Texas: I've never quite figured out why I like this place except that it is surrounded by a vast emptiness that has been grazed more prudently than public cattle country farther west. The history of Dalhart has a mythic touch. A couple of easterners rebuilt the burned state capital in Austin in exchange for over a million deeded acres near Dalhart. The easterners went broke trying to fence all that land. There's a metaphor of something grand here.

Finally to drive without destination is to accept your own fragility, the passage of time, with the miles ticking off the pace of your own mortality. Moving through the country you are moment by moment capable of topographically mapping your past, and more capable of a clear view of your future. This is as close as you're ever going to get to the life of a freewheeling migratory bird.

NATURE AND NATIVES

Occasionally as a writer you come up against a back wall that is far too sturdy for you to follow Dostoyevsky's dictum that you must dash your head against it over and over. Certain walls seem infinitely thick. Why should I spend what's left of my heart and mind, not to speak of my time, writing about environmental depredations when any person of average intelligence can look out the window except in very rare locations and see how we have maniacally fouled our nest? This perception is occasionally a great burden to some of us, as if we were doomed to carry a heavy and sodden knapsack of this knowledge throughout our lives. It can quite easily distort our happiness, our sleep and marriages, our daily walks, the possible grace of moment-by-moment reality. The knowledge is always encapsuled in the thrust of "what is" overlayed upon "what might have been." You have to squint in order to find love among the ruins.

In the past few years I have spent more time than I wished wondering how I evolved my notions of a land ethic that so troubles my sleep. Up above my desk I keep a small piece of paper that states, "You're just a writer," which is what a studio head in Hollywood barked at me years ago. This is an essential idea, though meant as an insult, in that it promotes the humility needed to function as a human being rather than as an ideologue, an altruistic ranter and raver, a religious lunatic who believes that God gave us the earth and we have metaphorically and actually chewed off the fingers and hands of the gift giver. Unfortunately with my overfed imagination I can see this vision in the manner of a William Blake or Goya painting. To return myself to earth I walk daily with my dog in empty areas that are naked, gutted, and blasted of their essential nature by our behavior. They are still beautiful, these mountains and valleys in the Southwest, or the rivers and forests of my Native northern Michigan. They would be much more beautiful if I didn't know what they could have looked like but then they will have to do because they're all that we have.

Naturally it's my parents' fault. When I was young and my father was the county agricultural agent in Osceola County in northern Michigan, I'd accompany him on his rounds of giving advice to farmers. This was early in my career as a bad boy, a mode of behavior partly caused by the evident trauma of losing my eye. He was easy for the farmers to accept in that he had grown up on a farm in the neighboring county and spoke their peculiar language of hard work and privation.

Now over fifty years later what I recall about those country drives is my father trying to teach me the names of weeds, bushes, trees, and wildflowers that we smelled or saw through the open car windows, or on walks when we'd take soil samples with an augur, collecting the specimens in small glass jars. I was a poor student and accumulated a smattering of knowledge that mildly increased itself by exposure to forest hikes, daily fishing excursions from our cabin, or longer ones to nearby trout streams and rivers. It was many years before I understood that the great amount of time given to me was due to my blinding that made me a berserk waif.

Added to these outdoor trips were books that he passed on from his own boyhood, by Ernest Thompson Seton, James Oliver Curwood, Fenimore Cooper, the redoubtable fibbers Horatio Alger and Zane Grey, Owen Wister, to which were later added the wilderness novels of Hervey Allen and Walter Edmonds, who wrote *Drums Along the Mohawk*. For the obvious reason of my disfigurement, I tended to be designated an "Indian" in childhood games of cowboys and Indians. This was further emphasized by my beloved Seton book *Two Little Savages*, which dealt with two white boys learning woodcraft while spending an entire month living as Indians in the virtual wilderness. The transition isn't entirely clear but I gradually came to identify with the Indians who stole the heroine away in romantic frontier novels, rather than with the courageous men who retrieved her. What a fine thing to have a pretty girl in my teepee, I'd think.

Perhaps everyone has seemingly smallish events in their childhoods that have disproportionate effects on the later lives they lead. I mean aside from obvious traumas of injury, sexual abuse, divorces, or deaths of either parent. I remember my stack of Audubon cards used for bird identification more clearly than the teacher who gave them to me. A neighbor boy is repeatedly patted on the head for his facility with numbers and later becomes an accountant. The most trifling event can become large. There is a deeply accidental and comedic aspect to how people become what they are that always reminds me of Aristophanes' idea that "whirl is king." I even met a man in San Francisco in the late fifties who told me that when he grew up on a farm in South Dakota his ambition was to become a big-city gigolo and pimp, a double occupation at which he was obviously successful.

Wordsworth said that the "child is father of the man" and it's probably a very good thing we didn't know this as children. Nowadays the concept is used to truncate the nature of childhood with excessive scrutiny and wild ambition in parents on behalf of their children. You often note the curious deadness in these miniature adults at their organized play. There are even lessons in stocks and bonds available to urban children.

I have to admit that my own lacunae in terms of good behavior may have come from my search and reverence for natural wildness. As a child I had read how the Natives of our Southwest favored beans, so soon after daylight I'd head into the woods with a canteen of water and a can of beans, and sometimes a bow and arrow. I'd build a fire to heat the beans but more often I'd eat them cold. So powerful were the sensuous impressions of these early hikes that it is effortless to re-create them over fifty years later. You were utterly without the opinions, attitudes, conclusions that so easily blind you to the nature of experience, virtually the nature of nature. "With all its eyes the creature world beholds the open, while our eyes are turned inward," said Rilke. When we are young in a natural setting our eyes aren't yet turned inward. It's extremely difficult but you can recapture this state as an adult.

Of course it's altogether predictable that the weight of the contents of your life would determine your later concerns, and you are quite helpless in the face of this accretion of memories and ideals. You know very well that only the stars are safe from our destructiveness on our own shortsighted behalf. We are but one of an estimated 100,000,000 species. It has given many of us pleasure to dwell upon our dominance over these species. In fact we have created aspects of religion to reassure us that it's fine to defile these other species as we wish. We have organized a virtual theocracy of land rape wherein all the steps of our iron feet are acceptable if not sacred. I am mindful moment by moment that this is the world I live in. I know the details. Nothing has changed since Mark Twain reminded us that Congress is our only truly criminal class of citizens. They have constructed their own game of canasta in which earth herself is scarcely a dominant factor.

It occurred to me that what I have studied about Native Americans throughout my lifetime has aggregated itself into an anecdotal mass, an unorthodox accumulation that wouldn't pass an elementary college course but nonetheless exceeds that of 99.999 percent of my fellow citizens who resolutely hide their faces from the sins of their ancestors against these people. We must accept the fact that most of us wish only to know what is convenient for us and educators have made only temporary inroads on this condition. I recently asked a Native American friend to what degree it distressed him that we apparently have never learned a simple fucking thing about his people. He said he wasn't distressed because accepting responsibility for wrongs is a religious idea and he hadn't noticed much religion "in motion" in modern culture. He added that without the element of goodwill all problems had to be approached legalistically because that was the only effective language for social change. How sad. No justice is possible without lawyers.

Days later I said to myself, "Get off your high horse," in itself an archaism. I'm a putative "white person" with all the inherent privileges that come with that, and the additional privileges of being a financially successful white person which puts one high in the first percentile worldwide. This does not in the least add a tinge of guilt because I did it myself by writing, an independent operator in a non-extractive industry. I drilled and mined my head, as it were. My problem is my sense of parity, which I acquired so witlessly and is not directed simply at the human race but at the other hundred million species. I actually believe that reality is the aggregate of the perceptions of all creatures.

I ruminated cowlike for a couple of days by the river running next to my cabin trying to figure out how to deflate this ruminative cow in myself that was driving me quite batty. There was a lot that was deeply comedic about the self-image of a man brooding thusly while drinking a thirty-dollar bottle of wine and pondering his own history and that of our first citizens, which is what Natives are called in Canada. Now we are back in the territory of noodling Hamlet but further down the food chain with "just a writer" falling deeply into the sump of all that makes a writer parodic. The father taught the child that we must be fair with the land, the Natives, and other species. The writer forgets that his or her calling is to write, and this doesn't include trying to identify with and imitate the often preposterously heroic characters that the writer has created.

Way back when, I envisioned that one could spread a thin cotton sheet over our country and its living history, then stand back and watch the locations where the blood soaked through. It's even easier to do with Europe's more recent history. We must consciously remind ourselves what happened at Sand Creek and Wounded Knee, to name two. Such events have never fully entered the history of the conquerors for the same reason that My Lai hasn't. You're scarcely going to see a Wounded Knee or a My Lai float in the Fourth of July parade. Come to think of it our so-called Indian Wars were, strictly speaking, mere real estate operations and conquests. This property is condemned for better use. Much later, it was Bertolt Brecht who said that whom we would destroy we first call savage.

What we lock in the closet forcibly away from public view invariably becomes ghostly and destructive. Nearly everyone is somewhat aware that it is the media rather than religion or a sense of national purpose that gives structure and credibility to their lives. It is the nature of diversion that frames our reality if you look at the amount of time spent. Who can forget Ronald Reagan speaking of "oil-rich Indians on their preservations," a notion gotten from several identifiable movies. When you go looking for accurate movie portrayals of Native culture you come up with only the recent *Smoke Signals* and, to a lesser extent, *Little Big Man*. Movies and television are largely to reality what fast food is to our bounteous crops.

In my own peculiar case, which proves not at all uncommon, I learned much about the habitat before I learned of the people who belong in it. The natures of our predecessors were only slightly taught in school, if at all. The information was out there but you had to dig, so I dug. It's unlikely I would have done so without my father's direction and the knowledge of how a relatively wild and natural habitat could be made livable without destroying it, and how Native religions could emerge directly from the earth that gave people life.

I'm dealing here with a world that is immensely susceptible to romanticism, the predictable distortions of ideologues, whether they are Rousseau or late-blooming hippies wearing turquoise with freak hots for peyote. We have to look at this world from the inside toward the outside, rather than the reverse. There can be no allowable concept of ethnic or genetic virtue, inevitably the major source of human butchery.

Here we run into the very thick back wall of xenophobia, of geopiety. I have seen countless examples of writers and critics acting somewhat scornful of one another on a regional basis. To a New Yorker much about Native culture of the northern Midwest all the way out through the Great Plains and Northwest is somewhat suspect unless the New Yorker goes out there and discovers it himself. A critic once visited the old ranch house I use as a studio near the Mexican border. He assumed it was part of a movie set. No, it's just an old ranch house near the Mexican border. The seven cow dogs in the yard aren't pets but are used to round up cattle in this rough country. This can go on and on. For instance, the peyote cactus is a fascinating hallucinogenic experience, but far more important the cactus is used by Native American groups to reinforce their tribal identity and as a powerful ally against alcoholism. When I saw an Assiniboine dance nine hours in a row at a powwow he was guided by a stronger impulse than aerobic exercise. Obviously, the converse is true. When writers west of the Appalachians complain that they are being ignored by the "Eastern Literary Establishment" I have to tell them there are at least thirty thousand writers in Boston, New York, and New Jersey who have similar feelings of neglect. The world looks quite different depending on where you stand and the nature of your self-interest.

Xenophobia is simply a biological part of the human beast and rarely transcended. Historically, minorities war for our attention. We have blacks, Jews, Mexican Americans, and Native Americans, all who have been profoundly traumatized by our history. I must say that largely speaking only Jewish intellectuals have been able to rise well above the problems of their own ethnic group and see clearly the torments of the others. The Jews, for instance, were fundamental in the forming of the NAACP. The ugly idiom "the squeaky wheel gets the grease" is more evident in Native Americans who have a cultural aversion against complaining, therefore it was easier until more recently for Congress and our populace to ignore them. The federal courts have even ruled that the Bureau of Indian Affairs must account for the billions of dollars of Native money that they have misplaced. Curiously, an issue as immense as this has gotten scant coverage. Clearly there are thousands like me churning in their own sense of injustice and squeaking with the wheel, "My issue is bigger than yours." It is quite difficult for a people to have a sense of history when so much of it has been banished from their sight.

Just the other day I was reading how the kestrel, commonly known as the sparrow hawk though it doesn't pursue sparrows, has a curious ability, because of the infinitesimal cones in its eyes, to perceive ultraviolet light, enabling it to further see the iridescent urine stains that voles leave in the grass, so it is able to better pursue them. This isn't a wonderful idea but a fact and it led me again to remember William Blake's "How do we know but that every bird that cuts the airy way is an immense world of delight closed to our senses five?" Whether you are reading E. O. Wilson or Jean-Henri Fabre you are drawn into ponderous delight of the smallest creatures. At this point it occurred to me that Native Americans spent a lifetime of attention to the natural world in order to survive. The fact that they no longer have to do so poses a series of enormous questions.

The poet Wallace Stevens made the statement "We were all Indians once" (current DNA studies say that further back we were all black). This seems technically true and led me to the uncomfortable conclusion that because of my familiarity with the natural world I identified strongly with those who until recently had depended on such familiarity for their existence. I had also long understood that my most intense pleasures came in activities such as hunting, fishing, and studying wild country that were the same for any Pleistocene biped. The essential difference between me and Native Americans was that my people never got the rawest of deals. My people were never reduced from a possible ten million down to approximately three hundred thousand between the years around 1500 to 1900.

I know men both white and Native who go into the mountains or forest, on horseback or on foot, to kill deer for their families. In impulse this is not unlike riding the subway to an office job. I have been told countless times that hunting is no longer a necessity for anyone in the United States, but that assumes you relish food stamps or the predominantly ghastly feedlot supermarket beef that oozes pinkish juice as if it has been injected with water. I've been to dozens of venison "feeds" in my lifetime, which are celebratory occasions where whole groups of families sit down and eat as much deer meat as possible. With the Chippewa (Anishinabe) you eat venison and corn stew at a Ghost Supper and afterwards go outside and throw some tobacco in a bonfire to say good-bye to your beloved dead whom you might have been clinging to in a mentally unhealthy way. It is believed that the dead wish to be relieved from our sorrow so that they may freely enter the next world. We can be taught by these ancient and traditional aesthetics of grief. I am amazed how throughout the United States the rich, the mildly prosperous, and those in cushy government jobs are eager to tell our dirt-poor Natives how to live. After being massacred at Wounded Knee the Lakota were forbidden even to hunt or dance.

At my remote cabin during my sixty-third summer I dreamt that after a lifetime in which I had spent thousands and thousands of days outdoors looking "at" nature I was finally inside looking out. The meaning of this was imprecise but the feelings have stayed with me. It became far simpler as a poet to imagine myself a tree or boulder, a creek or a field, and easier yet to imagine myself a fellow mammal. When Shakespeare said, "We are nature, too," he was making a leap away from the fundamental schizophrenia in Western culture that few have made. At my cabin made of logs there is less distance between inside and outside. You can smell the heart of the forest as you sleep and hear the river passing beside the north side of the cabin. At our winter casita near the Mexican border the walls are made of adobe, the dried mud of earth. This is comforting but does not discount the elegant imagination of man. I once spoke to a bedridden old woman in the immense bedroom of her hunting lodge in the

Rambouillet forest in France. The walls were of quarried stone and covered with ancient tapestries. Attached to the ceiling were hundreds of sets of bronze-tagged stag antlers, the history of centuries of hunting. The property had once been owned by Charlemagne and the lodge itself seemed to grow out of the forest. The inside and outside circulated freely among each other. I felt as comfortable as I had sitting in the doorway of an abandoned hogan on the Navajo reservation watching dawn, which seemed to emerge from the ground and into the sky.

We have lately received a terrible lesson that emerged partly from trying to historically put all the nations and peoples in the Middle East into our giant dim-witted Mixmaster and ignoring the potage except for "Just sell us the oil, folks." We did largely the same thing from the time we got off the boat in regard to Native Americans. Over five hundred tribes were reduced to one name, savages, Injuns, redskins, whatever. Even cursory reading, let alone travel, reveals unique differences, but there never was much cursory reading. Though they live in the same area the Hopi are as different from the Navajo as the Finns are from Italians, perhaps more so. And the Utes are as different from the Ojibway as the French are from the Germans, and so on. Never in our history has the public perception differed so profoundly from reality. Native history is still often taught as if these people were all currently dead.

I had no right from the beginning to identify with the Natives rather than the conquerors. It was an accident and in describing the accident it is appropriate that I feel a little foolish. They've received nothing from me except a number of novels in which I've dealt with the curious world of the mixed-bloods. I've consciously stayed away from areas where I don't belong, which are many. There are a couple of dozen Native Americans writing fine novels now, a specific renaissance that takes place too far from New York to be much noticed.

In my own case and others there is more than a bit of the fool in a poet's calling. The metaphoric jumps of poetry are also biographical. Wordplay was big in my life from childhood onward. Jim Pepper, a Native jazz musician, sang a beautiful song that was mostly a recitation of tribal names, a song that should be played in every school in America. If I list tribes I've visited or read about I'm swept away by the beauty of accumulated names and images, also the sorrow of our implacable cruelty: Acoma Zuni, Kiowa, Apache, Mescalero Apache, Arapaho, Pawnee, Miami, Arikara, Potawatomi, Ponca, Haida, Blackfoot, Lakota, Minneconjou Sioux, Omaha, Cheyenne, Chippewa, Ute, Cree, Havasupai, Papago, Pima, Mohawk, Mandan, Kwakiutl, Mohave, Crow, and so on.

What I have received from these cultures can't be numbered in the manner of our late addiction to hokum lists surrounding the millennium, which reminded me of a linear row of bowling trophies. Life is inevitably holographic and thousands of brushes have painted us inside and out.

I have learned from Native Americans that we prove we belong where we live upon the earth only by carefully using but not destroying our house. I've learned that you can't be at home in your body, your truest home, if you wish to be somewhere else, and that you have to find yourself where you already are in the natural world around you. I have learned that there are no specific paths for me in my work as a poet and novelist and that I write best calling on my boyhood experience as a faux Native setting off into country where there were no paths. I have learned that I can't have a viable religion by denying pure science or the conclusions of my own attention to the natural world. I have learned that looking at an upland plover or sandhill crane is more interesting than reading the best book review I've ever received. I've learned that I can maintain my sense of the sacredness of existence only by understanding my own limitations and losing my self-importance. I've learned you can't comprehend another culture unless you can stop your moment-by-moment mental defense of your own. As the Sioux used to say, "Take courage, the earth is all that lasts." Few of the hundred million other species can talk, so we must speak and act in their defense. That we have failed our Natives should urge us on, on both their behalf and that of the earth we share. If we can't comprehend that the reality of life is an aggregate of the perceptions and nature of all species we are doomed with the earth we are already murdering.

III

THE REST OF LIFE

GRADUATE SCHOOL

When I was fourteen and involved in an extended religious fever a group of us in our early teens were driven into Lansing one early June evening to attend "Youth for Christ." There were literally thousands of us singing and praying and I received a special recognition for leading the team that won the countywide elimination contest in the Bible Quiz championships. Since I was a mediocre athlete and student except in literature and history it wasn't difficult to find the time to memorize much of Corinthians, Colossians, Ephesians, Acts (of the Apostles), and the Gospels, though I preferred the word music of the Old Testament Isaiah, or the dire portents of Revelations. In the East Lansing library I even sneaked looks at the forbidden and blasphemous Apocrypha, a thrilling moment indeed.

But that hot early-summer evening at Youth for Christ a southern evangelist preached eloquently on how sex could lead us to spend eternity in hell. He asked us to imagine that each grain of sand on all the beaches in the world was a year, and when all the grains were used up eternity was just beginning. The preacher cared for us so much that he virtually sobbed out his sermon. We were all quite stricken and very aware that the lust in our hearts could doom us. When the "invitation" arrived at the end of the sermon hundreds came forward to rededicate their lives to Christ and a life of purity until they took their marriage vows and proper sex could be consummated. I had come forward in our own church months before and decided to do it again that evening but only if a red-haired girl from Charlotte, a town about thirty miles distant, did so and then I'd follow her up for the breathless pleasure of being close to her. I restrained my imagination about her to the level of the ethereal, though I knew this state could plunge in a trice if I wasn't careful. I stared at the back of her neck

while the audience sang, "Just as I am without one plea . . ." At the
end of the service she put a foot on a chair to tie her shoe and I could
see well above the knee on the other leg. My doom arrived in the
form of a hard-on that brought me to tears.

The next evening our Bible club had a picnic and swimming party.
We had a long water fight with the girls mounting the boys' shoulders
in the chest-deep water. It was impossible not to notice the palpable
warmth at the back of your neck. My partner was Evelyn, our minister's
daughter, which made it doubly confusing. When we'd flounder in the
water it was apparent that Evelyn was less interested in holiness than
in me. French kissing and discreet fondling underwater are alarmingly
potent. In discreet fondling you're pretending you're not aware of what
you're doing and all the touching is quite accidental.

That night I prayed on my knees on the metal floor register in
order to stay alert. I was keenly aware that spending an eternity in
hell was a long time. There was still sand between my toes from the
swimming party. My burbling prayers rose upward, and naturally when
I slept my dreams were riddled with sex including the image of a girl
I'd seen emerging from the baptismal tank in a wet white dress that
clung to her pink butt. O God.

The other evening while making notes for a new novel I wondered
again about this Christian idea that God is keeping a sharp eye on
our genitals and the possible consequences of our fear over spending
eternity in hell. This form of indigenous Calvinism made much of
time, thrift, hard work, and good works. I've never missed a plane
and was rarely if ever late for work or a meeting. To not be on time
and not get your work done is unthinkable. It is also maddening and
easily lapses into obsessive-compulsive behavior. It is an often manic
attempt to have some kind of control over swiftly passing time. I've
watched midwestern farmers carve up their days milking the cows at
five A.M. and five P.M., then supper at six sharp, hungry or not. Early
after our arrival here Native Americans noted our preoccupation with

time and how we are not able to eat until a bell is rung and then we quickly sit down and eat. Once a producer asked me when I would finish a new screenplay assignment and I said I would FedEx a draft on the fortieth afternoon. He laughed, then was quizzical about my seriousness. I admitted my behavior might be vaguely clinical. I've tried to blame it on my Swedish half. Once in Minnesota I saw a Swedish folk dance and noted that the dance steps had all the spontaneity of barbed wire.

Curiously this time obsession deals only with the continuous present and the future. I've often noted that I can keep track of the past only by what dogs we've owned at the time. My books and even screen projects surround the dogs, who are now permanently sleeping dogs except for Mary and Rose. We share in common the beginnings and ends of our stories, a slick statement not the less true for being so. It is the middle that stretches us thin with all the attenuations of time, the essential but still inscrutable component of the universe, the question mark that enshrouds us all and about which no one appears to have a clue. Even our cells change every split second.

Luckily for us we're only occasionally aware that we are caught up willy-nilly in the violent storm of time. Our biological imperatives both blunt and save us. It's easy to imagine Pleistocene man looking up and thinking, "Either those stars are moving or we are or both." Perhaps these larger considerations are too grand for us to deal with except momentarily and then rarely. The young man, really not much more than a big boy, hitchhikes to New York City to be a poet and then forty-five years later as a geezer tries to deeply consider what has gone on in between. There have been over fifteen thousand nights and days in between. Always the willing victim of his own polarities he's had no middle ground for rest. The somewhat desperate sense of time has been so all-enveloping he never has truly noticed its fragility or his own. The hubris is seemingly mixed in his marrow and seeps outward from there. He's a bright enough boy to know that to write something truly durable owns nearly the same odds as a plow horse winning the Kentucky Derby, but why should that deter him? He's a clumsy old breed of terrier and with the deaths of father and sister, those he loved most, when he was twenty-one he no longer had the slightest reason to be careful, to hold back. When the father and sister die you follow your heart's affections in their honor.

I bought Linda a thirty-dollar wedding band and went through a painful cycle of improving my behavior. Our life together, which began under difficult conditions, continues until today. Only the most outlandish romantic love could sustain us and that is what we managed. Our implicit coda was to avoid psychodramas and maintain ordinary etiquette and we've mostly succeeded. She is also the least defenseless woman I have ever known.

I discovered rather early in life that a bottle of beer made me feel better, not a promising sign if carried to a built-in, specious conclusion. What saved us was poverty. Growing up the way I did gave supporting a family precedence over any and all personal desires. After rent and food and gas for the car, the spare dollar would afford one five-ounce draft beer, or a bottle of Gallo burgundy, which was just under a buck in 1961. All of those who have been involved know the potential soddenness of student and graduate student marriages. The late Raymond Carver was the absolute master of this subgenre, the search for balance in an environment of near squalor. I had to finish nearly two years of college in one, plus work forty hours a week to get a B.A. After that an eminent scholar, Russell Nye, a friend of my in-laws, wangled me a graduate assistantship, which paid a little over two hundred a month, enough for rent and groceries but not much else.

The birth of our daughter, Jamie, somewhat healed the rift with my in-laws. Few can resist the glory of a first grandchild. I immediately became less of a monster. I still regret that my pride kept me from accepting any money from them, which I now see as false pride, a meaningless arrogance, what we used to call simple "asshole" behavior. While much nonsense is made of America as a classless society my real difficulty with my in-laws was that they came from well up the ladder, above my own parents and relatives. Linda's father, William Ludlow King, had gone to Dartmouth and briefly Harvard, and came from a family of Cornish copper-mine owners in the Upper Peninsula. It was in my father-in-law's ancestral home that my wife found the nineteenth-century journals of William Ludlow, which gave me the base for *Legends of the Fall*. He was a kindly man, a nearly antique gentleman, and I had no experience dealing with someone like him. Linda's mother, however, was clearly daffy, very intelligent but emotionally mercurial, partly from losing a baby who had gone nearly full term. It was from her that I heard on many late evenings some of the curious aspects of her husband's family, including the tale of a cousin who had donated a chair at the University of Chicago but lived in Paris with her lesbian lover. This kind of information thrilled me as it was so exotic compared to anything in my own family's past. My wife's grandfather once came to dinner refusing to acknowledge me as Linda's husband, sitting there drinking whiskey in an English tailored suit and wearing a seven-carat diamond Masonic ring, a problematical man who had squandered much of his wife's money, some of which had come from Mexican silver mines in the nineteenth century.

It is difficult at certain times to see your life in the comic terms it so amply displays. Graduate students are in a peculiar area, essentially noncitizens. It will be the only time in life when the pecking order is totally based on how vividly the intelligence is enacted, who controls the discussion at the table during thousands of cups of coffee, group budget meals, beers that are stretched as long as possible. In married-student housing, ours was called Spartan Village, there's an air of exhaustion, the parking lots full of unwashed used cars. In the students in the humanities the life of the mind has overwhelmed all other considerations. The wives tend to envy the wives of the science graduate students who live more orderly lives and have larger stipends. The wives of graduate students in English and American and comparative literature are fatigued with their babbling husbands, the after-midnight calls where it is asserted that Henry James might very well have been masturbating when he wrote *Portrait of a Lady*, or that Edmund Wilson isn't nearly as bright as he thinks he is, or that when read closely William Dean Howells is fascinating.

Friday night was a dangerous time of frayed nerves, the spending of the carefully saved beer budget, the spaghetti or pizza dinner, balcony vomiting, inconclusive fistfights, smarmy flirtations, and excitement over nothing in particular. It was a musical comedy with very loud Charlie Parker and ubiquitous rhythm and blues on the Inkster radio station out of Detroit. At night we tended a tiny marijuana plot hidden in a field near the apartments and were horrified during one night's party to see squad cars of the university police roaring across the field. Pot wasn't taken very seriously by police this early in the sixties but we could still envision the end of our noncareers. The squad cars, however, were ineptly chasing an escaped bull from the ag department's dairy barn, and one car hit a bank and ditch, became airborne, and pancaked, utterly destroying itself. We cheered the bull's escape.

At the time I was a terrible mishmash of divergent obsessions, from left-wing labor and civil rights politics to an aesthete's fascination with ballet, opera, the nether corners of art history in which I had temporarily majored, French Symbolist poetry, Rilke, and my dominant hero, James Joyce, not to speak of Dostoyevsky's diaries which were a daily missal. All of this didn't build a pleasant person. Added to this was the sliver of the faux Indian who ordered one hundred peyote buttons from the Smith Cactus Ranch in Albuquerque, New Mexico, a legal purchase at the time. I organized a hokum ceremony for my friends and gobbled a dozen or so of the buttons. I remember that this visionary experience was inconveniently concurrent with the Cuban missile crisis which by itself was cramping my toes and didn't need hallucinogenic fuel.

But I did at the time. I ate peyote twice and it reconfirmed my faith in my calling. It also scared the hell out of me in that you sensed specific dimensions in your mind that you were less than sure you wanted to be there. Years later when I read R. D. Laing's statement "The mind of which we are unaware is aware of us," my memory immediately revived the peyote experience. Of course peyote is a foreign substance and its mind-altering capacities are in themselves a kind of poisoning but then so are alcohol, tobacco, and coffee, not to speak of marijuana, cocaine, and tranquilizers.

I pulled way back from this experience out of a vaguely commendable fear that I might fail as a husband and father. Always a theoretic nitwit, I decided I must abase myself before the ordinary aspects of life, a gimcrack theology drawn from Dostoyevsky and my new obsession with Kierkegaard. I might have paid attention to the fact that I was gradually flunking out of graduate school where I did well in what interested me but was childishly unable to fake interest in such subjects as linguistics or Edmund Spenser.

On Saturday mornings I'd take our daughter, Jamie, about two at the time, on visits to the farms run by the agricultural department of the university. Together we studied pigs, cows, chickens, and horses. Of all farm animals horses have the best natural odor. It was pleasant, albeit melancholy, to see these animals anew through a child's eyes and fantasize about living on a small, remote farm where I'd make a simple living and study my Rimbaud in peace. Never at the time could I admit my unlikely candidacy for marriage, the statistically pathetic chances for success when a young man just shy of twenty-one marries a girl two days short of nineteen. At the time our main instruments of survival were a profound sexual happiness and the fascination of caring for the child. There was also the growing interest in something good for dinner every evening, keeping in mind the minimal budget which in itself promotes good cooking. Over the years I've noted how rarely divorce occurs when a couple happily cooks together, which also promotes a free sensuality in the bedroom, or wherever for that matter. Making love in a car, a pine grove, or a pasture did wonders for what they insist on calling "mental health."

* * *

Once when I was working for a book wholesaler in Boston I was asked by the management to look at a "flowchart" they had devised. To me this reflected something mysterious in the manner of Alan Watts and the other material in Tao that I had read, whereas what the company was looking for was an easier way to get the books from the second floor to the first floor. When I came down to earth I was quite helpful.

The study of Eastern literature, where flow rather than whirl is king, is wonderful if you're not obligated to function in the West other than nominally. In my college years I was apparently willing to accept any advice if it was well written. My coda was found in the great English prose stylist Sir Thomas Browne, "Swim smoothly in the stream of thy nature and act but one man." Since I thought of myself as a poet and nothing else I was obligated to behave as a poet though I had no firm idea what this was. At nineteen in New York City I was obedient to Rimbaud's notion of the "*dérèglement de tous les senses*" (the purposeful derangement of the senses) to break down and through conditioned perceptions. The tool at hand seemed to be alcohol but then I could afford only a few beers a day and anything more than that tended to make life sodden. In a Boston rooming house I shared a bottle of gin with a poet friend now dead, Peter Snyder, and we both managed to get the dry heaves. My first marijuana came in San Francisco in the winter of 1958 but this drug seemed mostly a soporific and also made one uncontrollably hungry. A few afternoon tokes with other beatniks in North Beach and then we'd line up at the back door of St. Anthony's mission for the monks' after-dinner food handout. This embarrassed me though I still remember a Swiss steak sandwich with gravy in a loaf of French bread. The other options were a fifty-cent bowl of noodles with pork and vegetables in Chinatown, or the thirty-five-cent plate of macaroni salad at the Co-Existence Bagel Shop. The anthems at the time were Allen Ginsberg's "Howl" and Bob Kaufman's "Abominist Manifesto." The graceful and delightful hangout was Lawrence Ferlinghetti's bookstore City Lights, which still survives.

Back in married housing I'd read *Pat the Bunny* to my infant daughter, and then read Sufi literature or Gurdjieff and Ouspensky, Vyacheslav Ivanov, Yesenin, Apollinaire, and Faulkner, none of which made me an acceptable graduate student but which promoted the kind of arrogance that irritated all of my professors except my mentor Herbert Weisinger, who could disarm me in a moment with his sharp Brooklyn wit, his soaring knowledge of all world literature, art, and history.

I was sympathetic a year or so ago when reading why the Yale graduate assistants had gone on strike. In my first year of graduate school my assistantship required four hours a day of research into foundations giving to the liberal arts during which I kept remembering my father's populist idea that foundations represented unpaid wages. My own wage for the supposed honor of being a graduate assistant was only a little over two bucks an hour. This did not compare favorably with the five an hour I had made as a shovel man on construction sites. The second year was even more problematic. I taught English as a foreign language using an improbably inept text program of simple repetition. My one class of twenty included students who spoke seventeen different languages, including a German with a dueling scar who had spent two years at Oxford and spoke better English than I did. Regulations forced all foreign students to take the course despite their proficiency. He already had moved from a dormitory to an expensive hotel suite. The real problem, though, was that I could barely understand any of the students, who would faithfully bray back the inane sentences I read aloud. I threw all of their test papers in the dump saying that they were being saved for research. I was a vocally nasty twerp to the professor who directed the department. Later when I needed a recommendation for a job he gave me one but I held it to the light and saw the word "arrogant" so I threw it away.

As a college senior I had finally heard my first poetry reading, with Galway Kinnell reading "The Avenue Bearing the Initial of Christ into the New World," from his recently published book. I was overwhelmed but my own capabilities were so far from his astutely lyrical cityscape that there was nothing more to imitate. I heard the Mexican painter David Siqueiros speak and regretted again that I had no talent as a painter. I talked a number of times in a smoke and coffee shop with Abe Rattner, an abstract expressionist, about his car trip with Henry Miller. After an hour Rattner asked, "Why do you stay here in Michigan? There's nothing for you here." I said I had a wife and child and he only nodded.

All my friends read Henry Miller in the manner of getting a blood transfusion. We were not all interested in academic poetry but we certainly read Robert Lowell's *Life Studies*, though I much preferred Frank O'Hara's *Meditations in an Emergency*.

When I think of my friends at the time I am struck by the mortality rate of young poets. There were three eventual suicides: Steven Gronner, Larry Baril, and later, John Thompson. There was also the mortality of people who didn't quite persist after promising early work, like J. D. Reed who published *Expressways* with Simon & Schuster, and David Kelly who published with Wesleyan. I also knew Tom McGuane slightly but he was in another group primarily interested in fiction and their own more advanced misbehavior, which included, to our envy, a bevy of Lansing secretaries. Richard Ford would appear in another two years. I also met Dan Gerber who would become a lifelong friend and publish fiction, nonfiction, and poetry. McGuane's neighbor, Bob Dattila, whom we viewed as a mysterious Sicilian from Queens, would become the only agent I've had in my long career.

Meanwhile I was flunking out during my second year of graduate school and obviously having a total nervous crack-up. I hitchhiked to New York City and stayed one day and night with my old friend the painter and art critic Gregory Battcock, who was gay. He was a pal, as was the young sculptor Italo Scanga. At Battcock's, while he was out to dinner, I was quite amazed looking at hundreds of photos of nude young men who were Gregory's sexual conquests. When I awoke in the morning on a mattress on the kitchen floor I was looking up a slip at the nude bottom of a lovely English girl who lived

with Gregory. Gregory was later murdered in Puerto Rico on a balcony where it was said that a sea breeze made a rose of his blood on
a stucco wall.

I returned home in a state of teary penance. My father's unexpected reaction was that since my heroes such as Faulkner and
Sherwood Anderson hadn't graduated from anything maybe I'd be
better off with a job. I was so disgusted with myself I threw away a
bunch of Jackson Pollock's clothing had been given to me years
before by his brother Charles who taught art at Michigan State. I
meant to become absolutely normal. Unfortunately I couldn't have
offered up a fair description of normal that wouldn't have yielded
projectile vomiting.

It was spring and I was wandering the campus aimlessly looking
at the stunning gardens that had been organized by the horticultural
and grounds departments. There was a particularly lovely garden behind the library that abutted the Red Cedar River where I first read
Joyce's *Finnegans Wake* in my freshman year, and where I also had read
Lorca, Jimenez, Hernandez, and Neruda, whom I discovered through
Robert Bly's *The Fifties* magazine, which later became *The Sixties*. In
this garden I also was drawn to the poems of Sergei Yesenin. My latest
discovery during this morose graduate student period was the work of
Rene Char, including "To a Tensed Serenity" ("A *une sérénité crispée*")
in the latest *Botteghe Oscure*, Marguerite Caetani's magazine, which
was published in Rome. Both Yesenin and Char gave me hope as both
came from rather humble beginnings out in the country. I was busy
filling sketch notebooks with images and observations but was still well
short of my first poem.

That June I convincingly flunked out of graduate school but we were
able to keep our apartment. I had now managed to organize an absolute loathing for academic life though I dimly understood that I was
temperamentally unsuited, which was scarcely the university's fault.
There was the question of whether I was suited for anything except
the manual labor I continued to enjoy on the horticultural farm.

I entered a paralyzing depression, with "paralyzing" being a euphemism. My memory, which normally is irrelevantly acute, fails me now though I recall that bureaucracy moves slowly and we were able to keep our married-student housing apartment until that fall. It always has struck me that summer depressions are worse because the weather isn't cooperative. Cold, wet snow and dense clouds are rather soothing to the depressed while bright and sunny summer weather with profuse flowers and greenery is abrasive.

My gentlemanly unobtrusive father-in-law sent me off on two expeditions to find work as a technical writer, a possible job category for me that he had researched with friends. The first trip was to Detroit and an interview at the Chrysler Tank Arsenal. I felt congested and my eyes teared when I looked out across a huge hall where five hundred men were writing specifications for armaments in waist-high steamed-glass cubicles. The interview went well but on the way home I pulled into a rest stop between Detroit and East Lansing and disposed of the sheaf of application papers in a trash barrel. I doubted anyway due to my radical political activities that I could pass the minimal security clearance. I still envisioned myself as a member of the Young Progressive Socialists, whom I had signed up with in New York City when I was nineteen. At a civil rights picket in front of Woolworth's I had been amazed when our campus police busied themselves taking our photos for their subversive files. I was offended many years later when under the Freedom of Information Act my state police file revealed that I was considered to be a harmless poet.

Washington was discouraging in a different way. One of my father-in-law's Dartmouth classmates was a hotshot in a big company. Our interview was a lovely lunch at the Mayflower Hotel but the upshot of our chat was that I was emotionally unsuited to be a corporate employee. I didn't show up for three other interviews but spent two entire days in the National Gallery, the splendor of which only recalled my freedom in New York City when I had spent dozens of days at the Met and the Museum of Modern Art, which back then was sparsely attended. Several years ago Anjelica Huston told me that a month or two before her father died she had pushed him through MoMA in his wheelchair when it was closed to the public so he could see the paintings he loved for the last time.

During this questionable period I was able to mildly endear myself to my mother-in-law through my willingness to play bridge whenever she wished. Part of my so-called obsessive-compulsive tendencies was to throw my entire being into activities not related to my graduate studies. I was a whiz at bridge, pool, and poker and had taken up golf partly because a student could play all day at the fine college course for seventy-five cents. I had played some as a fourteen-year-old caddy at a country club where we were allowed to play free early on Monday mornings and wealthy men we caddied for would loan us their clubs. At the university, though, I was able to ruin golf for myself in a few months. I would cut all of my classes and spend the entire day on the course, once playing three balls for fifty-four holes between dawn and dark. I had to tape my hands which were a blistered mess. I quit the day after I got a thirty-eight on the back nine from NCAA tees. In short, I was nuts.

By October we were evicted from student housing and moved in briefly with my in-laws, at a loss for what to do next. I was now prepared to take any job but a B.A. in English and Comparative Literature is a virtually worthless degree. I even took a test and had an interview for one of those gimcrack finance companies that prey on the poor with eighteen percent interest. I was proud when the interviewer told me I got forty-nine out of fifty questions correct. Unfortunately, they didn't want anyone that "smart," or so he said, though I suspected that my blind eye made me look too shifty. This was early in the morning and I walked down the street to Ellison's bookstore where I read the entirety of Nabokov's *Lolita* by midafternoon while standing up, not being able to afford the book.

A week later I was a leading candidate for a job that would later remind me of a Kurt Vonnegut novel. The job involved traveling around and visiting farmers and giving speeches to farm organizations on what to do to protect farm animals in case of atomic attack. Seriously, I'm inventive but I couldn't have made this up. There were

many candidates for this decent-paying job and the fact that my father was an agricultural professional got me into the top two before
the ax fell on my cringing neck.

Now it was into November and I was improbably anxious to get
out of my in-laws' house for reasons of friction. Linda and I drove up
north to Manton into a landscape I loved in my youth to interview
for an English-teacher position that had opened due to medical reasons. I didn't have the papers to entitle me to teach school though I
had taken a particularly wretched education course, but this was
deemed an emergency. The superintendent with a wonderful name,
I believe it was Hessel Shotwell, asked if I minded "knocking heads"
as there was a discipline problem with north-woods louts. I said I was
capable and I was hired on the spot. On the way home we were mildly
excited because with the job came a very spacious apartment above
a store for only a fifty bucks a month. We'd pack up and move north
in the coming week right after the Thanksgiving weekend. While
the job certainly wasn't appropriate for a "thief of fire," the ancient
notion of the poet, it would be good indeed to escape the confines of
the Lansing area for the Great North, where I could resume my early
passion for trout fishing.

A day later my world imploded. I had thought of going back north
with my father and sister to deer-hunt for a day but finally rejected
the idea in the midafternoon. For some reason my sister Judith gave
me her teddy bear that I had also owned as a child. My father said
that they were going to hunt behind Uncle Nelse's shack. As ever
we kissed good-bye and I apologized again for holding them up before I could make a decision, a matter that would haunt me ever
afterwards.

That evening I was back at the Kings' and I think we had just
finished a card game when the phone rang. My father-in-law answered in the kitchen and I could see by his stricken look it was
very bad news. He gestured to me and my mother told me clearly

that Winfield and Judith had been killed in a car accident. Bill King drove me the five miles home and I sat up with Mary and David who were twelve and eleven at the time. My mother spent most of the night washing the dishes over and over. We talked to my brother John who was in Cambridge, Massachusetts, working as a librarian. He drove straight through, arriving the next afternoon with his wife, Rebecca.

It has often occurred to me that surviving family members meet violent deaths in an enduring state of recoil. Forty years later the mood, the ambience, can return as if someone threw a shroud over you. It was already obvious to me that I didn't understand life processes, and I understood death less. Maybe none of us has a clue though the religious have their assurances. I have talked to veterans who say that even on the battlefield there is no emotional preparation. Death leaves you speechless, or at least verbless. You simply become a howling primate, audibly or not, with your bloody heart in your hand wondering how it continues to pump. The word "love" becomes mortally imprecise when the objects of love are torn from us and our love whirls off into the void on their invisible track. Luckily we weren't a TV family because the accident had been announced on the late-evening news before the state police had arrived to tell my mother. Before running out of my in-laws' house I had told Linda that Judith was fine, not being able to bear the whole truth. During the many raw moments that followed I even wondered if it would have been more bearable if we hadn't been such a vitally close family. We never missed kissing each other good night and now two of us were forever missing.

Soon after the funeral we moved in with my mother, Mary, and David. Startlingly enough while reading and working late at night I began to write a couple of finished poems, the first of my life despite my years of ambition to do so. I judged them a little less than contemptible but there is a pleasure in completing a poem no matter that it seemed a mere exercise noting that you were alive. I kept trying to get my little brother, David, to talk but he would continue to have problems doing so in the months ahead. Meanwhile I had refused to honor my agreement to teach in Manton mainly because I privately doubted that I was sane enough to do so. I continued to work on poems late at night and then sleep late in the morning to everyone's dismay. In my family's ethic it was unthinkable not to have a job, but then I felt so generally benumbed I wondered if I could do anything but construction work and in midwinter those jobs were in short supply. The most solid effect of the deaths that I could touch upon was that I must answer to what I thought of as my calling since nothing else on earth had any solidity. I made one of the most grievous errors of my life one day at a lawyer's office when we were discussing a lawsuit over the accident. I was the executor of the minimal estate and had distributed the death certificates, both of which read "macerated brain." That day when I entered the lawyer's office I had noticed him shoving a folder of photos under a sheaf of papers and when he stepped out of the office to speak to his partner I was fool enough to glance at the state police photos of the accident. I had known but it was hard to imagine how a deer rifle in the trunk had broken in half. Now I understood. The other driver was drunk and traveling over eighty on the wrong side of the road, and after dodging a car he thought was backing onto the highway he hit ours head-on. The photo images were from the farthest rungs of hell. I still wonder what compelled me to reach across the desk.

Soon afterwards everyone in the family but myself talked about what should be done with me: my older brother John, my wife Linda and her parents, and my mother. They decided I should be shipped to Cambridge where it was hoped that my brother would have the authority to get me on the right path. It is unpleasant long afterwards to admit the degree to which my paralytic disease was harmful to others. All of the mythologies of manliness that I had instilled in myself from childhood onward were utterly swallowed by the truth of my fragility as a human being. The closest I could get to day-to-day reality was when I held my daughter Jamie on my lap and read her children's stories, which allowed me in a peculiar way to begin to start over.

The day before I left for Boston I was sitting in a snowbound thicket beyond the swamp behind our house and found myself studying a quarrelsome flock of crows. The cold was sharp but bracing, and my wet feet returned me to a time when I had found crows quite fascinating, and now suddenly they were again. For moments my mind became light and airy and I felt thankful that I lived on this earth and still had a wife and daughter whom I loved.

BOSTON AND KINGSLEY

In the late sixties when I first fished in the Florida Keys I was puzzled when I met men who had recently mustered out from service in Vietnam, sometimes fighter pilots at Boca Chica who had done a couple tours and were trying to get back in touch with their stateside existence. These men often had a thousand-yard stare as if they were wild animals still hearing the hounds of war in the distance. They were generally restless within their skins and redefined one's notions of free-floating anxiety. It was immediately perceptible when they were able to shed the past and were simply men fishing or playing pool, walking the beach, as if they had quite suddenly discovered the totality of where they were. One day, as in Phil Caputo's *Rumor of War*, you're unloading a few bodies and hosing blood out of a pickup and then not that far in the future you're walking down Rush Street in Chicago. Quite a jump to fully absorb.

In Michigan I had painted my entire surroundings with my own often selfish grief and when I boarded the Greyhound bus for Boston I was at the very least plucked from ruins from which I wasn't capable of salvaging anything. My brother John, though quite scholarly and with a wide range of interests, was also utterly pragmatic. When he picked me up from the bus station he jokingly said, "I think I'm doing everyone a favor by getting you out of Michigan," a statement that in itself was a lithium bath.

John and Rebecca had a spacious apartment in Cambridge on Kirkland Street just down from the Swedenborg Church and the Peabody. John worked at the Widener Library at Harvard as the circulation librarian, which offered me the immediate delight of access to the truly vast Widener stacks. Michigan State had an adequate library but the Widener was the very best and it was quite impossible to come up empty-handed when looking for an arcane title. I found Blaise Cendrars's *Transiberian Express* translated by John Dos Passos, which William Carlos Williams, a favorite, had mentioned and which Henry Miller had written about in *The Books of My Life*. There was also an exhaustive collection of French and Russian literature in translation which thrilled me but probably didn't add a whit to my sanity quotient. I had learned to love the French Symbolists at a seminar taught at MSU by the Canadian poet A.J.M. Smith, certainly the most influential course of my college years.

Cambridge was a place where it wasn't awkward to think of oneself as an aspiring writer. In the Midwest to set oneself aside as a poet held peerlessly comic, not to speak of pathetic, potential and having revered Hart Crane and researched everything about him tended to make me wary about my so-called roots. As an instance my first weekend in Cambridge we drove out to Concord. When I was a senior in high school and John was in the navy he had sent me a collection of Emerson's essays, which I had devoured with energy. Thoreau was one of my father's enthusiasms. On that cold but sunny afternoon in Concord it meant a good deal to me to see the landscape from which these indisputably great men had emerged.

Within a week I was homesick for my wife and child though I knew Linda was not yet "homesick" for me. I became quite ill for a month which was unsettling but a good transition. When I recovered I'd read the help-wanted columns every morning in the *Boston Globe* with a set of feelings that have been experienced by hundreds of thousands of liberal arts graduates. In short, no one wants us, or not very badly. I also visited employment agencies, which were significantly unthrilled by everything I offered.

I was very lucky to have my brother who was gruffly encouraging. In contrast to the squalor of my first Boston visit I had a surething bed and a guaranteed supper. My dad had commented when I returned from one of my trips and had gone from my normal weight of one-seventy to one-forty that if I had stayed away longer I might weigh nothing. Here we're back to the young poet who sets himself aside from a culture but with scant interest on how to maintain himself from day to day. A few days without enough to eat and he thinks, brilliantly, "Maybe I should get a job." There's an endless suscepti- bility to the parodic, especially within a Midwest backdrop where all good things come from hard work and grit. For a change I was eager to work if only I could find a job that paid enough to support my wife and child. The countless listings for "management trainees" were quite beyond my ken.

Meanwhile I had found a wonderful hangout in Gordon Cairnie's Grolier Book Shop on Plymton Street. Poets visited daily, actual poets rather than the sort of student poets I was familiar with back home. I recall meeting Bill Corbett, Paul Hannigan, Steven Sandy, my future publisher Sam Lawrence, Desmond O'Grady, the small-press publisher Jim Randall, the Harvard class poet Bob Dawson, the printer and poet Bill Ferguson, and the future literary agent An- drew Wylie. One day Robert Lowell and Peter Taylor peeked in and nodded hello. Of course I was a complete nothing but then so were many of the others and being mutually nothing didn't seem to affect our camaraderie. Gordon Cairnie, an old Scotsman, was a rough and taciturn man but a capable though hesitant gossip, full of personal lore of every poet who passed through Cambridge.

Once at midmorning when I left my brother's apartment on Kirkland I saw a few police cars down a side street, and a black lim- ousine out of which emerged Jacqueline Kennedy, the president's wife, who was there to visit her friend John Kenneth Galbraith who, along with Charles Olson, struck me as the world's tallest brilliant man. Seeing the president's wife in an absurd way reassured me that I was in the actual world rather than trapped breathless in a mid- western academic milieu. At the end of my brother's hall lived two daughters of the Nicaraguan dictator Somoza, but they were goofy and pleasant.

Olson, whom I was to meet a number of times in the coming year, held a specific fascination for me though I had noted he wasn't held in any especial esteem at the Grolier Bookshop where the East- ern Academic poets were generally favored. My own taste ran toward farther west, to James Wright, Robert Bly, and to California with

Robert Duncan and Gary Snyder, a disparate group with no association but in my own mind. Even then I had begun to understand how
much taste is based on xenophobia. As far as I remember I never met
another writer at the time who had been in northern Michigan.
Another caveat I felt with regard to the Grolier is that no one was
more than vaguely interested in fiction, and though I hadn't written
more than an occasional trial page I had never fully separated the
two arts. You could say, "Melville, Whitman, and Faulkner," but you
couldn't then add another name of any of the living. Later on I was
occasionally tempted to add Nabokov and Saul Bellow but by then
the game had no particular meaning.

By spring and after three months in the Boston area I felt I was near-
ing the absolute triumph of getting an adequate job. Of course this
was closer to a mere intuition and in my life I've had very few accurate intuitions, but then every morning I would dress in one of my
brother's nice suits, because I had none myself, to "pound the pave-
ment" as they say. After a long day and evening designing a sample ad
campaign for BBD&O I had narrowly missed by a single other candidate getting a good position as a copywriter. It later froze my soul to
think of what emotional trouble my verbal abilities would have gotten me in at a big ad agency. It seems that so much of good luck and
bad are accidental and that the chance meetings that Pasternak had
been criticized for in *Zhivago* are in fact the core of life.

I didn't have time to be disappointed about not becoming an ad
copywriter because two days later I accepted an offer to become a salesman for a book wholesaler, Campbell and Hall. The idea of being a
salesman made me nervous in that I couldn't make good eye contact
what with my blind left eye drifting off at forty-five degrees. The manager, Luther Gosney, who hailed from the Carolinas, assured me that
my eye wouldn't matter because book people at libraries, schools, and
stores were already interested in talking about books so it wouldn't be
like selling cars or real estate where customers are indecisive.

* * *

While flying home to pack up my family, my first time on an airliner, I made notes in a journal about the utter haphazardness of events, perhaps aggravated by the idea that the plane might crash before I had the opportunity to reunite with my wife and daughter. You can find out odd details about people's character by asking them if they think a plane is more or less likely to crash if they are on it. I remembered a Twain scholar telling me that the phenomenal man had said, "We're never the same at night." On certain days, hopefully rare, our brains are as naked and accessible as they are at night, wide open to abrasive distortions and the kinds of questions that swallow the questioner whole. If I had made up my mind about hunting with them a minute earlier, five minutes earlier, moments earlier, my father and sister would have avoided the collision. They would have been ten miles, five miles, a single mile away from fatality. I had also read perhaps too deeply in literary biography and the biographies of painters to know how totally ordinary the struggles of my life had been. Everything in a culture mitigates against the fruition of the individual artist who has been foolhardy enough to set himself aside to answer what he thinks of as a calling. Even apparent encouragement can be a disaster during this early limbo before the heart and mind have achieved their own peculiar balance. The twenty-dollar used typewriter my father had bought me when I told him I intended to be a writer held the possible terror of any blunt instrument, a sledgehammer, an ax, an involved gun that you didn't yet know how to aim. And now I was going home to pack up for Boston, a place never mentioned in the dreamy talks my wife and I had when first married. Since then we always were where we always were because we hadn't the wherewithal to be anywhere else, certainly a condition that half the population of the United States finds itself in, a fact I know from my own humble background. Much later, when Ronald Reagan fatuously said that people in areas of high unemployment should simply move he was evidently ignorant that a mere visit to a doctor and the price of an antibiotic brings many families close to financial disaster.

Meanwhile the poet who has written very few poems and a five-page short story but has stuffed his brain to the cracking point with

the best of American, English, French, Russian, and Spanish literature is going home to load their possessions into a U-Haul trailer,
gather up his wife and daughter who are thrilled to be fearful, and
move east to Boston. They are a few steps up from the Joads but certainly not out of danger. They are most of all deeply involved in the
facts of survival. More than with poetry the mind spins with the question of whether the car will make it pulling the heavy trailer. They
are any young couple on the move, and even the peculiar ambition
to write poems and novels is scarcely extraordinary, and the driver
knows and repeats over and over that only the made thing, the work
done, finally matters, that intentions in themselves can be a crippling
disease, and that ambition bears no more weight than wishing yourself well when you get up in the morning and check in the mirror to
see who you might be.

At this point, I want to stop and describe an experience I had recently
that offered up a punishing metaphor. It had snowed down here in
Patagonia, Arizona, the day before. The area is in the middle of various mountain ranges near the Mexican border, and it was coolish
when I set out quail hunting with my friend the novelist Phil Caputo,
who wrote, among other things, *Rumor of War* about his wretched
experiences as a marine officer in Vietnam. Over the years hunting,
quail hunting in particular, has become more for me on the order of
an older urban man going to a gym in the mostly vain effort to keep
the body limber and operable. There is also the pleasure in watching
a bird dog work the cover where you witness a skill and intensity rarely
seen in the human species. A good dog doesn't have concentration,
it *is* concentration as it fairly floats along with a physical stamina
known only to the best of our athletes.

I knew soon after four-thirty it was time to turn back but then
Rose found a covey that wild-flushed and we stupidly pursued them
rather than turning back to the car, an hour's walk in the opposite
direction. Quite suddenly everything was against us, most dominantly
the improbably rumbled topography. The drainages, the washes or

arroyos that fan off Mount Wrightson in the Santa Ritas, have dug themselves deeply over the centuries, some of them virtual canyons. We didn't have time to backtrack before dark and not being goats we couldn't move laterally across the arroyos to the car. I chose to head southwest along an arroyo called Temporal, but I was one canyon too far to the west, a smaller one that narrowed and was still full of snow in some places, which radiated cold. Just before dark through the narrowing open sky of the arroyo I caught a glimpse of the distant mountains that are south of our casita on the creek where my wife no doubt sat with Phil's wife in growing alarm, in no little way because their husbands are far from youthful and to say the local terrain is treacherous is an understatement.

It became too dark to gamble on walking any farther though I knew we were an hour or less from my kitchen with our usual lavish supplies, including a fresh shipment of French red wine I especially pined for in the now freezing canyon. For the first time in decades I was pleased that I still smoked in that there were two lighters in my pocket. In the pitch dark we were able to gather a bunchgrass called saceton and plenty of kindling from the dead branches of hackberry and mesquite trees. We started a modest fire and in the light it cast we were able to gather more and larger pieces of wood including an enormous log Phil dragged from the wash. Now we had a true bonfire that heated our clearing in at least a twenty-five-foot radius. Rose, who is a bit petulant when not hunting, became overwarm and moved off into the grass for a nap. Before we had started the fire she and Phil's setter, Sage, were still looking for quail in the dark.

The fire meant safety in the same manner it did to Pleistocene man. My geezer body, exhausted by over five hours of rough walking, drew in the heat with the intensest of pleasure, my butt quite cold but my chest, face, and legs gloriously hot with dense sweat of exhaustion drying into the air. I can't say that we were truly comfortable but our bonfire was so reassuring that notions of true comfort were irrelevant. I curled up with Rose who was willing but irritable, the latter possibly because she had been lost three nights in December in a large area empty of people but thriving with the creature world. Rose is what dog trainers call a "competitive bitch." If she is let loose in the field with four male relatives she wants to beat them to the cover. It is a similar impulse to when you're hunting morel mushrooms or wild berries with friends and you very much want to find the mother lode before they do.

Suddenly the dogs perked up their ears at a sound, a resonant coughing, well up in the canyon to the north. It was a mountain lion coughing up a hairball gotten from grooming like a house cat, and abetted by eating furry creatures and swallowing stray hairs. It brought one to attention but not to any fear what with shotguns leaning against a log. There was also the total unlikelihood of the lion's interest in us. In their increasing contiguity to us through no fault of their own they have been known to pick off house pets, a few children, and the occasional jogger behaving like prey. Our alertness was simply a possible genetic reaction similar to hearing rattlesnakes rattling, a grizzly grunting, the twilight howl of a wolf.

Snuggling there with Rose, a very poor substitute for my wife, I attempted to locate myself in the general picture, something I do before sleeping and when I wake up. Members of a number of Native American tribes do this, and the innocent procedure was also advised by Dogen, the fabled Japanese philosopher of Zen. In short, you must find yourself where you already are, obvious but not so easy. I have long been a preposterously inept Zen student, somewhat in the manner of my failed graduate studies. I suspect this Zen oaf thing comes partly from Charles Olson's notion that as artists we should only "traffick" in our own sign, or Robert Graves's dictum that our poet fidelities must not be spread beyond the poem. In my prolonged debut as a geezer I have apparently not settled into wisdom. Every single answer seems umbilically connected to a multitude of questions. When younger I seemed to need a whole fresh metaphysic to get up in the morning. Now a bastard mixture of a few old ones will do.

Where am I? In a cold canyon near the border with the grass in the firelight marbled by snow patches, my left hand on the heartbeat of Rose. I'm looking at the best shadows in years flickering with the strength of the fire off the mesquite and hackberry. At the top of the canyon the strong

*light of the moon spills over the rocks like milk. I am a lost man of sixty-
four curled on the ground with his dog staring up at Orion whose stars in
the clear air are sparking, vivid, incomprehensible.*

Well, we were back in my kitchen at midnight drinking Bandol,
a Provençal red wine I strongly favor, and cooking up some quick
knockwurst and sauerkraut. A helicopter found us, manned by two
men from the Arizona Department of Public Service who were also
paramedics. We gave thumbs-up and tried to wave them away with
their powerful searchlight for fear they'd crash. Caputo, who has had
a great deal of experience, said our LZ (landing zone) was too small.
They finally landed on a nearby ridge and made their way down a
steep slope to us, having directed by GPS a game warden in a pickup
to a nearby trail. So we were "rescued," though I was slightly mourn-
ful as our grand fire was put out with shovels and water.

Years ago I wrote, "How can I be lost when I've never been found?"
A poignant question, but this was a case of cold, clear, lucid *lost*. Usually most of us are lost in the often suffocating effluvia of our lives, or
in the zoolike constructs built around our lives as protective measures,
made by ourselves with ample help from the culture. It's so hard to know
when to jump ship, bail out, cut and run, slide through the bars. Few
things are painfully simple though much is made of simplicity. Getting truly lost only offers up the metaphor with the clarity of a rising
moon, a lion's cough, the heartbeat and snore of a dog, the stars that
drew much closer than was their habit. I am haunted by a story told by
a rancher I know of how someone cut his fence and thirty cows got
loose. A kindly neighbor found the cows and drove them back into
another pasture, only this one was without access to water. Eight of
the thirty cattle died of thirst while gazing at a mountain lake a few
hundred yards in the distance. Over the years troublesome stock tends
to get culled out for practical reasons. A smart and pissed-off cow can
cause problems, a bull even more so. In earlier times the Mexican long-
horns in this area of the Southwest charged contingents of the United
States Cavalry. We love to look for wild animals that our ancestors so
resolutely exterminated with their habitat in a lust for profit. We can
easily love the idea of freedom and wildness but few of us have the power

of our children who might occasionally skip school for a movie, a ball game, or to go swimming. It is strange indeed how the most wild-eyed artists I have known can trip themselves and be lost within themselves. The basic romantic notion that we can always "liberate" ourselves is corruptly optimistic.

After my experience, which in the manner of a true senior I suffered without embarrassment, I said to my wife, "Isn't it wonderful to live in an area where you can get lost." There was no comment. After all she was the one who truly suffered with the idea that her husband might have pitched off one of a thousand available cliffs in the darkness. It's never the conclusions, it's the story, the experience.

Back to Boston and finally not lost like the perpetually unemployed, mildly exultant with a job and a paycheck, not much of one at first but I got a fifty percent raise after three months for accidental reasons. On my book route I visited a partially completed new school but the librarian wasn't there. In a long empty hall a well-dressed man was practicing with a fly rod and we began talking about trout fishing. I politely observed that he was turning over his wrist at the end of each cast, which had the effect of throwing a loop in his monofilament leader. He turned out to be the superintendent for three new schools in the area and the upshot of our fly-casting chat was an order for three complete school libraries partially funded by a government program. This accident overly impressed the manager and owners of Campbell and Hall and I had the fresh experience after a black-sheep existence of being admirable and, along with it, a new Ford station wagon to drive plus the hefty raise.

We had stayed in Cambridge with John and Rebecca a few days and then found an apartment over in Allston on a cusp between Jewish and Catholic neighborhoods near the Brookline town line. We were in a fourth-floor walk-up in a group of buildings called the Longfellow Apartments, a name that gave me some pause after being forced to try to memorize parts of his silly "Hiawatha" in grade school. Even after my solo shot of lugging up our meager belongings and twenty cartons of heavy books I loved our vantage point, from which so much of Boston was strikingly visible. No one thinks, "Boston: Land of Enchantment" in the manner of the *National Geographic*, but in the early sixties it seemed a lively place with a great deal of what is called "intellectual foment" arising from the many colleges and universities in the area, so that after the senescence of the fifties you could almost imagine from the rooftop the clouds above Boston to be clouds of ideas.

My book routes on varying days took me from Newburyport to Fitchburg to Providence in Rhode Island and to New Bedford, which as a Melville addict I loved. The area was storied in the oldest sense and while I was driving place-names would find their coordinates in my reading, and not always pleasantly. Driving across a bridge in Waltham I became certain that it was the bridge poor Quentin Compson had flung himself from in Faulkner's *The Sound and the Fury*. With Hawthorne north on the coast I couldn't help but wish that he had had the sense to escape to the early prostitutes around Scollay Square given that his wife was a cold-hearted virago.

Frequently I completed my rounds by midafternoon which allowed me to write, nap from a long writing night, or take my daughter Jamie for a ride or walk. We would stop at an old-style delicatessen on Brookline Avenue and share a platter of herring to the admiration of ancient Jewish men who would pat little goy Jamie on the head for eating her herring and onions.

As a midwesterner I have always been quite the fool for self-improvement schemes, an impulse that becomes nearly liturgical in more isolated areas. In Horatio Alger young men were bent on "improving their lot." You are either exercising yourself to a frazzle using the "dynamic tension" of Charles Atlas, improving your word power, saving your pennies in a big jar, making use of every minute, studying treasure maps, or reading biographies of men who made it "up from the depths." This kind of inane bullshit later exfoliated into Vince Lombardi's notion of toughness and the kind of rabid Americanism that was bent on punishing any form of dissent. On my sales route in the Boston area this penchant took the form of selecting a novelist or poet to meditate upon each day during the humdrum struggle with traffic and unknown roads. There were separate days of William Carlos Williams, Melville (especially *Billy Budd*, which confused me), Kierkegaard, Turgenev, Dos Passos, Rilke, Lorca, Céline (who didn't produce a good sales attitude), the journalist Dwight Macdonald, Steinbeck, and many others. I had been rereading the unfashionable Steinbeck in honor of my dead sister since he was her favorite author. My father had given me *Grapes of Wrath* when I was about twelve and it had produced so much sorrow in me in the manner of an American Dickens. In Boston I thought that Steinbeck like Mark Twain might have been generally denied a higher place because he was insufficiently puzzling to produce a goodly number of professional jobs like Eliot and Joyce. I was meditating on Steinbeck the day I walked into the Hathaway Bookshop in Wellesley and the stock clerk told me John Kennedy had been shot. This produced mutual tears as we sat there in the basement among the book cartons drinking coffee and listening to the radio.

I have long supposed that the central value of this very ordinary job was its settling effect on the enervation of unemployment and death. Driving solo can be soothing like gardening, fishing, or hunting. Where can we run from the knowledge and wisdom that we think we have but which is actually crippling our imaginations? The sedentary life often leaves us with no room for surprises while the movement of walking alone or driving can stir our neurons to unexpected life.

We had bought a couch at Filene's on layaway, the first big purchase of our marriage, and when it was finally delivered we had a party and the couch received its first red-wine stains. I continued to go to Grolier Book Shop on Saturday mornings and there is the question of how young, unfinished poets can talk at such endless length about poetry. The immense pink-faced bartender at Jake Wirths where we'd take the subway for lunch would shake his head, being more accustomed to sports fans. My old college friend and poet J. D. Reed had moved to Concord with his wife, Carol, so we saw them and the poet

Bill Corbett and his wife, Beverly, plus my brother John and his wife, Rebecca. We all drank too much except my brother and his wife, but then for an all too brief period in anyone's life alcohol can be quite forgiving. Since my job included lugging cartons of books I stayed in fine shape but my morning head was often fuzzy. On the way home I'd grocery-shop, particularly at a budget supermarket in Waltham where fresh scrod came as cheap as nineteen cents a pound. Only someone from the waspish Protestant Midwest can appreciate with enthusiasm what was available in Boston, from cheap ethnic restaurants, to delicatessens, to a grand fish store on Brookline Avenue, to the delicacies at Sage's in Cambridge.

I continued to write slowly under the cautionary onus of having read fine poetry in great quantity. In the spring of our first year I had ten completed poems and wanted to get back in touch with Galway Kinnell, who had been quite encouraging in a conversation we had had when he appeared at Michigan State. He had been subletting Denise Levertov's New York City apartment and that was the only number I had. I spoke with Denise whose work I knew quite well and she suggested I send some of my poems to her. I did so with a great deal of nervousness because no one but my wife, Linda, still my first and most valued reader, had seen my poems, certainly not my fellow unpublished poets. By common unworded consent we took the private high road, mostly out of the fear of judgment. As any scam artist knows you maintain your credibility by keeping others in the dark, and there had always been a tiny nodule back in my brain telling me I was a fake. For survival a young artist boundlessly inflates his ego hoping very much that the evidence will naturally follow. This was frankly a period in my life when I spent as little time as possible in front of a mirror.

It was in a little more than a week that I got a fat letter back from Denise, which I assumed contained my poems. Instead it was a ten-page scrawled letter saying that she had recently been appointed the consultant for poetry at W.W. Norton and if I had a manuscript of the same quality as the ten poems I had sent her she could certainly get me a contract for publication. Naturally I was dumbfounded

and fearful. This was absolutely my first approbation from the world
outside and it unnerved me. I had inherited a deep and unpleasant
maudlin streak from my father that told me nothing ultimately good
comes from anything. Wine might be good but the only thing you
could rely on was God's water. That sort of thing. I shared Levertov's
letter only with my wife for fear it would be bad luck to tell my fellow scruffy poets. I then set about mining my notebooks for unfinished work, false starts, bits and pieces, unruly longer poems that had
left me wondering what I had been attempting. A month later I sent
off the completed manuscript and settled in for what I assumed, having heard the war stories of poets at Grolier, could be a long wait.

I don't want to make too much of this experience but it is the
writer's first book in which are encapsulated the aggregate of his
dreams from the entire life he has lived to this point. Thus far, in my
case, I had not a printed word to offer up. I had had certain experiences that confirmed my grandmother Harrison's often repeated
notion that "life is a vale of woe." I still give biscuits to stray dogs to
placate the gods, identifying absurdly with stray dogs and wishing
them to feel better. Ultimately we want a measure of vindication for
all of the passionate energy we have given our art, a dangerous state
of mind in that the craving for vindication leads to a blinding self-
importance, the flip side being the self-pity that occurs when the
vindication is never commensurate to the effort. I have often told
young writers that if they depend on the collective media for reassurance they will be lost in the long periods when the media totally
ignores them. I keep remembering a strange experience I had with
my father about which I had written a short story in college in a faux
Flannery O'Connor–Eudora Welty style. It was a very hot summer
morning with the air looking yellow and an impending but as yet
invisible storm, which often followed extreme heat. We visited a
young farm family, a couple with a child who was severely impaired.
We sat at a table in an airless room with worn linoleum and the child
sat on the floor with its strangely shaped head pressed against the cool
chromium skirt of a potbellied stove. The mother told us proudly the
child was smart enough to keep its face cool. This was "the dark and

troubled side of life" mentioned in a song we sang at school with a refrain of "keep on the sunny side." This vision of the child has always been an inscrutable parable for me, a verbless image of reality forming a solid holographic picture.

Meanwhile, I waited with my wife not all that long, and then the unquestionably good news came on W.W. Norton stationery. So there I was thrust into "success," which is what getting a New York publisher is considered by poets. I couldn't help but feel giddy and uncomfortable, the latter emphasized when I entered Grolier to spread my good news and sensed that I was no longer the same member of our group. We all became even better friends but I was no longer allowed the easy camaraderie of the woebegone. I did not fully understand this until later in my life when I suddenly made a bunch of money from Hollywood and I was no longer "Jim" who drove an ancient station wagon with mouse nests in the back. A new deference entered the air and I uncomfortably became "Mr. Harrison" to many.

Despite the artistic light at the end of the tunnel (I liked it a few years ago when James Hillman said the idea that there is light at the end of the tunnel has been mostly a boon to pharmaceutical manufacturers), after a year in Boston we were getting homesick for the country and a more familiar way of life that would, of course, exclude the academic. I drove all week long but still tried to summon the desire to get Linda out of our congested apartment neighborhood one day of the weekend. Our favorite route was west where we'd eat splendid fresh fried clams in Hopkinton, and then drive east from Holliston toward Dover. Several times we attended horse shows, as Linda had owned horses since she was seven right up to the still questionable moment when she married me. The horse shows, English style, were very fancy compared to the midwestern variety. We even attended a polo match up in Beverly, a sport that is unrecognized in terms of its superb athleticism. The gentry were quite friendly compared to what I thought one might expect. Of course this was 1963, before the overcrowding in the Boston area made everyone more reticent and wary. I must say that I don't recall any snobbism around Harvard to an outlander poet. Years later at a reading and dinner there I was seated next to its president, Derek Bok, who asked me if I might like to come there for a year but though it was tempting to be around so many brilliant people I was doing too well in Hollywood at the time and also depended on my hunting and fishing. After a couple of years at Harvard's Widener Library my brother John moved on to become the science librarian at Yale and when visiting and doing a reading at Yale I found the aura to be much more abrasively snobbish than at Harvard. Further down the economic food chain Boston could be amusing. I've always been inclined toward the Irish and Italians and once when driving around a hellish Dorchester rotary a cabdriver started yelling and screaming at me. I pinned the cab to a curb with my car but when I walked up to his window my anger was disarmed. "Where you from anyway? You're not supposed to get out of the car when you're pissed off." The local bar in Allston had a line of half a dozen pay phones and when I asked the bartender why he said, "Where you from anyway? You stupid? The phones are for the fucking bookies." He was ceaselessly amused by my Michigan farmer's slow speech, an accent he compared to that of the comedian Herb Shriner.

Our favorite outing, usually overnight, was to Halibut Point, where J.D. Reed and his wife Carol, a fine painter, had moved from Concord. The summer of '64 in Boston seemed brutally hot and Halibut Point, a promontory into the Atlantic, was deliciously cool with its ocean breezes. I remember stooping with my daughter Jamie to gaze into a tidal pool and being struck by the profligate fertility of salt water compared to fresh, the tiny creatures with bizarre shapes crisscrossing the trapped water between tides. In Gloucester you could also buy a submarine sandwich stuffed with fresh lobster. J.D. had gotten to know Charles Olson and it was electrifying to spend time with this great man, one of the most fascinating poets in our literature. J.D. was a very large man, about six-four and three hundred pounds, but Charles quite literally dwarfed him. Both J.D. and Charles had been banned from a number of Gloucester bars for bad behavior so we always settled for a

Portuguese bar whose single food item was "pussy stew two bucks," a wonderful fish and shellfish stew. Charles was a hypnotic talker who urged me to read dozens of books, including Robert Duncan who later became a friend and mentor though I was totally unlike him as a poet. Eventually Robert was beside Charles in a deathbed vigil and wrote me a long diary-letter surrounding that sad event.

The Boston area was lively with poetry in those days and I suppose it still is. I remember the exotic and brilliant Garett Lansing, the waif John Wieners, James Tate, Fanny Howe, Michael Palmer, Clark Coolidge, and many others. Denise Levertov was in temporary residency at Radcliffe and introduced me to Adrienne Rich. I've often thought that these two fabulous women never got their due, say compared to Anne Sexton and Sylvia Plath, who became famous for basically sociological reasons quite beyond their own control. I saw the same thing happen to Kerouac, also my friend Richard Brautigan (who loaned me enough money later to write my novel *Farmer*), and more recently to Jay McInerney. The media at large seizes these people to exhaustion and it is difficult to survive the misunderstanding of the actual work. The attention always seems anterior to the art in the case of Robert Lowell or Allen Ginsberg.

Things were going well but we were getting fatigued with city life and had the sure understanding that we didn't belong there. I had a number of poems accepted by *The Nation* and *Poetry*, the first appearances of my work. I was chosen for the YMHA Discovery Series, which was my first public reading and for which I took the train with Bill Corbett and J.D. to New York City. Corbett was a dapper Connecticut boy and was quite critical when I wore a black shirt to make a courtesy visit to George Brockway, then the president of Norton and a very imposing gentleman.

By spring we were simply sick of urban life and I turned in my resignation. To this day I'm not sure what we had in mind other than the disastrously uncertain future of moving to northern Michigan where a college friend of mine, Lisle Earl, lived. I had a painful lunch at

Lockeober's with the owner of Campbell and Hall, Bushrod Campbell, an old New Englander out of Bowdoin who thought it was incomprehensible for me to leave with my "bright" future in the business. As a fibber since childhood I went to cowardly and unnecessary lengths saying my wife was having mental problems. A few months later when we were living in a junky thirty-five-dollar-a-month house in Kingsley and I was doing menial labor for two and a half dollars an hour I received a letter from National Shawmut Bank in Boston offering to fly me out to interview for a position as a trust officer because one of their clients, Bushrod Campbell, had assured them that I was the man for the job. I was troubled rather than tempted. While mixing cement on a freezing dawn I wondered how I had managed to give this evidently convincing impression of competence. Of course many poets are "shape changers," to use a Native American term. Wallace Stevens is an obvious example as is Ted Kooser, one of my favorite American poets, who was a vice president of an insurance company in Lincoln, Nebraska. And I've often thought that many of the poets I've known who are so brilliantly voluble would have made very good criminal-defense lawyers. Nonetheless, while trying to convince many that I was a poet, I had convinced the book wholesaler's owner that I was a whiz at business.

We loved the Kingsley area where we had towed the usual U-Haul trailer but not the macaroni-type diet that befell us. Kingsley is now mostly a suburb of sprawling Traverse City but in the midsixties it was a totally rural village surrounded by forests and not very prosperous farms, and two very good trout rivers, the fabled Boardman and the Manistee. The heart swelled with the beautiful landscape that would appear nondescript and scrubby to those who favor the cordillera of the Rockies but to me it was homeground, similar to the terrain around Reed City where I had grown up. Unfortunately the heart that swelled easily contracted at the prospect of making enough money for food and shelter. I was taken under the rumpled wing of Pat Paton, a part-time brick and block layer and builder who also worked the night shift at a factory in Traverse City, some twenty miles distant. In the morning we'd do everything from trimming Christmas trees to putting in foundations of houses and other cement work to roughing in and roofing houses. This didn't quite add up to a living even with our cheap and drafty rental. The main trouble was in covering the monster fuel bill and still having something left over for groceries. I also wrecked our car so we were left on foot. Once in the middle of winter it was below zero and we ran out of fuel oil with no money to buy more and our savior Pat Paton hot-wired a fuel truck and gave us a free tank full.

Another fool's paradise was the twelve weeks that I collected fifty bucks for unemployment. Still, we were happy to be out of the city, though even with my writer's efflorescing ego I could clearly spot doom on the horizon. The high point was in November when my first book, *Plain Song,* arrived. I smelled it for its new-book smell. I pressed it to my bare chest and had a drink. Pat had given us some venison and we celebrated with a half gallon of Gallo burgundy, a mainstay in those days.

Our marginal lifestyle wasn't frowned on locally because so many people in the community were equally poor. A friend, Jon Jackson, who later was to become a successful mystery writer, was trying to subsist on cabbage and potatoes. He stopped by on winter mornings with the newspaper hoping for a fried egg or two. Jamie was quite happy in kindergarten with plenty of friends so it would have been quite idyllic with the paycheck that I couldn't muster. Tom McGuane, visited with his wife Becky to fish and we had a splendid time. They were fresh out of a year in Málaga in Spain and headed for Wallace Stegner's esteemed writing program at Stanford. We began a mostly literary correspondence that continues to this day, in addition to becoming close friends. Sad to say the poverty that year in Kingsley became what is called "grinding."

If you think very deeply about your past you are back against Dostoyevsky's wall in reverse, the wall as thick as your life has been long. Your duty to dash your head against this wall is neither here nor there because that is what you end up doing anyway. There is no more disarming absurdity than asking, "What if I had . . ." because it invariably deals with key events that affected every single day, however slightly, in the life that followed. Each day, let alone hours and minutes, owns its fatality and this is no more grim or not grim than any other natural biological fact. We don't need clocks to tell us that. The old Zen man who said, "Throughout the body are hands and eyes" knew his own phenology and the sun's descensions draw us surely on with our increasingly melancholy birthdays. I can't mentally withdraw that day I made an abysmally stupid decision because how it affected the rest of my life is clear to me, and the life I have lived since carries the weight of that inevitably forgivable stupidity. That's life, we wisely say.

I brought us from Boston to Kingsley out of that fated Portuguese notion of *saudade*, the place or person that draws out of us our most extreme and improbable yearning, no matter that it is a homesickness for a home that never quite existed, a longing for a prelapsarian, Adamic existence that the mind creates out of filaments of idealized memories, as if by finding a similar landscape I could return myself to a state before everyone started dying.

In short, I am no less a fool for recognizing how foolish I was. When it was twenty below in Kingsley I could run a finger along a crack of the shabby wooden wall beside the bed and feel the nature of the outside. I would time the starts and stops of the decrepit furnace which could barely bring the house to sixty degrees. I could envision the nine dollars in my wallet. I would listen to the breathing of Linda and envy her acceptance of things as they were. I didn't recognize it at the time but I was lucky that my upbringing cautioned strongly against self-importance which is the flip side of self-pity. I brooded with amazing competence and it had already occurred to me this might be due to the fact that I was half Swede. Of course I had read all of the fabled Strindberg, Sigrid Undset, Tomas Tranströmer the doomed Stig Dagerman whose suicide was incomprehensible because he had been living with the beautiful actress Harriet Anderson. I easily dismissed this genetic fancy as I viewed myself as a totally free man though studying Camus so strenuously in college had taught me that personal freedom could be problematic. I knew that in Kingsley we were living as well as my mother had lived with her sisters and parents. As a child I had carried my hot flat stone wrapped in a towel up the stairs to the unheated room that still held the steam trunks of the passage from Sweden. It is scarcely privation to feel the delicious warmth of a rock in a cold bed. We weren't living as well as my father had provided for us but we weren't all that far off the mark. I was understandably embarrassed when we visited my rather elegant in-laws in East Lansing, but when we got in the car to drive back north Linda was quite happy to return to the thread-bare life I had unwittingly chosen for us. Love doesn't conquer all but it conquers a lot. Romantic love has suffered a great deal of ridi-cule in recent decades but however illusive or illusionary it main-tains the vigor of marriage. The fact that holding your wife's hand after forty or so years of marriage sometimes sets your heart thump-ing suggests that together you may have done something right.

In Kingsley I was often referred to as "Shakespeare" though not derisively. What else were they to think in this humble village with a New York-published poet in their midst, no matter that he was a construction worker who liked to hang out in the tavern with his friends. My boss and friend Pat Paton called me "Jim Indian" be-cause my dark complexion became very dark with outside work. Oc-casionally in college I'd say I was part black to catch reactions. In recent years some actresses and other well-intentioned nitwits have taken to claiming they are part Cherokee but I've supposed that this is because Cherokee is the only tribal name they likely know. Ac-tresses and others are much less likely to say that they are part black. Americans in particular regions are so often of mixed blood, partly because of the limited talent pool for their affections. When I saw Dorothy Dandridge in the movie *Carmen Jones* I was immediately in love.

Sad to say, widely parodied aspects of the poet's character seem as soundly based as the "mad scientist," or the crazy painter, but then single-minded, obsessed people are susceptible to parody. If alcohol is the writer's black lung disease, this seems particularly true of poets. When you add alcohol to other eccentricities such as logorrhea,

womanizing, often more than a touch of manic depression, you easily come up with a wildly colored dodo bird who might benefit by
being hosed down with lithium every morning. I've become a bit
reclusive over the years and no longer travel in poets' circles so I
can't say if this behavior still persists but it was certainly true in the
sixties and seventies when so many poets were bent on following
the fatal example of Dylan Thomas. Years later while doing readings in the Minneapolis area in the winter I was shown the site of
John Berryman's suicide and told that in his not very birdlike leap
from the bridge he had managed to miss the water and hit the shelf
ice. I'd like to make an exception for myself but I can't. I was an
"excitable boy," worse than most but not quite as bad as some. You
can't make much that is less than comic out of men who when traveling are perpetually at their first night of the convention. Point
the way to the good times and they'll be there first no matter that
at dawn they're bleating and eating the rug. While writing this and
straining to come up with exceptions I think of Robert Duncan who
came closest to the term "naturally high," or Gary Snyder who had
a unilateral stability despite any amount of drink, while Charles
Olson, Theodore Roethke, Robert Lowell, James Dickey, and James
Wright seemed set on some predestined self-destruction. James
Wright appeared to suffer from a unique demon that he subdued
well before his death.

Trout fishing and grouse hunting maintained my often slumping
spirits when nothing else would work except possibly my daughter
Jamie and an English pointer puppy we had gotten from the dog
pound. Though I've never cared for deer hunting, it was painful to
miss an easy shot in Kingsley because of the lost meat involved. My
cold evenings in a study I had set up in our attic were problematic in
that I had begun to study fiction in the same kind of long process
required in the writing of my poetry. I had stacks of "vignettes" but
not much more, just as with poetry I had subsisted for years in the

scraps of lines. When you are reading only the best the openings seem
quite limited. What could I learn from Faulkner's *The Sound and the
Fury*? Nothing that would work for me.

In the spring of that year I went down to Central Michigan
University to do a reading and the trip was difficult. The only sensible route would lead me past the site of the death of my father and
sister. Luckily I took another shirt because I soaked the one I was wearing with the coldest of sweats, and the highway had become a swirl
of images of that final moment. Along with my mother I had attended
several legal meetings dealing with the lawsuit over the matter, end-
lessly delayed by insurance lawyers in their usual war of attrition. Our
suit requested only the lost wages of the innocent father but that
doesn't mean a great deal in lawyer circles. We ended up settling for
far less because my mother, simply enough, found the idea of going to
trial unendurable. When I summon up the recollection my face still
burns with the verbal filth and sheer trickery of this legal language. The
fault was never in question, only the manner in which they could wear
us down and send the widow home with as little as possible. Even at
that our lawyer blithely took nearly half of what came our way. Later
when I was called up for jury duty my normally sturdy stomach churned
with nausea as I entered a courtroom where the strong so frequently
grind the weak under their expensive boot heels.

After the Central Michigan reading I had a perception that has
stuck with me ever since which was not without the cluttered ironies that abound in our lives. Literature teachers whether in high
school, college, or at the graduate level look at you shrewdly, apparently judging whether you should be accepted into a club in which it
is unlikely that they themselves will ever be members, but because
of their affection for their own literary favorites they view themselves,
perhaps properly, as guardians of some thoroughly imaginary gate, forgetting that time herself will tell, and not all that accurately in the
short term. It is startling indeed to look at old anthologies or see prize
lists in almanacs and see the "disappeared ones," not from political
terror but by the way time stretched them thin to the point of invis-
ibility. About the time I was in Boston, Conrad Aiken, a friend of

Gordon Cairnie, the proprietor of Grolier, had said that he had acquired a major reputation without being caught in the act. Not really. An amazing number of literary professors, especially along the Atlantic, seem irritated that the long-dead Steinbeck slipped through the gate without their permission. Poor Tu Fu never published a book while alive.

Late in the winter I seemed to be slipping toward depression because my own romantic delusions about life in the North had left us literally cold. Herbert Weisinger came to my rescue, summoning me down to East Lansing for a meeting at which he proposed that I write a master's thesis on how I wrote my first book of poems, *Plain Song*, and then he would facilitate my getting a degree which would allow me to find a "proper job." The department now looked at their black sheep as white though only a few of them were outwardly friendly. If I had been them I'd also have gotten rid of me.

I wrote the paper, which was eventually published in a book of my nonfiction called *Just Before Dark*. I never looked at the long essay myself, leaving the proofs to my oldest daughter, Jamie, who edited the book. Herbert used his power as chairman of the department to waive certain exams, not wanting to gamble on me taking a test or flying off the handle again, as it were.

The degree was awarded, a pure acknowledgment of the power of New York publishers, and Linda and I headed farther north to Northern Michigan University for an interview and I was promptly given a job. It was early summer now and the Upper Peninsula countryside was wild and beautiful. We were a bit unnerved but encouraged though we failed on that first visit to find a place to live. It turned out to be lucky that we didn't sign an apartment or house lease because a scant week later Herbert called to say he had accepted the position of chairman of English and hoped I would join him as his assistant at the State University of New York at Stony Brook out on Long Island. Herbert would get me out of the contract I had signed with Northern Michigan University.

Normally poetry and fiction, not unlike painting and sculpture, are considered to be solo acts but I've been forced to note recently how many others have had some specific influence on the occasionally helpless arc of my life. It seems that I can effectively deal with practical problems as long as I'm not actively writing poems or fiction, but if I am my good sense is confined to that "métier," and I can't deal well with anything outside the arena of the imagination. This is embarrassing to admit for someone who grew up in close confines with the iron-hard facts of life as it suggests the somewhat mysterious experience of "possession," of the creative (loathsome word) act as a seizure. I'm afraid so, though it makes me uncomfortable to think about it. The material at hand slowly takes over the brain and other considerations fall away. Certain friends and acquaintances have noticed this failing and have moved politely toward solving the messes caused by my ineptness.

I had known Herbert at Michigan State where I was a prominent, if obnoxious, student in comparative literature after abandoning English and American literature as too small a piece of the pie. Even then nationalism in the study of literature seemed to truncate possibilities. Herbert Weisinger, though from Brooklyn, was in the grand tradition of European scholarship that saw its full flowering when refugees from World War II joined the faculties of American universities. Herbert still is the most brilliant man I've ever known, quite at home as a scholar of Shakespeare, a mythographer, an expert at art history, and apparently familiar with the semi-secret corners of world history, not to speak of anthropology, and the history of science. He had studied at the Warburg Institute in London and also spent a year at the Princeton Institute for Advanced Study.

We had stayed in touch and after the death of my father, Herbert did his best to help me. His best friend other than his wife, Mildred, was a Canadian poet of some repute, A.J.M. Smith who had known Malcolm Lowry of *Under the Volcano* fame. Being around these two men made the world of literature close to home, though not quite as close as I felt in New York. Both men understood that I felt "called" to be a poet rather than a scholar though we never talked about it and I had nothing to show for my intentions except a notebook from which I read to my father a single time a month before his death.

Herbert was able to get a collar on me with great subtleness so that I was nearly unaware of his concerns. His old friends like the Panofskys at Princeton, the critic Kenneth Burke, Joseph Campbell, or the anthropologist Loren Eiseley had their names arise only in the form of diffident witticisms, not name-dropping. He was not quite shy but certainly avoided being forward. I was a very late bloomer and Herbert quite naturally stepped in when I lost my father. From the time I first met him we had spoken jokingly of my self-improvement binges. When I was mentally troubled I would read Karen Horney, Adler, or most likely Jung, while Herbert was more of a Freudian. He did not discount Jung but reminded me deftly that I had to function within the realm of the ordinary. When I expressed nervousness about helping him run a large English department he assured me that I would find it "nearly child's play" now that I had published one book, which had done well enough in terms of attention that I had a contract for another. Herbert's faith reminded me of that of Bushrod Campbell at the Boston book wholesaler.

When I drove out east for my perfunctory interview I spent the night in Branford, Connecticut, with my brother John and his family, then drove early to catch the ferry from Bridgeport to Port Jefferson on Long Island. It was a warm August morning with the sea calm, the air clear and delicious. Despite relentlessly battling my superstitious streak I felt the omens were auspicious. Traveling toward a new job by boat seemed vaguely mythic and I felt a surge of optimism that hadn't been there since I held my first book in my hands. The meeting with senior professors was pleasant and brief and I returned home to gather up my family.

We naturally make much of our survival dramas. The fantasy of having the rest of your life off to simply write becomes transparently silly when it happens, and you lapse back to your childhood dreams when you wished to be an Indian, a fireman, or just a plain old hero. At any age you can wish for a miracle that life is ill suited to deliver. When you look at the billions raked in by state lotteries where the odds of the big prize are fifteen million to one your mind softens toward the sheer goofiness of human behavior.

Good luck and bad are confused notions. I was very lucky to come to Stony Brook, to be dropped into, for rather haphazard reasons, an academic and literary atmosphere far more intense than anything the Midwest could offer. Working for a book wholesaler had given me an abrasively raw look into how the end product of publishing works. This was an eventual advantage as I didn't indulge in wasting time with the unrealistic expectations of hinterland writers. On my first day on the job when the department had gathered for the new semester I was introduced to Alfred Kazin and Philip Roth. Since I had read everything they had written this was a rather heady experience. I can't say that either was very friendly at the time but then I was the new kid on the block who might eventually have a real influence on what they taught and their schedules. There is also the point of Buckminster Fuller that a "high energy construct" doesn't waste time. Being brusque with a tinge of politeness is mostly a way of saving your sorry ass from the multiple demands of people trying to get you to do what you don't want to do.

Stony Brook could easily draw on so many first-rate people because New York City was only sixty miles away. I had known Herbert Weisinger for years but wasn't prepared for the delight I took in being around so many Jewish intellectuals who spoke about ideas as if they were living organisms. In contrast to the laid-back, soporific Midwest, ideas became part of the day's contents. I remember Kazin, Peter Shaw, Vivian Gornick, and Jack Thompson, who was part of the Trilling group out of Columbia, wrangling about a literary point in the hall outside my office at a level that made anything similar I'd heard before look amateurish. This was at a time, 1966, before poets and novelists had become accepted fixtures in English departments.

* * *

At last we were living in a grown-up house, a bit run-down but in a pleasant neighborhood with less than a block to the Long Island Sound from which our daughter Jamie would return with horseshoe crabs. I quickly became friends with Robert White who taught in the art department. Robert White was the grandson of the architect Stanford White and lived on the beautiful wooded and expansive family compound in nearby St. James. One day soon after we met, Bobby asked us over to dinner with William and Rose Styron and Deborah and Peter Matthiessen. Again, this was a startling experience because I had read the work of these literary giants. I had heard that Bobby White "inspired" Styron's *Set This House on Fire*. I also noticed that people drank a great deal so I felt right at home. Later on, after living quite remotely for over thirty years, it occurred to me that this social contiguity among writers tends to matter more than it should, or when people pretend that it doesn't matter they're speaking either innocently or falsely. I'm not absolutely sure that when I eventually had lunch with Kazin at his club in New York and we had a drink with Gordon Ray who was president of the Guggenheim Foundation that it had anything to do with me getting a grant but I don't discount it.

I was back writing at night as I had done as a book salesman but the Stony Brook atmosphere had enlivened me so that I wasted far less time brooding. It is often a good idea for a writer to move to the country but it's probably a mistake to do so too early. It was a comfort to write at night knowing when the furnace came on that I could pay the fuel bill, and a greater comfort yet to know that the furnace would rouse the house to a livable temperature. If only our dog Missy hadn't eaten my *Collected Yeats*, my Christopher Smart, and chewed on a number of others.

It's hard to step back from the incalculable messiness of life. In fact, the messiness *is* your life into which you hope to install a perceptible narrative line. Since childhood I've loved to watch birds and I've imagined when buried in my own mess what it would be like to be a bird with high human intelligence, with the ability to see life topographically and to see time holographically. Amid the welter you'd always be able to grab the main chance like an avian predator, say like a goshawk with its unique degree of concentration and irritability, but then as a human your total perspective most likely arrives when you're sitting in the confined environment of a bathtub.

Way back when I used to jokingly quip to whining fellow writers, "Tell it to Anne Frank." Over thirty years later I can look into the tiny sunroom of the house in Stony Brook from which I could see the moon and stars around leafy or bare trees when I wrote at night. The dog was apologetic about eating books but the damage was done. The corners of a volume by Mandelstam were also missing. At the time I resented the idea that my early religious passion had merely been taken over by literary passion because it stole all possibilities of cool sanity from my endeavors, of stepping back far enough to design a less confusing life.

The inventor of Parcheesi was doubtless enthralled by the life steps that led him to his discovery. In the seventies in Montana at McGuane's ranch in whatever drug and alcohol haze we used to read to each other from a biography of the inventor of black-velvet painting who made the breakthrough in the South Seas while on the track of the spirit of Gauguin. The wild humor was in the vast distance between the flowery and pompous language and the end product, which you can still find at yard sales and certain stores. How can you measure banality when looking into your own heart and mind? What was Timoshenko really thinking before his maps of war? Had Henry Kissinger finished his orange juice that morning when he made the phone call that cost the lives of another hundred thousand Asians? Of what precise concern is the recent interest in the sexual behavior of Picasso and Einstein? Many appear to have a deep interest in it. For our immediate purposes how could Mandelstam have continued writing so beautifully as he faced his gruesome concentration camp death? What is poetry that we continue writing it as history unravels around us? Of course it was always thus. I think of the careers of some of my favorite Chinese poets, the obvious Li Po and Tu Fu and the transcendent Su Tung-p'o, who suffered war, exile, imprisonment, and the deaths of two wives, and it seems unimaginable that they wrote this immortal work. It continues to be a mystery as does the scientific fact that birds rehearse their songs and vary them during their dream life. We can't stop.

Back to the confusion and living within the confines of our fragile minds. One day recently I learned that my last book of novellas, *The Beast God Forgot to Invent*, would be published in Thailand. A half hour later when I arrived at my studio at the Hard Luck Ranch I found out that my favorite cow dog had died suddenly while choking on food. I went out in the backyard and wept because I loved this girl who had lived only a single year. Every morning on hearing my car she would run up the road a few hundred yards to greet me, then pretend she was leading me into the yard, trotting smartly and making sure I was following. Naturally I gave her biscuits as a gesture of our not very deep understanding of each other. It is in the nature of the human mind that in the future when I think of Thailand, see my Thai book, or eat Thai food, I will most poignantly remember Mary. We can scarcely extricate ourselves from our own true nature.

I wasn't very long at Stony Brook when it occurred to me that the English department had all the charm of a streetfight where no one ever actually landed a punch. Intelligent people have greater powers of contentiousness. The nexus of difficulty was that many faculty members who had been there for a long time and lived locally resented the newer members, referred to pejoratively as the "stars" who commuted from New York City. The stars preferred or tried to insist on teaching on Tuesdays and Thursdays which would offer them four-day weekends for their "research" or whatever. Tempers flared when crossed, the kind of ice-cold verbal tempers that I wasn't used to. I had been a straw boss of large labor crews on the university horticultural farm but this didn't quite prepare me for telling a New Yorker that he had to commute three days rather than two, or informing an old hand but lesser scholar that the new Yeats man would be teaching a coming graduate seminar. Herbert had a propensity to shove difficult problems my way, including those with the graduate students, most of whom seemed to live as I had as a graduate student—in a perpetual state of anguish. I tended to favor younger and brilliant assistant professors over the kind of old grumps who had tortured me at Michigan State. I was also there at the indulgence of Herbert and totally immune to power plays. Absolutely everyone was "working on a book" and thus wanted to teach as little as possible. How was I to deal with the accusation that the New Yorkers weren't taking part in the evening intellectual life of the college community when it wasn't apparent that there was such a thing? In somewhat quarrelsome meetings it was easy to see that most problems were considered problems of language and that once you got the language right it was presumed the actual problems would go away. There's a torpid subgenre in fiction called the "academic novel" but if you read Mary McCarthy or Randall Jarrell on the subject you need go no further in this fulsome area of the human comedy. My very gradual solution over my two years at Stony Brook was to become more autocratic, not a very popular way to be but then none of the professors seemed prone to act out of anything but immediate self-interest. I had studied the salary schedules and the pay was ample. Herbert's wife Mildred redefined the tough roots of feminism so we as quickly as possible equalized the salaries of male and female professors of equal rank. This was an important point and it was easier to see that later in the history of the feminist movement equal pay for equal work should have been the primary point.

Late in high school when I read Pasternak's *Doctor Zhivago* I was distressed to see that "garrulity is the refuge of mediocrities." I hadn't yet met a single living writer and was hoping to talk to number of them. A few years ago when John Updike reviewed a volume of Edmund Wilson's diaries in *The New Yorker* he isolated a passage wherein Wilson regretted the thousands of hours of literary social contiguity, the drinks, dinners, assignations, events, meetings, award ceremonies, lectures. Of course much of literary reputation is based on social contiguity though not in the longest haul. It is alarming to see how this year's flavor can quickly disappear. I know that some enjoy intense activity and find memorable what is essentially the gossip of past years in memoirs, but then social laundry lists quickly pall. From my own point of view I would have preferred social grocery lists: a case of Domaine Tempier Bandol Tourtine, twelve veal chops, two lobes of fresh foie gras, three tins of duck confit for a salad for twelve, the oldest Calvados affordable. That sort of list, rather than that of the insouciant Mimi, or Bob for that matter, who screwed their way to publication by Knopf, then got tenured jobs at an ivy-strewn Eastern Seaboard campus. Last year a friend sent a memoir by the writer Frederic Prokosch that was densely lumpish with meetings with every famous writer here and in Europe between 1920 and 1940, resolving questions that no one has ever asked and reconfirming the tenuousness of reputation. Literary ice is thin indeed and nearly everyone disappears in the same manner as a coal miner, a farmer, a disenchanted realtor. Long ago I made one of those daffy bargains with fate that I would ask only that my books remain in print. I'm sixty-four and they all are. What more?

Once while doing readings in Minnesota I idly stopped by an ice arena in Minneapolis and watched a group of young men and women practicing speed skating. I was fascinated by the swiftness, the synchronized birdlike waving of arms on the straightaways, the tuck of the inside arm on curves. The technique seemed monochromatic but accomplished and the speed generated quite stunning. At the time I was a woebegone poet drinking too much and struggling with a crack-up. I was lucky that a local New Directions poet, Carl Rakosi, who was also an analyst, had the time and inclination to spend an evening talking over my stalled trajectory. The problems slowly disappeared but the image of the speed skaters stayed with me.

Well before the first year was over I perceived I was by temperament well out of my element at Stony Brook despite the engaging
life of the mind. By nature I'm a semi-recluse, a tad melancholy as a
balance between frightening extremes with an avowed intent of not
sticking my neck out which, conversely, always happens. Just the
other day the writer Charles Bowden told me that if you move a
local black-tipped rattler over two miles it dies. Within two miles,
however, it lifts its snaky head, observes the landscape, and makes
its way home.

The metaphor of speed skating is enviable partly because I am a
poor skater and it was utterly out of my realm of capability. When
we played hockey I was the goalie. A public job such as I had at Stony
Brook was continuous tripping and learning how to fall without dire
injury. One day a professor specializing in Alexander Pope stopped
by my office to tell me that I was "certainly an interesting regional
poet," a matter I had already noted in my journal, to wit, everything
written outside the confines of New York City is "regional," even
William Carlos Williams in New Jersey. Another emotional pratfall
came at Christmas when Linda and Jamie went home to Michigan
and I had been asked to do the preliminary interviewing at the Modern Language Association in New York City, the annual national
Christmas vacation cattle call for candidates for jobs in English departments. I had wide experience in being unemployed and it was
painful talking to thirty or so male and female recent Ph.D.'s who
desperately wanted to join Stony Brook faculty for reasons of high
pay and closeness to Gotham, the nearly pathetic silliness of Stony
Brook having become a "hot" place to teach. This was hard to perceive as I had observed that all but a few students were surly and
muttonish for reasons of temperament and hormones. The high point
of MLA was walking over to Schine's, where my college friend Bob
Dattila had told me his father worked. This very large and imposing
Sicilian made me the thickest rare roast beef sandwich of my life,
which, with a couple of ample whiskeys, allowed me to proceed with
the maudlin interviewing. Later that winter we even turned down
Stephen Spender. Everyone wanted to teach at Stony Brook but no

one wanted to live there. The closeness of New York City was not an unreasonable goal.

I didn't skate, I began drinking too much, the only one in my larger family to do so except my uncles Walter and Artie who had World War II to blame. Naturally I didn't think I was drinking too much because my cronies, J. D. Reed, Gerry Nelson, and Jack Thompson, were drinking more. On the White estate Bobby would shoot an arrow straight up and then all of us drunks including Bobby would run for cover to avoid being killed by the arrow, a sensible and artistic form of Russian roulette.

One of our biggest family expenses at Stony Brook were the phone bills generated by my talking to Tom McGuane out at the Stegner program. George Brockway at Norton had suggested I think of writing a novel and I had no idea where to begin save with a pencil and tablet as advised by Faulkner in his interview in the *Paris Review*. I certainly wasn't going to write about my current experiences. I was supposedly writing a television play for NBC about a man whose favorite moment in life (it's still up there) was giving dogs fresh bones. I gave a reading at the Guggenheim Museum in New York or maybe that was later. I gave a reading for the Academy of American Poets but maybe that was later. I hosted seemingly countless readings for poets like Robert Lowell who definitely didn't seem to care for me when we had lunch with Jack Ludwig. After a James Dickey visit my wife Linda said "that man" wasn't going to enter her house again. James Wright was totally wonderful but by then he had quit drinking. We kept the atmosphere subdued because of Wright's nervous condition. My mother who was visiting at the time was thrilled by the courtly way Wright quoted her so many poems from memory. A few months later I was seated between Wright and W. H. Auden at a dinner at Drue Heinz's palace on the East River. I kindly enough changed seats with Wright who wanted very much to be next to Auden to talk about Edward Thomas and other English poets. Wright had seemed upset that I was talking to Auden about his gay poem "Platonic Blow," which had nearly gotten him arrested before Mayor John Lindsay had called off the blue dogs. Auden, however, didn't have a filament of the bourgeois in his system and his pecan face further cracked with laughter.

The finest experience with a visiting poet was the appearance of Robert Duncan whom I'd never met and now is having a resurgence long after his death. Duncan was a bona fide genius without so much as a simple B.A., and though from San Francisco he had no particular interest other than icy wit in the Beat-academic controversy. During Duncan's visit I took him into a graduate Joyce class and he promptly without notes filled three blackboards with speculations on the structure of *Finnegans Wake*. Herbert Weisinger whispered in my ear, "Double his fee." Both of them had known the great medieval historian Kantvoritz. John Cage was visiting the music department at the time and it was a pleasure to see these two geniuses together at a party at our house. Robert was fretful about missing his vitamins and Cage took Linda aside and said that a couple of aspirin would work. A few years later when I visited San Francisco and stayed with Duncan and his long-term partner Jess I was struck by what was certainly the finest private library I had ever seen.

Maybe I was trying to skate in my bare feet. My truce with the real world was my family, and the ambience of my job was beginning to draw off all of my energy though I had finished a second book of poems, *Locations*, that was soon due for publication. My fantasy life surrounded a fishing trip to Michigan's Upper Peninsula that I had taken with my Kingsley friend Pat Paton the summer before when we had spent time in the truly wild Huron Mountains and seen no one else for days. But meanwhile my mind was also enlivened by a friendship with an instructor, George Quasha, who had a marvelously fertile mind and still does. The second year at Stony Brook I taught a course called "Modern Poetics," which had an assigned reading list of one hundred and twenty books that served to get rid of an overflow of students. I also spent a lot of time with my prized student, Eliot Weinberger, whom I later learned wasn't even enrolled. Aside from his own work Eliot later translated the work of Octavio Paz and many other Spanish-speaking poets of note. Another bright student was Geoffrey O'Brien who currently edits the Library of America. An additional boon occurred late in my first year when Herbert and I decided we needed a reputable poet and hired Louis Simpson away from Berkeley. Simpson was widely thought to be "academic" but it was impossible to think so if you knew the work or the poet. He was wry, laconic, quite playful, and imminently knowledgeable, part Caribbean by birth. Once I had lunch with Louis and Derek Walcott at a German restaurant up near Eighty-second Street and Walcott told me—we were all in our cups—that as opposed to Simpson nothing would come of either of us. A few years ago I was seated next to Walcott and Rose Styron at the head table of my only PEN dinner and I reminded him of this. He said he didn't remember, though it was possible, then teased me into lighting a forbidden cigarette with the effective prod that I was "bourgeois" if I didn't. I did so whereupon hundreds of others took my cue. Future historians studying the media record of our age will come to the unavoidable conclusion that tobacco is the largest issue of our time.

My frequent trips to New York City would leave me exhausted but satisfied. It has dawned on me that my next thirty years spent as a home cook in the hinterlands were largely spent trying to re-create the food that is readily available to New Yorkers every single day, from French to Italian to Chinese to German to soul food and so on. The only item unavailable is first-rate BBQ, especially Texas-style beef brisket, a singular gift of that state that is currently haunting us with sword rattling and grotesque malfeasance.

I did a number of haughty reviews for *The New York Times Book Review*, so pompous that they embarrass me to this day. I attended meetings of the Coordinating Council of Literary Magazines, and one of the first Associated Writing Programs meetings wherein R. V. Cassill was impassioned about getting poor poets and writers jobs at universities. Now, of course, the effort has flowered into something resembling a Ponzi scheme as such programs are producing many more writers than there are literary readers or jobs for that matter. Once book jackets would advertise that the writer, say Marvin Schmidt, had been a "hod carrier, waiter, cabdriver, septic-tank pumper, lifeguard, toe freak, and private detective," and now the items have been reduced to "MFA, Southwest Missouri State University." I haven't yet come to any relevant conclusions on the matter though when I met Ann Beattie years ago and complimented her on her first book she said she was still waitressing.

Now my skater's feet had grown tiny and raw, and the only carrot left was the poet Dan Gerber offering us a house on his property back in Michigan. He had visited us in Stony Brook in his own plane and on the way home made a foolhardy attempt at bypassing a thunderstorm, which caused him to give up private flying. The dim light at the end of my own confused tunnel seemed to be more than a few drinks at the end of the workday. I couldn't get the hang of local saltwater fishing. I didn't have the time or money to hire a boat though one lucky evening on an inlet I caught a shad and a small striped bass, both of which were delicious. Quite suddenly two good things happened. Tom McGuane, who was exhausted by failure, had sent me the manuscript of his first novel, *The Sporting Club*. I gave it to Alex Nelson, married to my instructor friend Jerry, who worked at Simon & Schuster as a junior editor. She in turn gave it to Richard Locke who was farther up the ladder and within a week Tom had his acceptance, plus the agent Candida Donadio. I must say that shepherding a manuscript never worked that well again in my life but this single success was utterly thrilling on behalf of a close friend.

The other wonderful event came with a call from Elizabeth Kray who ran the Academy of American Poets and wanted me to have lunch in New York with her and Carolyn Kizer. I did so and Carolyn told me that it would be announced in a month or so that I was getting a National Endowment grant, which in those days, before congressional interference, was enough to take a full year off. After lunch I called Linda from a pay phone, then broke into a dreamy trance on the train back to Stony Brook, imagining a whole year back in northern Michigan where I fully intended to fish every day and hopefully see a wolf in the Upper Peninsula.

I think this was in March and I entered a definitive manic phase that would last until we left the village of Stony Brook in June. Simpson and I had unwisely secured partial funding from the National Endowment to host an "international poetry festival." I was questioning the wisdom of this one day when Professor Wang, who won the Nobel for parity physics in his twenties, entered my office for novel-reading suggestions. He did this occasionally and I was reminded how frequently scientific geniuses are interested in the humanities as compared to the reverse. Louis Simpson followed Dr. Wang and wondered idly how we hoped to handle a hundred American poets and twelve foreign all at one time. Good question. We looked at the wall separating my office from the departmental secretaries, Cecilia Grimm and Lilian Silkworth, hoping that they would pick up the ample slack though they had no authority to do so. I had long been convinced that women should take over all offices of government and there would be far less bleating, farting, bragging, and bluster. This could be thought of as a simpleminded solution to world problems but I'm still convinced it's true.

Of course 1966 and 1967 were radical years politically. Even to faculty members demonstrating is more interesting than the day-to-day torpor of university life. Louis Simpson, J. D. Reed, and I flew down to Washington on a La Guardia shuttle for a writer's march on the State Department against the Vietnam War. My student Eliot Weinberger had already been beaten black and blue in one demonstration so we felt both timid and obligated. Solidarity is a rare feeling for writers but we marched along led by Norman Mailer and Robert Lowell. J.D. and I were at the tail end sipping from a flask of whiskey talking about Bachelard whom Quasha had introduced us to when a group of American Nazis began shouting anti-Semitic epithets. We were joined by Robert Bly and charged the Nazis who fled because we were larger. We were then collared by our parade marshals who said we would be asked to leave the protest if we couldn't behave.

This was one area where I favored the tactics of Malcolm X over those of Martin Luther King, Jr. and Gandhi. I'm still not sure who is right but I had never heard such violence in ugly language, even in the moments preceding a bar fight.

We had student strikes at Stony Brook and in imitation of Columbia the administration building was seized. John Toll, the president of the university, called our house and my self-possessed wife told him I was taking a nap before my sacred poetry evening. This didn't work so I drove over because I had been told that my students were some of those involved. I met with the president and two deans and suggested, since it was a cold night, they have the power plant turn off the heat to the administration building, and also the phones and electricity. This worked by dawn but I ever after felt like a turncoat with these pragmatic midwestern gestures.

The International Poetry Festival with its dozen international poets and its hundred American poets is safely tucked away in hopefully unrecorded history. Many were inspired. Many mostly drank and threw unknown objects out of windows. Naturally I handled the food and wine and liquor of which there were enormous quantities. There were assignations in the bushes, also I tripped over a coupling couple in a midnight parking lot. Poetry can evoke the basics. After I escaped the area I was informed I had overdrawn the budget by thirty grand or so. Navy blue shame filled my noggin and I retreated even deeper into the woods. Often in my life I've reminded myself of one of those dreamy midwestern dolts who slide through the novels of Sherwood Anderson and Willa Cather and who, standing on the tracks, discover that the approaching object and loud noise is actually a train. Despite my sorry departure I was soon informed that I had been promoted to an assistant professor from my position as a mere assistant. The department meeting in which this was decided was supposedly confidential. Many were evidently against me but Alfred Kazin overwhelmed them and won the day by dint of authority and eloquence. Despite this kindness I knew it was unlikely. Linda and Jamie had happily flown ahead by a couple of weeks. Linda had begun to feel trapped by the fact that Long Island was an island, and had been having nightmares of burning sheep in burning boxcars rolling slowly on tracks in the night, with apocalyptic escape available only through congested New York City. My own departure in our old Ford with a dog and an irascible cat for company was more literary with my trying to remember a Duncan poem, something about Roethke breaking down, falling to pieces within the deceitful coils of an institution, ending with the line "What *is* hisses like a serpent and writhes to shed its skin." Self-serving but appropriate.

NORTHERN MICHIGAN

Nothing is less interesting, except to his future scholars, than a writer in the midst of a productive period. "He or she wrote." There you have it. I'm sure it was embarrassing to any writer who watched *The Way We Were* to see Robert Redford sitting there before an old Remington, partially typing a page, then ripping it from the carriage, wadding it up, and tossing it toward the wastebasket. Such scenes are mercifully short. Now that the computer has replaced the typewriter the scenes will be even more banal. A few years ago a friend from the *Chicago Tribune*, Bob Cross, stopped at a public campground to type up notes on his old Olivetti and several curious children dropped by to watch. None had ever seen a typewriter.

I call this memoir *Off to the Side* because that is a designated and comfortable position for a writer. In situations where you are inevitably the center of attention there is a feeling of restless discomfort, maybe even inappropriate behavior. When someone wishes to "give a dinner" for me I invariably turn it down. I like to go to dinners if I am off to the side where I belong. How can you observe the vagaries of human behavior if you're the target? This constitutes the inevitable and profound unpleasantness of book tours. It's the school carnival all over again and you're the man with his head stuck through the canvas hole. Others are throwing objects either softly or hard. This is not a plea for sympathy but a statement of the obvious, at least for those in the trade. Except with friends you make people a little nervous. If you're curious, which I almost always am, they have a trace of the feeling that they have become a work in progress. The bold ones in the upper Midwest say, "I'll tell you my story and we'll go halves on the money," or an approximation thereof. I've been teased with sentences such as "I knew he was dead because the snow had stopped melting on his face," or even "There were three of them sitting on the couch, all naked and pretty darn big, but those ladies were a feast for a logger's sore eyes." In Hollywood you're even further off to the side because the Powerful Ones seem never quite capable of believing that they have to depend on a guy who drives an older brown Camry to create a movie idea and a script for them. A man who makes over twenty million a year stares at you with bleak cynicism because it is you who has a "stable of gold" in your lips, as Rimbaud not Rambo said. We could go further, or perhaps closer, afield by imagining what it is like to fly a single-engine plane across the Matto Grosso at night, but it is still the sedentary tablet, typewriter, or computer that is the undramatic center of the writer's life. As a child when I was trying to learn how to milk, my Swede grandfather offered me a dime if I could fill a big pail. I sat there on the milk stool pulling the teats until my arms and hands were numb and hot with pain. He steadied the cow so she wouldn't kick me but allowed her to swat me with her tail. That's a bad day at the tablet.

The stone house on the farm or the high hill a few miles from the village of Lake Leelanau struck us as paradise. From the dining room table we could look off to the west at Lake Michigan and see the green Manitou Islands, and sometimes South Fox forty miles distant. The farm was mostly a cherry orchard with a wide hillside field in alfalfa, and other fruit trees near the house, apples, peaches, and pears, and a garden spot. We had found the place by running an ad in a local newspaper with the usual "writer on grant needs house" and we were a little dumbfounded by the results, which included nice carpeting, and staring at sunsets, and the passing iron-ore boats out in the Manitou passage.

Leelanau County in the mid-sixties was short of the hordes of tourists who currently afflict it. The county is a hilly and verdant forty-five-mile-long peninsula jutting out into Lake Michigan with general agriculture to the south and mostly cherry and apple orchards past the midpoint to the north. To the west along the coast the gov-

ernment had nearly completed a seventy-mile-long national lake-
shore that gave the public access to a grand block of water and hilly
forests. Our entry into this splendid world was a seventy-dollar-a-
month rent and my help in hitching up farm machinery as the landlord had arthritic hands. I was also asked to help with the Mexican
cherry-picking families who were coming soon after my arrival. Most
of them were arriving from Texas as they had done on this farm for
several decades. They lived in quarters out back and during harvest
I was enthralled sitting on our porch and listening to the guitar playing and singing in the evening. When we first moved in seven-year-
old Jamie sat me down and said she was tired of changing schools and
could we please stay in this place? I said yes.

The trouble in paradise was absurdly obvious but I was slow to recognize its ramifications. You finally open the cage for the animal and
it's not sure it wishes to leave. I had been churning along like a burly
terrier with working and school since the age of fourteen. Only lately
have I noted the limits of tenacity, the lack of subtlety in my direct
approach. A year's freedom was beyond my ken and then it had acquired all of the muted and questionable colors of an answered prayer.
The deep maudlin streak I had inherited from my father mixed nicely
with my notions of "terrible freedom" that I had adopted from my
study of Camus. When I had read Milne to my daughter and come
upon the character of the donkey Eeyore ("All I get is thistles") my
ears tingled with embarrassment.

I fished. I ran our dog Missy who recaptured her essential English-
pointer wildness in the country. When called back to the yard she
often elected to jump over the hood of the car in the driveway.
I fished again and again, traveling south toward Kingsley to the
Boardman and Manistee rivers to fly-fish for trout. I hiked the coastal
shoreline, lay in the sand pockets of the huge dunes, and wondered
what came next and whether my scattered mind was capable of a
novel. My proper sense of intimidation came from having read the
best. When you have relentlessly fed yourself on Dostoyevsky,

Turgenev, Melville, Faulkner, Stendhal, and so on, you have climbed on a very tall horse that is difficult to dismount in order to find your own proper size. I was also mindful of Pound's dictum that writers fail when they start from too narrow a base.

An idle man can generate immense quantities of hubris in his daydreaming. I kept remembering Ungaretti's line *"voremmo una certezza"* (give us a certainty) when I should have known that matter is better cast aside in favor of Keats's "negative capability." "Being right" is better left to lawyers and businessmen whose livelihoods depend on it. Ironies abound and proliferate much faster than answers. The questions grow even more immense while answers tend to diminish in power. Sinclair Lewis could write properly and correctly about the inhabitants of *Main Street* but it also makes the novel one that you didn't care to reread, while you tend to return again and again to the mysteries of Faulkner. Being right in fiction also presupposes that you will inevitably be vindicated as a writer, in itself a far-fetched proposition.

So a glorious summer began to move along quickly and my mind was like a sparsely attended restaurant where the service is always slow or downright bad. The solution that arrived was one that a nitwit could have come up with: travel. When your mind is suffocating in its own sludge, move it. I returned to the Upper Peninsula with Pat Paton and this time we took along Dan Gerber. The trip was nearly a bust with especially rank weather but served to remind me that I had found a retreat that has lasted until this day. Gerber and I had been planning a literary magazine to be called *Sumac*, innocently unaware of the ghastly amount of work involved. Reading the submissions reminded me of the trunk full of student papers I had taken to the dump back when I taught English as a foreign language. We persisted through nine issues and twenty-one books including Duncan's *The Truth and Life of Myth*. We published a number of fine poets including Robert Duncan, Charles Simic, Hayden Carruth, Gary Snyder, Galway Kinnell, Richard Hugo, Diane Wakoski, and James Welch but were finally worn out by the process and besides, I had to make a living, which required all my time. I had also become a little puzzled when publication in our little magazine was being used as a credential by poets working in college English departments.

When we returned from our week's trip to the Upper Peninsula Tom McGuane called from Montana offering a horseback trip with a rancher he knew into the Absaroka Mountain wilderness. All we had to do was help the rancher-guide check out his elk stake camps for the coming season. Ever foolhardy I agreed. McGuane and Gerber were experienced riders but I hadn't been on a horse in a very long time. It was a splendid, occasionally frightening trip. Of the ten days out several were spent encamped in areas where Yellowstone Park dispatched their troublesome grizzlies. More unnerving to me were the skinny trails across the precipitous scree, knowing that if my horse, with the unlikely name of Brother-in-Law, tripped I would become an especially bruised form of mincemeat. Let's just say that I was a brave man with a very purple ass from the riding in which I learned to stay saddled while Brother-in-Law took his pleasure by jumping over every log or deadfall he could locate. Halfway through the trip I ran out of cigarettes and whiskey, a form of suffering meaningless to the body-Nazis who now infest America. Naturally when we got back to Livingston we headed for a saloon and then to a cathouse run by a wonderful woman named Sally Dollarhide, and where I eventually met the governor of Montana. I'd feel much better about politicians if they spent less time counting their extortionary soft money and more time in whorehouses. The real value of the trip other than the purging effects of wilderness was the relentless talk about fiction with McGuane, continuing our marathon talks between Stony Brook and Palo Alto. Wanting to play from strength I was yet unwilling to admit I intended to write fiction for the reason that I was feeling cramped in poetry and writing from my own viewpoint. I was frankly withering waiting for the next poem to edge over the lip of my consciousness. I liked the idea of becoming many people by writing a novel, and when I wore out one set I could invent another.

*   *   *

In the spring of my first year of liberation, and with my National Endowment grant running toward its end, we traveled down to Summerland Key in the Florida Keys where Tom and Becky McGuane had a
rental home. McGuane's novel, *The Sporting Club,* had just come out
to good reviews and I had wangled the chance to write about it for
the *Detroit Free Press.* We thought we'd write the review together in
the grand tradition of Walt Whitman writing his own best reviews.
A certain modesty crept in and we were paralyzed. Richard Locke,
Tom's editor, thought it the muddiest notice the book received.

Summerland began my lengthy love affair with the Florida Keys,
which ended only in the early nineties when Key West became too
crowded for my taste. It was mostly the splendor of flats fishing, poll-
ing the skiff in the shallow tidal flats surrounded by mangrove islets
while looking for tarpon, bonefish, and permit. The bird life and
marine life, the sweep and grandeur of the sea, seized your entire being
to the extent that you thought of nothing else. The hundreds of variations of turquoise and beige on the flats and the deep blue tidal chan-
nels became home for a month a year for twenty years.

Key West in the seventies and eighties was a bit of a literary
capital, so that you had the peculiar combinations of a first-rate sporting life in the closest proximity with a sprawling colony of writers
and musicians. Many of the major writers like Tennessee Williams
and Jimmy Merrill and dozens of others were gay but that gave the
air an energetic sense of rebellion before the revolution that was to
follow. I recall light and mutual teasing but nothing more. Once when
seated next to Tennessee on a flight to New York, fueled by morning cocktails, we talked very loudly and behaved badly but then several others on the plane were complimentary over the entertainment
we offered. I was impressed when two stewardesses sang a show tune
with Tennessee to cover his braying questions of whether I thought
cocaine was good for a writer's work. Years later when Truman Capote
made an extended trip to Key West and we spent time together he
refused to fully explain his long-term quarrel with Tennessee saying
only, "We're all vile." Since I have lived largely in remote areas

I've often wondered if there is that easygoing companionship between straight and gay writers in big cities like there was in Key West. It was a wide-open arena for questionable behavior on anyone's part. One evening someone had given me a garbage bag of Colombian buds, which I stored in the shrubbery before going into Howie's to hear Jimmy Buffett and Jerry Jeff Walker, both in the early stages of their careers. It was on my second visit to McGuane in Key West that I met Guy de la Valdéne and Jimmy Buffett, both of whom became lifelong friends.

We left Summerland with the creaky but familiar feeling that we were broke again. Linda took this more gracefully than her brooding husband. We flew to Lansing, picked up our car at my in-laws where there was the unworded question of what our next questionable move would be. We drove north in a nasty April snowstorm, stopping at the Lake Leelanau post office to pick up the mail. I remember looking at Jamie playing with her accumulation of Florida seashells in the backseat with piles of books beside her. Among the many letters in the backed-up mail was a critical one from the Guggenheim Foundation announcing I had been given a year's grant, effective immediately if I wished. I had expected a rejection based on my assumption that I was unlikely to get grants two years in a row despite the fine critical reception I had gotten for my second book of poems, *Locations*. Naturally we were enthralled, not the least for my promise to Jamie that she could stay in the same school. How clearly adults I've met remember broken promises from childhood. If you tell your child you're going to build a tree house, build it, or you'll live forever in modest infamy.

I had already begun my third book of poems, *Outlyer*, though it was going slowly as I kept being haunted by a Pasternak aphorism, "Despite all appearances it takes a lot of volume to fill a life." We had a pleasant trip to England with the Gerbers, my first trip overseas, which gave me a taste for more. We had a nice walk on Hampstead Heath with M. L. Rosenthal who showed me some Keats haunts. Since Keats was the first germinal poet of my life my skin tingled somewhat childishly to identify the critical "place" of the poet. I felt nearly the same in the Lake Country with Wordsworth whose "The Prelude" I worshiped.

I was, however, beginning to feel a little awkward with the professional poet's life. Once during an impressive lunch (the guests, not the food) in New York City hosted by James Laughlin I had looked down the table at Barbara Guest, Gary Snyder, Denise Levertov, and Lawrence Ferlinghetti and speculated idly on what everyone did all day every day. My own sidelines of fishing and bird hunting failed to answer Pasternak's aphorism, but then perhaps the two grant years I was indulged in at least gave me the time to sort out what might be my life's work. I'm mindful that few writers ever get that kind of freedom from immediate obligations. I had certainly found that the vaunted academic's life had left me less freedom in terms of time and enervation than working as a book salesman or as a hod carrier. Both jobs and grants buy time but the latter more so, pure and simple. Years later when Congress was carping about the National Endowment, and especially individual grants to artists and writers, it occurred to me that government funds had initially sprung me into a life where I ended up paying millions of dollars in income tax, enough to cover hundreds of their paltry grants. Patronage of whatever kind is critical if we wish artists of all kinds to give us a life generally above the sump of ordinary greed and political chiseling.

I must say I was never very good at the care and nurturing of a career. In New York City I seemed to favor saloons and restaurants over literary events and parties. That summer after England I made a mistake in judgment of sorts. Alfred Kazin was going to be in the Traverse City area visiting a friend and hoped I would have time to show him around the "landscape" of my work. If I had been more ambitious I would have hung in there for Alfred's arrival but instead went off to Montana trout fishing with McGuane. Kazin was offended and I never heard from him again except for a tersely negative note on my second novel, *A Good Day to Die*, suggesting that such characters couldn't exist (whacked-out Vietnam veterans had been arriving in Key West rather than entering academic life and I had written about one who tried to blow up a dam—this was in 1971).

I have no admiration for myself when I write about such matters but America is scarcely a classless society. I grew up in a family not all that far from the edge of poverty that was definitely there in my Swedish grandparents, and pretty close in my father's family. No one on either side of the family had been to college except my father whose original aim was to study cattle and raise them on his own farm, something he could never afford. When he died at age fifty-three I recall he was making a little more than nine grand a year, sparingly enough to raise five children. I have generally favored the company of so-called working people in the taverns of the places I have lived. I have a few comparatively rich friends who are all quite comfortable in the same taverns I habituate. Some of them are what a realtor friend calls "lucky sperm," people who are rich from reasons of parentage. I've never known an actor, a truly famous person, more comfortable with ordinary people than Jack Nicholson, who comes from a lineage of railroad workers and beauticians. I occasionally find it ironic that I've developed a taste for fine food and wine. I have gladly paid a thousand-dollar check for a meal for friends but I wouldn't go more than a few hundred bucks for a sport coat or suit. I don't see the point of making much of one's humble "roots" (maybe to win a boozy argument) because you're no more responsible than someone with inherited wealth. It's a little like people telling you all the bad habits they've given up. It's what you do, not what you don't do.

Lucky for me I fell off a cliff, or a near cliff, that autumn of my Guggenheim year while bird hunting with my dog Missy, really a high, steep bank of the Manistee River, the kind of bank where the clay looks dry but barely under the surface it's slippery and wet. I took a tumble ending up with my legs in the cold late-October water. The pain in my lower back was immediate and it took over an hour to crawl and stumble to the car. I would have stopped at a store for a pint of whiskey but I couldn't gamble on getting out of the car let alone back in.

I spent a couple of days on our living room floor drinking whiskey out of a hospital straw and crawling to the toilet. With my very strong aversions to hospitals coming from lengthy stays at ages seven and eighteen I created an intuition that I could recover in a few days on the floor. Linda got sick of it and quite suddenly our old country doctor showed up, shot me full of Demerol, and I was taken in an ambulance to the hospital in Traverse City where I was suspended in traction for several weeks, came home, and then suffered a severe penicillin reaction from the treatment of an infection. All my joints were swollen up with rheumatoid arthritis, which further aggravated the torn muscle in my back. I lapsed into a semi-coma for several days in which I was sure Gary Snyder had visited for a soothing chat though he remained in California. Snyder and I had done a college reading together and had had a grand time. I ended up losing nearly forty pounds because, ever the nascent gourmand, I couldn't bear hospital food. When I got out of the hospital for good it was suddenly winter and I definitely wasn't mobile. I had to wear an involved corset that stretched from my breasts to my hips and was overwhelmingly unsexy throughout the two years I had to wear it.

I say "lucky" in regard to this injury since I have doubts that without it I would have settled down enough to write novels. During the first week of my extended convalescence I spoke with McGuane on the phone and he suggested that it was time to write a novel since I could no longer do anything to avoid it. I already had been writing longer poems in the musical form of "suites" so I began by sketching a wordless, rhythmical diagram of the planned novel to be called *Wolf*, with the subtitle "A False Memoir" intended to throw off the obvious scent that the novel was helplessly autobiographical. Later on I read of the alarming surprise for the poet when he discovers that it's his own story that is true, though I mentally added that this story was something you had to get out of the way so you could proceed to more interesting venues, which meant other people.

Off I went typing with two forefingers on the old Remington my father had given me years before, and on which I had been reasonably adept before my work as a hod carrier had done something injurious to the tendons in my hands. Say the construction site is muddy, thus you have to wheelbarrow twelve hundred concrete blocks to the excavation site. That particular day you ended up handling thirty tons twice which is quite an aid to the appetite, also an inspiration to go back to the university, but your hands have become quite a mess and it is quite clear you'll never be a watchmaker or surgeon. This lack of typing ability made the process laborious because I first diddled with the sentences longhand and there was the poet's urge to make sure they had internal music. I was curiously without expectations for the novel so I felt a great deal of the pleasure of freedom which gave me additional energy.

When I finished the novel my grant was exhausted and we had no money to have a copy made, a dollar a page at the time. I sent it to my brother in New Haven on the eve of a mail strike so that the manuscript was lost for several weeks. Thankfully my brother John had an authoritative presence, to put it mildly, and the mail officials allowed him to dig through the mountainous bins at the New Haven post office and he found it, copied the manuscript, and forwarded it to Alex Nelson at Simon & Schuster and the novel was quickly accepted. I didn't have an agent and certainly learned how necessary one is. From then on I depended on Bob Dattila and learned there were advantages to having a Sicilian agent for reasons of tenacity and the ability to break ordinary rules in our favor.

There is an implicit deceit in events that from the outside seems to smother the interior origin of the event. You can listen carefully to what people are saying but you're missing a great deal unless you are speculating with concentration on why they are saying it. There is a wonderful "brainlessness" to novel writing. I mean that you are using so much of your mind you forget that it exists. You're balancing a construct that daily grows longer, almost unconsciously keeping track of a thousand pieces and gestures with no real eye on the last page because your immersion in the process is total. Beginnings and endings are the most artificial parts of the process. The expectations about publishing the results become far from the point because you are filled and fueled by memories, images, dreams, modest visions, the emotional content of your most passionate reading, all of which sweeps you away more deeply into your invention. When it is the first novel, and assuming you are not witless, you know very well that the odds of your work being published are ten thousand to one against, and even when it is published the reactions from friends and relatives are often puzzled and evasive. The hero of *Wolf* is not an altogether pleasant character. Full to the brim with social and emotional rage he camps out in the Upper Peninsula while looking for a remnant wolf (they were only rumored back in the sixties before numbers of them migrated from the west through Wisconsin from Minnesota, and across the ice in the east from Canada). My hero, Swanson, recounts his questionable life, which caused nervous unrest in many readers. After a couple of my novels were published my Swede mother asked me, "Why can't your characters have normal sex?" but then a few years ago before she died she said, "You've made quite a living out of your fibs." Norse compliments can be a bit thin and coolish.

The novel, however, did fairly well, going into two printings and offering me a smallish territory in the map of contemporary fiction writing where "poet novels" are rarely welcomed or seriously considered. Fiction writers tend to view themselves as made of rougher stuff, wry and cynical, striated with ironies, perhaps more manly and less capable of the ebullience poets can show in their life and work. I have found, though, that many fiction writers begin with poetry, or at least commit a few poems to paper, and this long list includes Faulkner, Hemingway, Mailer, and Matthiessen. Younger fiction writers fret that the genre is already overfull without the incursion of poets stealing the scant review space. There's a certain kind of writer who tends to think that anyone else's good review detracts from the future prospects of theirs. The territorialism of the creature world, say a pack of cow dogs, is equally present. I have noticed it moving back and forth

between the genres of poetry and fiction, sporting and nature journalism, screenplays, children's books, and food writing. There's a
specific resistance into letting you into the different clubs that is
sometimes amusing, sometimes not. Sniffs, growls, barks. Like the new
kid at school, the new dog is not always welcome.

Our stone-house paradise on the hill came to an end. Our landlord's
daughter and son-in-law were returning to the area and we had to
give up our home on relatively short notice. We were desperate, but
Dan Gerber stepped in with an offer to loan us a down payment on a
farm. We were mindful of our promise to Jamie that we would stay in
the same school district. During the search we lived in our friends the
Patons' garage down in Kingsley where our second daughter, Anna,
was conceived. We finally located a small farm, really the only thing
for sale in our price range. This house was more than a bit rickety,
but there was a fine barn and a granary that I made into a studio. The
monthly payments were ninety-nine dollars and forty cents, an
amount that was occasionally hard to muster. All in all, though, we
were quite happy in our first home. Linda had grown up fairly styl-
ishly but her hope had always been to live on a farm with dogs, cats,
horses, and chickens. The down payment was eight thousand five
hundred dollars. It is melancholy to think how far afield young writers must go now to live cheaply, though there's always Mexico, which,
notwithstanding its problems, I think of as a glorious destination and
culture quite without the backspin of living within the empire.

We were thrilled indeed when Anna was born. Under the assumption
that we would eventually afford to have another child we had waited
ten years and when the money seemed unlikely we went ahead anyway. I've always become quite irked when asked if I hadn't wanted a
son, partly because it was hard on my mother and her four sisters to
know that their own father had wished for a son to help on the farm.
The birth of a new child is an incalculable mystery that has nothing to

do with gender. His or her character becomes immediately permanent and you love him or her with your entire being. You simply don't even think of him or her being someone else. I suppose the anger surrounding this singular stupid question is similar to that of a childless couple who wish no children or can't have them and are frequently asked, "Where's the baby?" It is especially heartless when you think of the unwanted children in the world, born to be waifs, perhaps a billion of them.

Jamie at age ten was helpful as I had had to be with two younger sisters and a younger brother. Anna was extremely willful. We had to hold her down on the floor to give her medicine. She would eat or not eat her meals as she wished and there was nothing we could do about it. Her first words were to growl like our two Airedales, Hud and Jessie. She liked to go to the tavern with me where the owner, Dick Plamondon, would show her magic tricks. Once when she was about three we had dressed her in her Sunday best for a visit from the in-laws. She became naughty so I took her for a ride down to the beach. She wanted to swim and I explained, "Maybe in the afternoon" and she suddenly walked into the water up to her neck, turned back to me, and glared. Since it was anyway too late I thought, "Why not?" Both of our daughters, probably due to a strong mother and an indulgent father, have been feminists since birth, a charming but rather firm "don't push me, asshole" implicit in their attitude toward men, culture, and authority. With Anna this nonironical clarity of purpose gave her complete control over our dogs, something we were unable to manage. A terrier can behave beautifully at obedience school but bringing it back home to the property it believes it owns is another matter. That's when you need a girl with the character of a terrier and not a trace of the wishy-washy to take over the problem. Much later in life I thought of doing a piece called "Writers and their Bird Dogs." While we were hunting in Montana I had watched with amusement Richard Ford trying to catch his young Brittany but then a month later in Michigan I had broken my foot trying to catch my Lab. Neither Carl Lewis nor Michael Johnson can catch a bird dog. With a writer it's "Please come here, Rusty, I'm having a hard time today what with a dozen inconclusive faxes and e-mails plus a nasty call from New York. Rusty, today I was thinking of that Aldous Huxley character who had a soul like a 'tenuous membrane.' Maybe that's me but it's a bit self-serving. Rusty, I beg you!"

Thus at thirty I was finally launched in poetry and the novel with the firm but thoroughly unproven conviction that I could have an old-fashioned career as a full-time literary writer who didn't have to stray from his calling to make a living. It was a meaninglessly untried ideal drawn from literary history where you read of the victorious, not of the thousands who failed and disappeared. In admitting it there's a trace of a story my dad told me once while we were fishing about a yokel neighbor who had gotten up in a church meeting and had confessed with profuse sobs that he had burned down the school outhouse as a teenager thirty years ago before. After twenty-five books, a hundred or so essays, and numerous versions of fifteen screenplays, a profession I quit some years ago, I finally can make a good living as a poet and novelist just a year short of the normal retirement age of sixty-five. I don't offer any personal deference to my productivity because, having refused to do anything else, what was I to do with my time? Now it's a Newtonian principle where you can't stop the object in motion that wishes to stay in motion until it meets an immovable force like the grave, becomes a "dirt napper," an Arkansas idiom for the dead. I feel lucky after watching what happens to so many retirees. They become jumpy, anxiety-ridden, perplexed, apprehensive, flat bored until they find something new to do, much like a writer who finishes a grand work and reenters ordinary reality in the halting steps of a zombie facing imminent sunrise.

The years came and went as is their habit. It's hard to see a succession of yesterdays when it's clearly a continuum broken by nights of sleep. The fact that we spent nearly a decade more than a few steps beneath the median income no longer seems extraordinary when it is stretched out to more than a half a lifetime totally within a free-market economy. Right-wingers make a big deal about this but I haven't been able to isolate any pure virtue in doing what you want as opposed to doing what the culture thinks you should do. If the country is going to slide seven billion dollars a year to farmers why the relentless carping about one percent of that amount for the arts?

Living on the edge required more attention than I had left over from my writing. I had begun to write a few outdoor essays or columns for the back pages of *Sports Illustrated,* the intent being to earn free time for novels and poetry, but like any other family at our earning level we had deadly extra items like antibiotic prescriptions, flute payments for Jamie and eventually for Anna, a fender bender when the insurance had lapsed, vet bills for the dogs, cats, and our budget horses. I also noticed the time it took to research and write an essay required nearly all the money you got paid. This is the usual story I read about the American family below the median who are perpetually one paycheck away from disaster. I at least didn't have the temptation of credit cards because I wasn't eligible. Grocery shopping was a careful project but then this had the good effect of sharpening our cooking skills. Linda also kept a very large vegetable garden which I spaded in the spring. Mindless manual labor can be very soothing if some attention is required. You have to watch what you're doing when you hoe. And when you cultivate corn from the distance of a tractor seat a sex fantasy can tear out a whole row. The slightest good news would promote a celebration with friends, a paycheck, a good review, a few hundred bucks for a book of poems, and most of all an advance on a novel of a couple grand. When I did my first column on horse-pulling contests for *Sports Illustrated,* which was easy since I had watched them since childhood, the twelve-hundred-dollar payment seemed lavish. We packed the car and drove to Montana to fish and visit the McGuanes' small ranch.

Sports Illustrated also financed a number of my spring fishing trips to Key West. Guy de la Valdéne owned a skiff and had rented a house and we would fish all day thirty days in a row, often joined by the painter Russell Chatham from Montana who had become a friend. At the time McGuane had had some movie-business success and was directing a film from his own novel *92 in the Shade* so had to temporarily give up fishing. Key West had also helped Gerber, McGuane, and de la Valdéne to develop marital problems at the time. It was an island totally devoid of rules of behavior, a tropical island fueled by sunlight, dope, and booze, as far from Kansas as you could get in America. Later I noted that the movie business never quite equaled Key West for questionable behavior. McGuane wrote the liner notes for an early Buffett album that said Jimmy was "one of the last of the sucking chest wound singers to sleep on the yellow line." No one quite figured out what that meant but it seemed appropriate. We had a "social club" called the Club Mandible with about thirty members, which spearheaded our efforts toward unconsciousness, or a rather punishing form of consciousness. Drugs were virtually free because so many local friends were in the import business which was rather brazen in the Key West of the seventies and early eighties. Key West then was very much a seafaring town and a sailboat or shrimp boat run to Colombia or Mexico wasn't any big navigational feat. I remember a group of men testing a bale out of the back of a pickup on Simonton Street in broad daylight. They'd put a handful in a small paper bag, light the bottom of the bag, take a deep drag, toss the burning bag into the street, become contemplative for a few minutes, then make a judgment.

At that time it was nearly all a marijuana trade, a drug I've never cared for though I see it as far less injurious than alcohol. I remember the disappointment when a sailboat at Mallory Pier was busted with millions of Quaaludes, a pill very popular with young women. Naturally this open activity finally caught the attention of state and federal officials, partly due to a *Miami Herald* exposé, and the activity was partially suppressed, more by a vigilant Coast Guard than anything else. A number of local officials seemed to be involved but then Key West had always been a smugglers' haven and there wasn't any social onus to being caught. The end of the decades-long wide-open party arrived with the cocaine trade when things got real serious, including murder. The Colombians tended to scare the local "businesses" away. Several acquaintances were found limbless and headless, or torn to pieces by bullets. It all made writing as a profession quite appealing. People made millions of dollars but I don't recall anyone holding on to the money. Twenty years later it has the aspect of a lurid dream. You were pretty safe fishing for tarpon, permit, and bonefish though near one remote mangrove island in the backcountry we took polite rifle fire well in front of our skiff bow. Best to fish elsewhere. The other big item that subdued the party atmosphere was the widespread arrival of AIDS. Chatham and I picked up sandwiches for fishing one morning and there was suddenly that purple streak of Kaposi's sarcoma on a friend's face and a wordless yes in response to our wordless shock.

The obsessive nature of our fishing took place because saltwater fly-fishing could ascend to the magnum emotional level that we gave our work. You're essentially using the same tackle, only bigger, that you use for trout fishing, but the tarpon you cast to so lucidly visible on the shallow flats or channel edges might weigh more than a hundred pounds. To do it well you have to evolve a fairly high level of skill and when successful you release the fish. Nothing in my life has been quite so electric as a close-to-the-boat jump of a tarpon, or a marlin for that matter, the latter fished off the coasts of Ecuador and Costa Rica. Unlike the heavy-tackle deep-sea fishing that Hemingway favored it is a sport of finesse.

Fishing was mostly coming up for air after long periods of work, something to clear your mind for the next project, a sport that could wipe the slate quite clean. Guy de la Valdéne would also come to northern Michigan to hunt grouse and woodcock in October, and Chatham came for a few seasons, but Guy has missed only two years in thirty. Bird hunting can also lift you out of your humdrum work life but perhaps not as completely as fishing. How well the bird dogs work and how well you've all been cooking adds immeasurably. Jamie used to keep a food and wine diary of our Octobers before she left home and on reading it I was struck by how natural it was that I developed gout. When I made a good deal of money the food and wine obsession got further out of hand. You probably shouldn't eat grouse and woodcock, venison, a quail and dove pâté, abalone and oysters, caviar, calf sweetbreads, kidneys, liver, and ducks all during the same week with several cases of wine. That's a health tip. Finally, I couldn't imagine life without fishing. As Thoreau said, "The wildness and ad-ventures that are in fishing still recommend it to me."

Just yesterday it occurred to me that I may have made too much in my own mind of the financial difficulty of these years between thirty and forty, an elaborate mythos of near poverty. Not that there weren't grim periods but then the success that followed may have made me overemphasize the years of failure. This is scarcely original in terms of motive with a little "success guilt" thrown in, wherein the man with the full wallet gets wretchedly sentimental about the voyage up from the depths.

There was also the irony of travel. How could you complain at the tavern about being dead broke when the Gerbers had recently taken you to Africa? You also had flown home via Rome and Paris, and at the Excelsior in Rome you had stood there with your wife amused at midnight staring at your first bidet, after which you ordered up a bottle of wine and pasta to start making up for the bad food in Africa.

Sports Illustrated helped on my trip to Russia a few months later. The idea was that I'd try to do a piece on the suppressed sport of horse racing. Dan had a better grip on travel than I did, especially in Rus-sia, where I fell easily into the local vodka habits. We especially liked St. Petersburg, Leningrad at the time, where we stayed at the Hotel Europa. We were given grand quarters because Dan's father had sent over a lot of food-processing equipment during the famine after World War II and the Russians remembered the name. This made me a little nervous because we were traveling on phony "farmer" passports, hav-ing been denied writer visas. There was not a trace of a thaw in the early seventies and I had stupidly tried to call Voznesensky whom I had met in New York. Our private guide has also told me not to try to call Joseph Brodsky who was on the verge of exile. It was a case of "Innocents Abroad" and it later seemed obvious that the fancy women in gowns, rubies, and diamonds we took to dinner were KGB. Whatever, we were harmless poets visiting the spirit of places that produced my heroes Dostoyevksy, Turgenev, Yesenin, Mayakovsky. When you met educated Russians capable in English it was wonderful to see their great enthusiasm for their poetry, their ability, over drinks of course, to quote extended passages with great passion, something you definitely didn't see at the time in America.

After writing *Wolf* I published a book of poems with Simon & Schuster called *Outlyer,* and after that experience I chose to publish my poetry with small presses that would keep the books in print. With some notable exceptions like Knopf a poet is better off with a university press, or a small press like my current poetry publisher Copper Canyon, where there is an attention to details and the nature of poetry that doesn't yield up to the marketing methods of modern publishing.

After *A Good Day to Die,* a dour attempt at a thoroughly "noir" novel in an American setting, I wrote *Farmer,* somewhat based on my mother's family, imagining that her only brother who died in the 1919 flu epidemic had lived and I was simply writing his life. It was fairly well reviewed but the bindings were faulty and Viking withdrew the book, not to surface again for years because I turned down the one-thousand-dollar paperback offer. Fifteen years later *Farmer* had a fair resurgence in paperback, and a tasteful movie was made of it by the Brazilian director Bruno Baretto, starring Dennis Hopper and Amy Irving. This quiet movie was retitled *Carried Away* and drowned without notice. Inexplicably, the novel did well in France.

EARLY HOLLYWOOD

Our life seemed to be coming to an unpleasant head, the minor encouragement being a budget screenplay of *A Good Day to Die*, the first that I had written, for the documentarian Fred Wiseman who promptly got a stomach ulcer after visiting Hollywood. I also wrote a screenplay for Warren Oates whom I had met on the set of McGuane's *92 in the Shade* in Key West. Both screenplays paid me five grand, which was the same amount I was getting for a full novel but the screenplays took far less time. I confess that neither of them were any good. A good screenplay takes a sizable measure of talent and I hadn't yet studied the genre. Later on at Warners when I read a half dozen of William Faulkner's screenplays I was appalled and amused by how terrible they were.

Rock bottom was arrived at in 1977. I hadn't even filed an income-tax form for seven years, which was a felony, and we had no prospects whatever. I was owed money by Eliot Kastner for a screenplay I had done with McGuane but I never received the check. Jamie was a teenager by then and kept walking up to the empty mailbox for weeks. Guy de la Valdéne's mother, Diana, sent us a check which allowed us to scrape by. I had met her in France on my return from Russia when I stopped in Normandy to do a *Sports Illustrated* essay on stag hunting. Guy picked me up in Paris and we drove to the country up near the Rambouillet forest near Dreux. It was startling to arrive at his mother's home and discover that it was a grand château surrounded by a thoroughbred horse farm. Richard III had stayed there during his own Normandy invasion and a German general had installed central heating during World War II. In the breakfast room of the château there were many unframed paintings by Diana's cousin, Winston Churchill. Guy's beautiful sister Lorraine was there with her eventual husband, Christian, who arrived by motorcycle from Paris with a big package of foie gras. There were even very large pike in the moat that encircled the château and we fished for them without success. Everyone at the château was bilingual except me and the servants. I remember eating a baby wild pig called a "marcasin" liberally stuffed with truffles, and drinking some 1923 Margaux and some Armagnac from the 1890s. It was simply the most interesting food I had ever eaten. I had never remotely been exposed to very old money and noted that it seemed nonbourgeois as there was no TV, no one read newspapers, and when people argued the language was raw and frank. A year later when I returned to France to help Guy edit a tarpon film he had directed I slowly began to understand French foibles. We worked on the film, for which Jimmy Buffett supplied the music, at a studio in the Antegor district of Paris. The proprietress of a local bistro desperately wanted a flowery cowboy shirt I was wearing and Guy arranged a trade for a meal of *têtes de veau* for four, the brains, neck, and cheek meat of a calf. I have never been able to hold back from the basic food that many consider exotic.

Meanwhile back in Michigan I became quite paranoid about my tax situation and our financial distress. My impractical solution in 1977 was to begin writing a sequence of novellas, beginning with one called *Legends of the Fall*. No one was writing novellas at the time but I had enjoyed reading the novellas, or the very long short stories of about a hundred pages, of Katherine Anne Porter, Isak Dinesen, and the German writer Hugo von Hofmannsthal.

Legends of the Fall had a peculiar origin. I had been brooding about it for quite some time. My wife had been up in the Keweenaw Peninsula helping go through her deceased grandparents' home, a very large place with fourteen bedrooms and fireplaces. In an old trunk Linda had found the journals of her grandmother's father, William Ludlow, and on reading them I was amazed how a young mining engineer from Cornwall had traveled widely after the Civil War. He had been around the Horn to San Francisco, down in Mexico where his older brother owned silver mines, in Montana and Wyoming where he did surveys for the U.S. government. The trump card was delivered by my brother John when he found at the Library of Congress Colonel William Ludlow's report to Congress on the Custer expedition into the Black Hills in 1873. Colonel Ludlow had led the scientific part of the expedition and been accompanied by George Bird Grinnell. In his report to Congress Ludlow strongly recommended that the Black Hills be left the "sole province of the Sioux" but soon after the usual land grab and greed for gold followed.

I used only a small part of this recorded "reality" for my novella but the material was fabulously suggestive. Ludlow's intelligence was both literary and scientific. He and his men had lassoed a grizzly bear and inspected it, then "released the beast with some difficulty." They observed grasshopper plagues, and under the guidance of their Cheyenne guide One Stab had avoided Sioux war parties.

I spun my tale in nine days as if I were taking dictation from the past. Soon after I began writing another novella called *The Man Who Gave Up His Name*. We were now absolutely depleted financially and I fell into a clinical depression with the side effect of tunnel vision. The year before, I had met Jack Nicholson on the set of McGuane's movie *Missouri Breaks*. He had borrowed my motel room to take a quick shower before watching dailies and I think I gave him *Wolf* and *A Good Day to Die*. Later I got a postcard saying if I ever had any ideas for him to send them along but I never had any ideas, which he found peculiar. Meanwhile Toby Rafelson, whom I had met socially in L.A., informed Nicholson I was broke and he told her to have me come down to Durango where Toby was the art director on his movie *Goin' South*, which he was directing. Other than a few hours in Montana I had spent an interesting evening at the movies with Jack and Anjelica Huston the day after he received the Academy Award for *One Flew Over the Cuckoo's Nest*. It gave me pause at the theater in Westwood to see a crowd's reaction to "celebrity," which is at the same time apprehensive and eager. Nicholson, ever in his dark glasses, handled it with grace and was proud that both the entrance to the theater and the popcorn were free. Meanwhile I was so numb at the time of Toby's call I don't quite remember how I got the ticket, perhaps through Guy or my father-in-law, but through the efforts of my wife's cousin in Miami I ended up stopping in Cozumel for a few days to write a small piece for *Esquire*.

I flew on to Durango through Mexico City where I was picked up by Annie Marshall, Jack's secretary and friend, whom I had also met on the set of *Missouri Breaks* along with Anjelica, Jack, and their crony Sue Barton. We waited for a while at the Durango airport for Annie's cat Pinky, who had been shipped down from Los Angeles. Annie kept hissing at the baggage people, "Donde está my fucking gato vivo," a splendid introduction to the movie business.

I hung around the movie set and, of course, drank with the cast and crew, which included Mary Steenburgen, Danny DeVito, Ed Begley, Jr., Christopher Lloyd, John Belushi, and Jack's preposterous uncle Shorty, a railroad worker from New Jersey. The movie company had enlisted an officer of the Federales to guide me around, as I had had for several years the germ of a novella to be called *Revenge* and it immediately occurred to me that Durango was a perfect setting with its almost medieval social structure. It would certainly not be a healthy move to have an affair with a young wife of a rich and powerful local.

After about a week in Durango I was getting mildly nervous about what I was doing there, but then Nicholson drew me aside to address the problem. I was staying at his rental and every evening we had spoken about literature and movies until late, but now we were talking about money, which for me had always been a ghastly issue. I was put at ease when he merely asked about my debts and what I needed to come up with for a year of writing. When I got home two days later the check was already there. We had spoken about his having some share of the film rights of what I wrote but I did not realize at the time that this was usually a meaningless gesture. Our deal, however, turned out to be a substantial exception, but when the money fairly rolled in he would accept only the amount of the original loan. Many people can afford to behave this way but very few actually do.

*   *   *

Back home I spent a few days stunned and then the numbness of my depression began to lift. I finished *The Man Who Gave Up His Name*, and then rather quickly wrote *Revenge*, a story almost as wrathfully insistent as what I had experienced with *Legends of the Fall*. I've always been deeply cynical about any experiences that purport to be affected by ghosts or suchlike, but certain poems, novellas, and novels have resembled a seizure in composition, a somewhat demonic thrall where one's entire being is carried away in the writing and there is no alternative to working in three shifts a day, morning, afternoon, and often deep into the night. It is an experience that is both longed for and unpleasant.

When I turned in the manuscript to Dattila he thought it might be difficult to sell because "no one has ever heard of novellas." The initial response wasn't encouraging. Simon & Schuster turned it down unless I was willing to expand the title novella into four hundred pages or so, in which case it would be a sure-thing best-seller, an offer I rejected outright. Shortly afterward Sam Lawrence picked up the book for Delacorte Press, and then things began to move very fast, too much so for my composure. Clay Felker printed the entirety of *Legends* in *Esquire* and Rust Hills edited *Revenge* for the same magazine. The most startling event soon followed. It was still before publication and Linda and I had stopped in Palm Beach for a few days to visit Guy and Terese de la Valdéne on our way to Key West for the annual fishing vacation. I was already in an unnerved state because our daughter Jamie had won a National Merit Scholarship and we couldn't accept it because of my nonexistent tax forms. We weren't off the plane in Palm Beach for more than a couple of hours when John Calley, who was the president of Warner Brothers, called and made an offer of a hundred and fifty thousand a year for three years as an option on what I might write, not a purchase price but an option, sort of an allowance. Given inflation, and this was 1978, the offer would equal about two hundred and fifty now. I remember there was company around so I took the call in the backyard on a very warm night that somehow wasn't comforting. In any event Bob Dattila and I would go out there for a few days and talk it over. We ended up making a much better deal involving the novellas *Revenge* and *Legends of the Fall* with Warner Brothers, but Calley had definitely caught our attention.

I have often thought that if I had accepted the original offer of a munificent three-year grant and stayed away from Hollywood I may have been better off, a meaningless but interesting speculation. I was just short of forty years old and had spent a rather close-to-the-bone lifetime dodging disasters and acquiring a somewhat tenuous literary reputation with eight books of fiction and poetry. I had fallen short of a viable income to support a wife and two daughters, and though our mortgage payment was a scrap less than a hundred a month, it was sometimes difficult to squeeze it out from the average of ten grand a year. Nicholson's help had been pleasant relief indeed and now a scant six months later the antique idea of "the sky's the limit" was appropriate. There was certainly no one to ask for advice which anyway I wouldn't have taken unless it included "go for it."

Having been through all of it I have never been sympathetic to the woes of the American novelist in Hollywood. If your temperament is not suitable to teaching what gets you out there initially is a wish to make a solid living. A good break, a big one at that, and you are simply as susceptible to greed as a realtor, lawyer, stockbroker, doctor, or anyone else. In your lifelong study of world literature you have read dozens of tales of greed, not to speak of philosophical treatises and religious texts warning of the evil therein. No one in the history of either side of your family had ever made any "real money" and they all seemed to have become quite philosophical, if not serene, over the idea that they would never be rich and that "getting by" would have to be enough. And now the one-eyed goofy, the black-sheep poet emerging from this gene pool, has inadvertently struck it rich. After the first full year of this experience I was sitting on the porch of our recently remodeled farmhouse, triple the estimated time and expense and a thoroughly enervating and obnoxious process, reading the *Detroit Free Press* and noting that I had made more money in the last year than the president of General Motors, Harlow Curtis. I idly hoped he was happy in his work.

* * *

Now that I have the easy lucidity of distance I have begun to comprehend my illusions. First of all, literary writers aren't meant to make an ample living and if they do it is usually episodic, what my friend Caputo refers to as the rags-to-riches-to-rags story. Literary novelists can have a number of good years and then the air goes out of the tire with a perceptible hiss and squeal. You can hear it down the block. The recent Ken Burns documentary on Mark Twain was chastening, so much so that late at night I was talking back to the video, "Don't do it!"

Nothing is so murky as the issue of money except perhaps sex. When you throw Hollywood into the career it becomes even more problematic. Hemingway was inappropriately self-congratulatory about avoiding screenplay writing what with solid novel and short-story property payments, but most of all, he had his wife Pauline's allowance. Faulkner, for all the mythological smoke screen he established, was making as much as ten thousand a week in modern terms in the middle of the Great Depression, but then he was supporting a dozen people who all seemed eager to put Billy back on the train from Mississippi to Hollywood. Ray Stark told me that as a young agent one of his jobs was to try to get Raymond Chandler off the floor of his apartment where he occasionally slept fully dressed in a drying pool of his own vomit. I'm not sure if this is true but it sounds right. John Steinbeck went to Hollywood and fell in love, reasonably enough, with a torch singer. It is interesting to read that when Scott Fitzgerald went to the gold mine in the west he purportedly quit drinking but on further reading you see that he was drinking a case of beer a day, the same as a bottle of whiskey. When I read that Dylan Thomas wrote nineteen screenplays for the English film industry, I couldn't believe it, though half that number would tell a story. Closer at hand, my good friend Tom McGuane had done very well but his home life had dissipated. All of this is not to say that I identify with, or even mistake myself as belonging to, this grand tribe of writers, only that if I had cared to closely observe the readily available evidence I may have acted otherwise. Maybe, but probably not. Who doesn't at times feel like an exception to all general rules?

At first it's lots of fun to make money though "fun" itself isn't a laudable category. It was fun rather than pleasurable which is a word you might use to refer to a long hike in unknown territory, catching a marlin on fly rod, staring at a Caravaggio for an hour, a morning in the Musée d'Orsay in Paris, an evening of making love to someone you love. The fact that acquiring a bunch of money doesn't mean nearly as much as you thought it would is moot. You thought it would and it did very briefly, you spent most of it, and it was a little mysterious how quickly it could go away. I have watched with a specific awe certain friends and acquaintances who have either made a lot of money or inherited it and have been able to hold on to it. They seem to have a gene or a level of attention that is missing in me though in some cases it is what Nicholson used to call "dead money," a larger overflow that you have neither the time nor the inclination to spend. This is of course a level that only a few writers like Stephen King or John Grisham ever reach. I can't think of any literary writers who hold on to their money, though frequently their heirs do well.

McGuane used to compare the whole Hollywood experience to being on the high board, mostly at night, and possibly the pool below you was empty. I habitually think of it as being stuck on a shuddering elevator, always caught between one floor or another, always in transit up or down. When I was in Hollywood and attained a level of composure it was usually at the UCLA Botanical Gardens, kitty-corner from my old hotel the Westwood Marquis, or when I had moved up to Nicholson's on Mulholland after finishing my immediate business. In those two places, which formed my California *querencia*, a place to stand at full strength, I could relax and see the broadness of the comedy in which I had made myself the featured actor. To receive the fullness of this comic sense I usually had to be sitting in nickel-ante zazen at the edge of Nicholson's pool deck looking out and a little down at a broad green galley below, or at the botanical gardens, sitting on a park bench staring at the extravagant shapes of the Pacific-rim flora. It was then I was often struck by belly laughter. I could clearly envision the head shaking, the puzzled, smiling faces of my beloved dead.

What Hollywood *is* depends on what kind of figurative glasses you are wearing at a particular time. I have never been in another place that manages so successfully to conceal its essential character. Early on during the first trips you are wearing a bum's glasses as one of the countless thousands looking for work in the film business. On one of my very first trips I was driving with Dattila and Warren Oates on the Hollywood Freeway crossing the hill over toward Burbank when we stopped in traffic. I looked up at the apartment buildings stacked against the wall of the canyon and on a deck a young man was standing in an open robe whacking off and looking down at the traffic. I said, "Maybe he's looking for a Lamborghini."

Literary types and eastern snobs like to quote Gertrude Stein, "There's no 'there' there," but then there's plenty of there to any long-term residents who live in the dozens of neighborhoods. The incomprehension is the transient's problem and in my case, and with so many others, you are wearing the "looking for a job" glasses which are not all that pleasant in New York for a newcomer either. You're also wearing draft-horse blinders besides your glasses because of the singularity of your mission. After a couple of trips you perceive what Robert Altman later dramatized in his movie *The Player*, that Hollywood is made up of a few hundred "players" and then there is everyone else whom we might call the "scramblers." The players are also scrambling but rather gracefully and at a rate of pay that is virtually unknown to all but a few in our economy. It is very hard for a scrambler to get more than nominally noticed by a player. Lucky for me that I was a novelist and Hollywood has always had a yawning desire, an unpleasant necessity for stories, though there is a specifically discernible lacunae when it comes to Hollywood knowing a good story from a bad story, but then isn't this a problem they share with publishers? To be fair there are a few good filmmakers, producers, and directors, and a great number of bad or mediocre ones.

This was a couple of years before the big break and Dattila and I were staying in a small, inexpensive suite at the Sunset Marquis, a place habituated by the low- and midrange road kill. Our rooms were sandwiched between Kinky Friedman of the Texas Jewboys and Harry Reems of recent *Deep Throat* fame. By local standards they were both fine gentlemen though Friedman like all musicians played music on his tape deck at living volume. There were many beautiful young women at the Marquis, some of them stashed there by executives, also aspiring actresses to whom you were invisible because you weren't a player or even a near miss, or attractive enough to overcome barriers. You were supposedly writing a screenplay at the time for Warren Oates about a P.O.W. whose wife, believing him dead after a long absence, remarries, and then he returns home. For reasons I've never determined, actors like masochistic stories where they are beat around severely but then emerge as at least the moral victor. Maybe that's how they see their lives. I was having a hard time on a slim budget mostly because I would do any amount of cocaine that anyone kindly offered, and the additional problem with cocaine is that you have to drink a lot to subdue the edgy feeling. That factor shot the mornings and after lunch at Ben Franks I'd have a traditional nap. The writing in small quantities took place in the afternoons between countless trips to the window where you could part the drapes and look down a couple of dozen feet to the pool where the kind of girls rarely seen in the Midwest were sunning themselves in the briefest bathing suits possible.

On this particularly misty trip west Margot Kidder had taken Bob and me to a Director's Guild screening of *Shampoo*. I was a little confused when after the movie finished David Geffen and Warren Beatty, whom I later got to know, circulated through the audience asking people what they thought. Naturally I said it was wonderful but this experience referred me to a mental flaw that came up again and again in the next two decades. From my childhood at the Reed City Theatre onward I liked just about every movie I ever saw, especially those in Technicolor though some of those most memorable were in black and white, say Huston, Bergman, and Truffaut. The fact was that my omnivorous curiosity which helped build the novelist and poet within me also made me accept *The Egg and I* and *Ma and Pa Kettle on the Farm* or any of the Francis the Talking Mule series starring Donald O'Connor. Of course the 3-D craze passed me by because I was blind in one eye but just about any film experience left me fascinated no matter how banal. Naturally I liked the best movies the best but it was unthinkable to walk out of the worst because I had to see what happened, which made any crap passable. This kind of attitude made the intensely critical perspective necessary to being a good screenwriter difficult to muster. It would be embarrassing indeed to add up the money total it required the business to teach me how to write a good screenplay. The hardest thing for a novelist to learn is that you first have to see the frame and then let the words follow. So much of the novel is made up of what people are thinking and there the language properly comes first. Nothing else is possible. The mystery writer John D. MacDonald cautioned me that if a screenplay reads beautifully it's likely not a good screenplay. That's probably what was basically wrong with Monte Hellman's *Two-Lane Blacktop* and dozens of novelists' screenplays where the language is lovely and the movement is lethargic.

When a midwesterner is blown away he does his utmost to pretend that he isn't. I went west after John Calley's call but my agent and I had turned down, albeit nervously, the three-year option grant. I suppose that gave him the impression that we were difficult customers. Dattila, with both the demeanor and the thinking of a New York street kid, felt we would be stupid not to maximize this opportunity. After all, he had tried without success for nearly a decade to make me a living and we had spent an enormous amount of time on my visits to New York trying to figure our way out of the bind. Dattila also had my brother John's way of worrying about my tenuous sanity without coming out and directly saying so. He had convinced me to see a "mind doctor" while I was in New York and over twenty years later I still see Larry Sullivan, a man with an immense range of practical wisdom. Many writers have felt that even the most modest forms of counseling and analysis might steal their secrets, whatever that might mean, which means that art is not so much natural as it is the result of dark and unbearable tensions. I wasn't sure what my powers were but I was very sure that I wanted to stay alive and provide for my wife and daughters, and the effect of alcohol and drugs on my questionable sanity had become shameful.

When Hollywood wants to court you they do so exhaustively. When I arrived for my first meeting with Calley I was put in a five-room suite at the Wilshire used by Doris Duke or Barbara Hutton, someone like that. It didn't have the desired effect. There was an open and full liquor cabinet and I wondered how the hotel kept track. You could always drink a bunch and bring the bottles back up to level with water. Dattila arrived late in the evening and that calmed me down. I met with Calley for breakfast in the morning and was startled to see he was a nondescript man in a worn leather aviator's jacket. He was profoundly witty and soon put me at ease. I asked to be put in smaller quarters in the future so the next trip he rented me one of the discreet bungalows behind the Beverly Hills Hotel. Things moved quickly and we made a deal for *Revenge*, which Nicholson wished to star in, and also sold an option for *Legends of the Fall* for which only the day before we had turned down a grand offer from MGM because we were unsure of the people.

Off I went, as it were. I quickly wrote a passable screenplay for *Revenge* and then agreed as part of the three-screenplay contract to do a version of John MacDonald's Travis McGee series. I had spent time with MacDonald in Florida while working with Rust Hills cutting ten pages of *Revenge* for its appearance in *Esquire*. The Travis McGee screenplay didn't work out in my opinion because it was a generic approach to the series rather than settling on a single novel. I was working and playing overhard and was not a little angry because I couldn't get a release from my three-picture contract to write a remake of James Cain's *The Postman Always Rings Twice* for Jack Nicholson to be directed by Bob Rafelson.

I had been home from an exhausting trip to L.A. for only two days when Calley called to say that Sean Connery had read my novella *Revenge* in *Esquire* and wanted to discuss a project with me and Calley told Connery that they had me under contract. I flat refused, being of unstable body and mind, but Calley said Warner Brothers was trying to hook Connery for a Bond project, and he would send a plane for me the next morning and have it take me back the following morning. The fact that I agreed showed that there was no hope of getting off the toboggan more than momentarily. Margaret, Calley's secretary, then called to see what I wanted to eat on the plane and I said a corned-tongue sandwich from Nate & Al's, a Jewish deli in L.A. that I favored, a six-pack of beer, and a bottle of bourbon. Margaret laughed and said that wasn't the usual order. The next morning I boarded Warner's Hawker-Sidley, larger and more comfortable then a Lear, in my best Hawaiian shirt and off we flew. The meeting soon after my arrival was successful and I was taken home early the next morning with another Nate & Al's sandwich. My visiting father-in-law picked me up at the airport and was bemused to see how the black sheep was getting very white.

The project was a flop, partly because Warner Brothers couldn't legally secure the rights for a Bond project. I worked nearly a month at the Beverly Hills Hotel and ever after found its color of pink unendurable. Sean showed up bright and too early every morning but my nightlife had taken a toll and I was lethargic. One morning we had a meeting with Mike Ovitz and Calley. I said that my back hurt though in reality I had been doing coke and booze with two prominent ladies until nearly dawn. I got down onto the floor to stretch out and promptly dozed off in front of these three showbiz eminences. It was pretty impressive.

I was clearly on the shuddering elevator and the door was locked. It was difficult for me to write with anyone else around except back home with our young daughter Anna, and now I had Connery and a secretary in the suite. The distractions were too many. We would often lunch at the pool with bathing beauties idling around us and God knows where they came from. One day I lunched with Sean and

Jack Nicholson, who'd never met, and Sir Lew Grade from London appeared at the table, cannily observing that I had the attention of two bankable stars. He wondered if I had anything to sell and I said no. "Just make something up and give me a call tomorrow," he said. One evening I barbecued thirty pounds of prime beef ribs for a crowd including Sean, Jack, and Warren Beatty who all wore white suits. It was pleasant to destroy so much fine tailoring.

Just the other day I figured out the legend of the thistle for that period of my life. Up at the Hard Luck Ranch near the border town of Patagonia, Arizona, I remembered that the year before I had begun daily watering a backyard thistle in this semi-desert climate. The thistle grew larger at a startling rate, a dozen times the size of those that didn't get the daily watering. Within a month it was the largest thistle I had ever seen but then one day it toppled over from the weight of its unnatural size. I didn't fall that quickly. It was a slow-motion fall, mostly mental in nature.

One day at the Beverly Hills Hotel I got a poolside call from my father-in-law who rather dryly told me that he was dying and wondered how financially fixed we were. He probed a bit and when I told him the truth he whistled having closely witnessed our bleaker years. Shortly after this, my mother found out she had colon cancer and soon after that my brother John's daughter Gloria was struck on her bike by a car. My mother survived another twenty years but Gloria died in New Haven after being in a coma for a hundred days. My brother recited her grave service on an icy and windy day with the Long Island Sound glittering in the distance. Nothing is harder to deal with than a small casket.

The one sensible thing I did at this time was to hire a friend of my older daughter, Joyce Harrington, as an aide. After settling my tax debacle and its possible brush with federal prison (it's better to have the money on hand when you come forward) it occurred to me that we needed someone to help with the large part of life at which I was so dramatically inadequate. I couldn't type, entering a bank made me sweat, lawyers frightened me, and accountants addled me so that I couldn't write for a day or two. Despite learning how to make money I couldn't quite figure out that I had to, at the time, give half to the government. Joyce was one of seven children of a New York City meatpacker. She was much more functional and worldly than I. She pretty much took over all of my life except the actual writing, fishing, and hunting and over twenty years later is still with me. This worked fine because it has often struck me that I have no area of expertise in life except my imagination. I mean I'm a pretty fair fisherman and a moderately good dog trainer and bird shot but these talents are good in this world only through helping you avoid it.

I flew off to London where Nicholson was filming *The Shining* to discuss the *Revenge* project. This was a delightful intermezzo and I had packed along volumes of Keats, Christopher Smart, John Clare, and William Blake, all of whom were detrimental to my film career. Amid everything else I had finished a novel called *Warlock,* the only book I've ever written that I loathe, shot through as it is with ironies that continue to scratch their tired asses.

In London Jack lived on Cheney Walk on the Thames in a modest mansion that his English friends called a "raghead" house, usually rented by wealthy Arabs. Anjelica Huston and her sister Allegra, who later became my English editor, were there, and Harry Dean Stanton was also in London shooting the first of the *Alien* movies. Sometimes Anjelica and I would visit the set and then go to San Lorenzo's for a very long lunch, then we would have our naps and Jack would come home from his long day of work quite exhausted. I was there for only a couple of hours that day but Stanley had shot the scene where Jack chops down the door with a fire ax twenty-six times, tiring work indeed. Every morning Tim, the cook, would discuss dinner with me, then drive off to Harrods to buy our nonbudget victuals. It was serene compared to Hollywood, with very little cocaine, though once as a practical joke George Harrison was sent to my bedroom to wake me from my nap with a long line.

Stanley Kubrick was a fascinating man who utterly failed, to his disgust, to get me to learn how to play chess. He always had a newspaper stuffed into his red James Dean jacket which didn't quite fit his portly figure. The smallest lapse in conversation and out would come the newspaper for reading though I once noted it was several days old. There were any number of somewhat drunken parties with upper-crust English who had a capacity for booze that competed with that of the Russians. The high point came with the arrival of John Huston and a long meeting where we discussed our procedure for the screenplay of *Revenge*. His plan was oddly similar to that of Fred Wiseman for *A Good Day to Die*, where you simply take apart two copies of the book, paste the pages, and cross out what you don't like. He invited me to come down to his place south of Puerto Vallarta in Mexico which was approachable only by boat and where we could later work on the screenplay when the contracts were straightened out.

I went to London twice for several weeks though we didn't discuss *Revenge* all that much because Jack had total faith in Huston to lead the way. I felt the same. Huston was a grand character indeed, the most impressive of the many directors I met. He was thought to be far too arrogant by the studios, which he probably was from their questionable point of view.

Much of any writer's film job is waiting for the principals who are doing something else, and London was a splendid place to wait. I mostly walked, stopping at pubs like the Wharf Rat where twice I saw rock groups involved in rather ineffectual fistfights though they never managed to set their feet and slug it out. I liked a friendly musician named John Bonham who later died at age thirty-three.

One day on a long walk I stopped at a posh restaurant where the staff was hesitant to serve me. I told Anjelica and she said it was because of my dreadful clothing which I thought was rather nifty by

midwestern terms. She took to calling me "Walter of Battersea," which
referred to a lower-class neighborhood, so I wrote her a poem.

Walter of Battersea
for Anjelica

I shall commit suicide or die
trying, Walter thought beside
the Thames—at low tide and very
feminine.

Picture him: a cold November day,
the world through a long lens; he's
in new blue pants and races the river
for thirty-three steps.

Walter won. Hands down. Then lost
again. Better to die trying! The sky
so bleak. God blows his nose above
the Chelsea Flour Mills.

What is he at forty, Nov. 9, 1978, so far
from home: grist for his own mill; all
things have become black and white
without hormonal surge.

And religious. He's forgiven god
for the one hundred ladies who turned him
down and took him up. O that song—
I asked her for water and she gave
me kerosene.

No visions of Albion, no visions at all,
in fact, the still point of the present winding

about itself, graceful, unsnarled. I am
here today and gone tomorrow.

How much is he here? Not quite with
all his heart and soul. Step lightly
or the earth revolves into a berserk
spin. Fall off or dance.

And choosing dance not God, at least
for the time being. Things aren't what
they seem but what they are—infinitely
inconsolable.

He knows it's irony that's least
valuable in this long deathwatch.
Irony scratching its tired ass. No trade-offs
with time and fortune.

It's indelicate to say things twice except
in prayer. The drunk repeats to keep
his grasp, a sort of prayer: the hysteria
of the mad, a verbless prayer.

Walter recrossed the bridge which was
only a bridge. He heard his footsteps
just barely behind him. The river is not
where it starts and ends.

MIDDLE HOLLYWOOD

Quite suddenly John Calley retired from Warner Brothers and I immediately felt like a waif or orphan. In quick succession after his departure Warners rejected David Lean for *Legends of the Fall* because it would be too expensive, and refused to hire John Huston for *Revenge* because he was too difficult to work with. I was already somewhat deranged at the time but the news was a real stunner. It had occurred to me that Hollywood was a microcosm of the boxing world and I was Leon Spinks who had misplaced his teeth and was arrested with cocaine in his glove box, in short a very good fighter in the short haul but with no real prospects. Hollywood seemed to be in transition and I was unaware of the details. Only the year before when I had had lunch with Calley and Ted Ashley, the chairman of Warner Brothers, Ashley had said he thought it improper that a writer of my quality should be forced to work with an actor like Sean Connery. Now Hollywood was going through a period, however brief, when everyone was dispensable except bankable stars. In meetings there was no real point in bringing up quality filmmaking with people who had openly rejected the great John Huston.

Jack became cagier after this incident, saying that Orson Welles would be acceptable as a second choice. This was a matter of pouring salt in the studio's wounds but was quite wonderful for me as I had several splendid meals at Ma Maison with Welles. The meals were on Warner's tab and billed directly so I didn't have to use a transitional credit card that might have been questionable. I had become more relaxed in the berserk milieu and food had come to supplant cocaine as a primary morale aide. Welles called rather early one morning to say that he had "planned" a special meal for us that would include the freshest possible Atlantic salmon to be flown in that morning plus Patrick Terrail had managed to get hold of some French *agneau sel,* lamb that had grazed on the salty grass near the Atlantic, and so on, and on and on. I have no idea what this five-hour "business" dinner cost. I remember that I, with Orson's diminutive black driver, had to brace a foot on the rocker panel to get Orson out of his limo. A Hungarian countess friend of Welles lasted halfway through the dinner before she fled in disgust. Welles advised me to avoid hatcheck girls who would inevitably cheat on you with musicians. I filed this away with other advice I was unlikely to use. We became bleary and teary over the beauty of Rita Hayworth whose *Life* cover photo I had cut out and saved as a very young man. He and Huston had been close friends for many years and neither were particularly upset over their involvement in the *Revenge* disaster. He told me that when they dined together in France at expensive restaurants they would stick each other with tabs by feigning illness and on one evening both had simultaneously collapsed to the floor with fake heart attacks. With Welles I began to understand that the director's battles with studios could be more extensive and profound than a writer's.

It was gradually dawning on me that it wasn't a good idea to write several screenplays a year plus their revisions in addition to trying to hang in there with your calling as a poet and novelist. It was both exhausting and a little schizophrenic, though the poems and novels came from a different place and I needed only to "access" this region to be off and running. On a very creaturely level I was ruining my health and thought constantly of methods of escape though this was unlikely as the dominant element of sanity in my life.

The solution to this crushing sense of claustrophobia turned out to be ridiculously easy. I simply drove north one June day into Michigan's Upper Peninsula, the scene of my first novel, *Wolf,* and looked for a cabin, a retreat. Years before on a trout-fishing trip I had been curious about Grand Marais, a small harbor town on Lake Superior, because there were three trout streams in the area, the Fox, the Sucker, and the Big Two-Hearted, plus innumerable beaver ponds in the dense forest. After a few days of looking around I found a cabin on a tip from a local bar owner, Jerry Alverson. The cabin had been expertly built of logs in the mid-thirties, and the fifty acres were bisected by the Sucker River. I spent an entire ten minutes looking at the place then drove back to the tavern in the village, called the Realtor, and offered the asking price. I had no knowledge of real estate bargaining but discovered shortly thereafter that there had been a number of lesser offers so in being a bit of a fool I had won the prize. It was a little embarrassing when I drove home and admitted to Linda and my aide Joyce that I had neglected to go inside the cabin. I had to go back to L.A. so they drove north and actually went inside and told me on the phone it was fine.

At the moment I didn't have the cash to pay for the cabin so I called Ray Stark who had been trying to buy an option for the novella *The Man Who Gave Up His Name*. I named a figure and he said, "Why?" and I said, "Because that's what I'm paying for a cabin so you fucks won't kill me." As opposed to many in the community I liked Stark, who was an old-fashioned mogul, very much so. Once on a project he demanded that I appear in L.A. the next day and I said I couldn't because I had to go bird hunting with friends. "You're a fucking bird-watcher?" he asked. "No, I kill them and eat them." "Fine," he said, "just come as soon as you can." Later on when I was cornered again by the IRS Stark sent a check in twenty-four hours against a future project. Naturally you fulfill your obligations and do a better quality of work for someone with this forthright generosity. I was sure I didn't want to be on Stark's wrong side but then I never was.

I began to alternate weeks at the cabin and our farm and continued to do so from May through October for twenty years. One advantage of the cabin is that there was no phone service or electricity. I had a generator when I needed lights and the stove and refrigerator ran on propane. People who are driven batty by the phone should treat themselves to the pleasure of doing without one for a week at a time, especially in a place where all sounds not made immediately by yourself are natural, except for a very distant truck or chain saw. You heard birds, wind, rain, the river, coyotes, and, rarely, wolves. In late September and October you also heard the thudding roar of Lake Superior when the first northwest storms arrived, which often lasted three days, the worst of them I remember having winds up to ninety knots and the marine forecasts warning of seas over thirty feet. These storms were bracing and as far as I could get from the way I was making a living. One evening I saw a female wolf semi-crouched in the two-track leading to the cabin out to the main road. I had heard a wolf the two previous evenings but had despaired of seeing one. My bird dogs at the time, Tess and Sand, on hearing the wolf crept up to hide under the bed. I figured there must be something in canine genetic memory that told them this was a threatening sound. Years later while I was bird hunting with Rose, we discovered a wolf den and she hightailed it back to the car two miles distant. Rose is a bit neurotic and is also disturbed by the circular wail of a loon, and once on seeing a bear she leapt her seventy pounds into my arms. I didn't blame her having recently helped a bear hunter put over two hundred staple stitches in a hound after a fight with a bear smaller than itself.

While at my cabin if anyone in the golden West wished to reach me they had to call after ten in the evening at the Dunes Saloon. The cabin itself became an addiction and I even came to love the five-hour drive north from our farm, feeling safe when I crossed the huge Mackinac Bridge into the Upper Peninsula. One evening I was late for an "important call" at the Dunes and had to explain to a producer that I couldn't leave the cabin on time because a very fat mother bear was sitting beside my picnic table watching her two babies demolish my garbage can. Another time the producer Mark Canton was appalled when I told him that a large garter snake was living in my stove where it curled around the pilot light for warmth, and when I plopped down a skillet or turned on a burner the snake, who was finally caught and transplanted, would shoot out a burner hole which was startling. Canton said, "Don't talk about snakes, I'm Jewish." I couldn't help but add that I had shot a rattlesnake in the bedroom of our casita near the Mexican border, then couldn't get back to sleep for a while.

The cabin gave me a total retreat from a livelihood that I had shown no great talent for, but also added another illusion. For years I assumed that the cabin restored me from and for my battles with the "real world" where, in fact, it only prepared me for more time at the cabin. There was an often not amusing cultural shock in trying to track a bear across a grand sand-dune area of a dozen miles, and then twenty-four hours later being in a rancorous meeting at a studio where I had been told my latest screenplay was "soft in the middle," a less than helpful criticism.

During those early years in the great North I did manage, however, to devise some survival techniques, the first of which was to try to withdraw my combative emotions from the long and dreary meetings. The second was never to have a drink in daytime hours because it made me too agreeable. The last was to be in bed nine hours before a morning meeting. These rules were all dreadfully bourgeois but then I had a family to support and there was that curious feeling held by the Spanish that you didn't want to drop dead in the wrong place. Passing away in an English manse in Beverly Hills didn't seem preferable to toppling over with kerosene and Bordeaux stains on my shirt in the cabin clearing. I had loaned a couple hundred grand to friends and acquaintances, none of which was ever repaid except by the two poorest of them, one an Indian and one a laborer who in the summer worked sixteen hours a day when he was in his early sixties. Beyond a certain livable point for my family it was evident I didn't care about money, at least not to the obsessive point of many men I had met.

Freedom is time and it is significant for a writer when he earns enough to buy himself clear time. The beauty of the cabin was that it minimized interruption. I've always been a claustrophobe, sometimes to the panic level, even aurally with loud music. How much better to work in an area where mostly what you hear is the sound of a hundred or so species of birds. The dominance of creature life took me back to the cabin of my childhood. The rain on the roof that soothed me when my blind eye was a hot coal in my head now soothed self-administered injuries. If I sat for an hour or two on a log beside the river my concerns rather easily drifted away with the movement of the current, perhaps a main reason people fish for trout. If you spend a fair amount of time studying the world of ravens it's logical indeed to accept the fact that reality is an aggregate of the perceptions of all creatures, not just ourselves.

With mind and heart more settled I wrote a novel called *Sundog* which enlarged the field of vision in my previous work. I also, and not surprisingly, wrote a long poem, "The Theory and Practice of Rivers," which afterwards I recognized as being basically Zennist of an occasionally enraged variety. I had a dozen or so stumps in a twenty-five-mile radius of the cabin where I sat to compose myself during hikes. This technically wasn't zazen I suppose but then my effort was toward simple survival, and besides, there is evidence that the roots of meditation are to be found in prehistoric hunting techniques. You sit and wait without thinking about waiting or sitting.

I don't have a strong enough constitution to write about my long string of failed screen projects. After it was all over it dawned on me that the people involved would have done as well with my projects as the ones they ended up making. It was all a crapshoot and I wasn't a central player unless I could bring along a bankable actor. There were so many variables, some of which I didn't completely understand. For instance, I think the horse picture I wrote for Ray Stark and Marty Ritt, the wonderful director who had done *Hud* among others, would have been made if Ritt's heart condition hadn't worsened to the point that he couldn't be insured. The research in Lexington was pleasurable because I had to learn the intricacies of the thoroughbred trade in a month's time. My only previous exposure had been at Diana Guest's, Guy's mother's in France, but in Lexington I had to visit all of the main farms. Ray Stark, who was also in the thoroughbred business, came down for the Keeneland sale and it was fascinating to watch the very rich bid too much just to keep a particular horse away from someone else. It was a "dick thing," as the young liked to say a few years back. Ray took me to a lunch at Bunker Hunt's home. This was before his silver collapse and I remember being seated between

Phillip Niarchos and one of the Sangster group from Ireland, and across from a quiet sheikh from Saudi Arabia. It was a nonsmoking house except for an anteroom where I sat and had a cigarette with a group of burly bodyguards with whom I felt more in common. Several times when traveling with Nicholson, I suppose partly because of my poor tailoring and thickish appearance, I had been mistaken for his bodyguard. At Studio 54 in New York, for instance, the bouncers had insisted that I check my nonexistent pistol and I had refused for the fun of it, and at the Plaza Athenee Hotel in Paris the head of security took me aside for a brief meeting on how "we" were going to handle the paparazzi. I patted my nonexistent holster and he became quite upset, saying, "But we don't shoot photographers in France." Nicholson on one of our walks would hold up a bottle of Evian so the photos couldn't be used because they had become advertisements.

Part of my research for Ritt on the horse picture was to go to the track with him several times. Marty was one of the best handicappers in Hollywood, if not the top dog. I lost thousands on my "intuitions" rather than betting on his accurate tips. My real success was fixing a busted radiator hose in his Mercedes with electrician's tape. "You midwesterners can fix anything," he said. I had an embarrassing evening in Lexington when word got around that I was from Hollywood and I was guided to a restaurant where for my entire meal people leapt through a beaded curtain and sang me show tunes directly in front of my table at full volume. I've always found show tunes embarrassing, if not loathsome, and to hear "I'm as corny as Kansas in August" bellowed at you while trying to eat lamb chops is a difficult assignment. When I told Stark he thought it was very funny but then he didn't live through it.

Sometimes it was the travel that was the tonic. I worked on an unpromising idea (my own—you can't really dramatize an unbuilt dam in Central America) for Stanley Jaffe and his assistant Patricia Burke, whose offices were in New York City which meant I could stay at the Carlyle and walk down Madison to work in the marine combat boots Doug Peacock, the grizzly-bear expert, had given me.

New York employment also allowed me to see my mind doctor on a regular basis for symptomatic relief from the contemporary world. Like Ray Stark, Stanley Jaffe was a bear, a real tough guy, but we got along fine, probably because of my work ethic.

Another earlier project for Columbia and Taylor Hackford, a screenplay on the life of Edward Curtis, allowed me a large travel budget to visit many of the Indian reservations on the trail of Curtis. Still better for travel was Lou Adler's project in Rio de Janeiro. We met in New York but then Lou had a bad neck and perhaps several girlfriends, so I went ahead to Rio alone to look at the territory. My mission was to devise a screenplay idea, also to convince Sonia Braga to be vitally interested in this unwritten project. I was guided by a Brazilian, Christina Kler, who had rented us a lavish apartment with five servants right on Ipanema. The evening of my arrival I went to a rather frightening Umbanda rite in the countryside outside of Rio where the devils had been cast out of a black drummer and he had bounced around a garden on his back like a bullfrog. Rio in the weeks leading up to Carnaval is a lively place, a little too lively for my taste. My paranoia increased when Christina told me that when a Swede comes to Rio he never leaves. Sonia Braga was of surpassing loveliness though she and her friends were a bit cynical of me as a Hollywood emissary and I had failed to bring copies of my novels and books of poems to convince them otherwise. As a relief from Rio madness Christina took me north to Bahia, the most intoxicating city I've ever visited, with a large magic store next to the cathedral. Every street corner acoustic guitarists seemed the best you had ever heard and the women, often a mixture of black, Indian, and Portuguese, were the most graceful in the world. I hadn't quite recovered from the Umbanda ceremony of the first day where I had drunk a secret potion from a wooden bowl to level out my life, not an immediate prospect because Lou arrived and we went to seven grand balls in seven days, one of them on top of a mountain where my vertigo kicked in to a dizzying degree. Back at our duplex we were surrounded by heavily armed guards because the minister of the interior lived on the first

floor. During my first few days in Rio I determined that a couple of
plainclothesmen who followed me in my barhopping were there to
make sure I kept out of harm's way. I was convinced that our cook,
Sebastiana, was a witch, though a good and positive witch. Later back
at my cabin my sleep was full of lurid Brazilian nightmares and when
I called Christina about the matter she consulted Sebastiana who
instructed me to drop three lighted candles into moving water at
midnight. I did so and the nightmares vanished despite my cynicism
over the matter. Still later I rethought the potion I had drunk from
the wooden bowl because after the splendid Brazilian cocaine I quit
the drug forever soon after returning to America.

After trips to Brazil, Ecuador, and Costa Rica I became convinced that American literary critics had been amiss when writing
about supposed "magical realism." All of our life processes and the
natural world are viewed quite differently in South and Central
America. Borges, García Márquez, and dozens of others are decidedly not white Protestants and to refer to their prose as magical
realism is demeaning to them. It's simply their realism. As you sit
on a veranda listening to old sambas while looking at the warm Atlantic, including the old prewar samba "Estrella Dalva" (O morning star), the world becomes far wider, more haunted and timeless.
Even the ocean looks larger with Imanja rising from the sea like
Botticelli's Venus in her curved shell.

One summer morning in 1987 the director Hal Ashby stopped by
the cabin. I could hear his Corvette thumping its bottom along my
rumpled two-track for minutes before he drove into the clearing. He
had called the tavern the night before saying that he was driving from
New York to L.A. and would be in the area. This seemed to be a little
odd because the cabin was about a thousand miles out of the way from
a direct line between New York and Los Angeles. I knew from both
Jack and Warren Beatty that Hal was perhaps fatally ill and though
we were not close we had spoken any number of times of trying to do
a project together. We spent several hours pleasantly talking and he

said he understood why I loved the cabin. When he drove off I figured he was just saying good-bye to friends.

Despite my confusion I liked certain people in the film business very much. Some people despite their massive celebrity are very appealing on an ordinary basis. I was very sorry at the death of John Belushi who didn't seem all that crazy by Key West standards. One late evening while we were talking about teaming up for *The Confederacy of Dunces* he said he hoped he wouldn't have to gain weight for the role, and this after eating a massive pizza by himself. Belushi was either morose or soaring, a rare and true comic genius. I kept thinking of the Old West phrase that despite his evident brilliance he simply "didn't have a lick of sense." I also found Don Henley of the Eagles very amenable. I was always struck by the high price, their entire lives, that musicians of magnum success end up paying, wherein they are forced to become permanent spectacles like public monuments. This is not a matter of sympathy but truth. Rock and roll didn't really touch me like jazz and rhythm and blues, though I was quite overwhelmed one night at the Top of the Rox to hear James Taylor singing to five of us. There were many others I didn't know well but impressed me, like Bill Murray who seemed to have Nicholson's unilateral stability. The same with Danny DeVito. John Candy was wonderful but you weren't very confident that he would make it and he didn't. It's never been adequately explained why owning comic genius is the most grueling of all.

I was quite lucky to have the soothing company of both Lou Adler and Nicholson who handled L.A. as if it were their own personal birthday cake. Going to the Lakers games drew you away from the quarrels of meetings, in addition to just seeing splendid basketball, which never quite works on television. Jack and Louis had seats on the floor next to the visitor's bench where the game was improbably visceral and the subtlety of the moves detectable. They also co-owned a guesthouse in Aspen. Once at the foot of Little Nell in an apartment I sat all afternoon with Art Garfunkel eating cheeseburgers, drinking beer, and keeping track of the way skiers fell down. Later Arty stopped at our farm in northern Michigan on his meticulously mapped walk across America. I had studied the map in his New York condo, also the log of the books he read, which was chastening in view of my own sloppiness.

I've often supposed that my survival with a modicum of sanity depended on the way I continued fishing and hunting for two months a year, and often more than that, whether in Key West, Montana, Michigan, Mexico, Ecuador, or Costa Rica, though by 1990 Key West had worn out for me because I couldn't bear all the changes, the burgeoning tourism that was doubtless a good thing for some but not for me. My claustrophobia has predicated where I've lived and traveled, and the limitations could be irksome. Once I couldn't hang in there in New York for a possibly rewarding meeting with Harrison Ford because it had been raining several days and the relentless beeping of cars and cabs drove me batty. Under usual circumstances both New York and Paris are made tolerable by my walking several hours a day. Paris has made legal inroads on the beeping problem but not New York. In the eighties and early nineties my sure cure for claustrophobia was long driving trips, usually solo, but sometimes with Dan Gerber until a painful divorce dug a three-year hole in his life. He has since recovered. Divorces can be harrowing for friends who are invariably asked to take sides. For a couple of years I carried a dog whistle and when people would talk about their divorces I'd blow the whistle loudly.

Miserable projects were often leavened by the steadiness of the people involved. I worked well on a dead-end project with Sydney Pollack and Mark Rosenberg. I had come up with a story about a group of sixties radicals who went to a university together and reunited while trying to get their old ringleader out of a Mexican prison. I knew the material well and thought I had written a good version but Sydney didn't like it. Mark liked most of it and had a broad background as a student radical. It was a loggerhead situation, which reminded me of the time Taylor Hackford wanted Edward Curtis to shoot someone in my screenplay, something I couldn't do with a historical figure who never shot anyone. As the years went by I blamed Taylor Hackford less and less because the connection between movies and reality is questionable at best, and the pretension of biographical reality should be avoided because those who are knowledgeable or directly involved will yell foul. Something similar comes up in literature in translation when someone expertly translates the sense of a poem but then it's no longer a poem. With Sydney and Mark it became evident that the material was still too raw to deal with. At the height of the noontime quarrel one day Bill Murray burst in the garden door of Sydney's office, sat on Mark's lap, and began eating his lunch. Mark was a glutton like myself and his feelings were clearly hurt, but at that moment I figured out what was wrong with my screenplay. Ordinary radical leaders are boring. A week with Ralph Nader would leave one comatose and wanting to wrestle with the Sex Pistols.

On trips to L.A. after completing three or four days of meetings during which I'd stay in a hotel I would move up to Nicholson's for a few days of cooling off before going home. I learned to do the same thing in New York, spending at least an extra day merely walking, eating, and spending time with friends. If you want your marriage to last you don't want to come home with the acrid smoke still coming out of your ears. At Nicholson's I'd swim for a couple of hours and then follow whatever the program was. Dog paddling always seemed my most appropriate Hollywood stroke. One day we went over to Mike Eisner's for a fund-raising lunch for Bill Bradley who was my favorite politician well before I met him. Bradley had ended up marrying Ernestine Schlandt, a Ph.D. in comparative literature and a colleague from my days at Stony Brook. I later went with Jack to a fund-raiser in New Jersey for Bradley, and few years further down the line I went to Washington to do the early *Charlie Rose Show* and to spend an evening with Bradley, for whom I was writing some environmental piths, gists, quips for his speeches. The Eisner lunch was a preposterous case of a writer being off to the side, as I certainly didn't belong to the group of hotshots and moguls. I felt as addled as I did one day in a cabana at the Beverley Hills Hotel and a mobster offered me a true bundle of cash to write a screenplay for an unnamed star and I asked where do I put the cash? Under my daughter's bed? Eisner is a man who, like Barry Diller and David Geffen, is able to see the entertainment business in the manner of what John Huston prescribed for directors: topographically, with the large view not preventing the consciousness of details. I sent Eisner a copy of my novel *Dalva* when it was published and within days I got a letter back explaining why it wouldn't make a movie though he liked the novel. The busiest people seem to have time to get everything done. This is only offering respect to a kind of person with abilities remote from your own interests.

Nicholson more than any other major star I've met knew how to protect himself, how to live a private life with his books and paintings away from the public eye. It was a matter of controlling all incursions whether in Beverly Hills, New York, Paris, or London. This requires a good deal of precision and energy, of knowing what you want to a degree that I as a writer found forbidding. Of course I saw this kind of social pressure only at a distance, and when a certain amount of it arrived for me in France I mostly wanted to run for the cover of Arles or Marseilles, whereas famous actors and actresses have to cooperate to a certain extent because it's part of their livelihood. Nicholson also used his place outside of Aspen as a retreat. Aspen people like Parisians tend to leave their noteworthy citizens alone. One morning in Aspen we looked at stacks of possible screenplays for hours and our reward was to go to a fashion show about which I wasn't enthused until I learned that our seats would be backstage where the ladies changed outfits.

Even at a goodly distance of time I've not been able to draw specific conclusions about show business except minor ones, like certain actors and producers are spectacularly good drivers. Jack, Harrison Ford, Sydney Pollack, and the producer Doug Wick always amazed me when driving, partially because I'm so lousy in traffic. Having only one eye doesn't help. In fifty or so trips to L.A. I tried to drive from the airport in a rental car only once, a shattering experience. After rush hour I could drive locally though not well in Beverly Hills and environs though other cars would beep at me for driving too slow.

Once during a long stay at the Beverly Hills Hotel Jack had loaned me an older mint El Dorado convertible, but after a few days I found the car decidedly unliterary, filling me with anxiety over wrecking it. I felt like a goofy showbiz pimp which may have been close to the mark. A number of times I asked studios to have a five-year-old brown Taurus station wagon sent to my hotel but they were never able to deliver.

Having two daughters made me a little more aware of how actresses are treated. The situation comes close to the inscrutable in that actresses are rarely as "bankable" as actors but nearly all producers and studio powers are male, hence the movies that get made tend to be male-oriented. Maybe it's an insuperable "sexist" problem (a foggy word). I think of actresses I have known, some of them only slightly, and none of them seem to fit the overweening media renditions of actresses. Jessica Lang, Madeleine Stowe, Deborah Winger, Michelle Pfeiffer, Anjelica Huston, Lauren Hutton, Winona Ryder, Amy Irving, Jeanne Moreau, and Catherine Deneuve have struck me as far less impulsive and ditzy than an equally long list of their male counterparts. Perhaps I become jaundiced by the fact that actresses are far more interested in literature. For instance, when I had drinks with Lauren Hutton at the Top of the Rox we talked about William Carlos Williams. I'm not saying that these women are "bookworms" but that they were far better read as a group than any other save English teachers. All of them seemed to have a somewhat melancholy awareness of how brief the industry, if not the public, would find them acceptable on the screen. Curiously, two of the oldest, Moreau and Deneuve, struck me as the sexiest, but then there is a necessary defensive posture among actresses to keep the usual mad dogs off their tracks. The sheer fact of male-female desire is always there but both magazine pages and movie screens are thin indeed. I've always been irritated when occasionally angry readers think that I personally represent the hundreds of characters in my novels, some of them fulsomely unpleasant. Of course it's impossible for actresses and actors to avoid public identification with their roles, which are just that, roles. It seems far-fetched but way back in my early time at the Sunset

Marquis I talked with Arnold Schwarzenegger about German literature while he was eating an entire wheel of brie from our refrigerator
after pumping fifty tons of iron in an hour at Gold's Gym. Go figure, as
they say. If you think of Hollywood, in toto, as a huge, whimsical Tro-
jan horse moving through time it's not surprising that the culture is
largely ignorant of the nature of all the people inside the horse who
make it move, make it function.

GETTING MADE

My fifties were a blur of work partly due to a television program. One evening after an ample dinner with good wine my wife and I began to watch a program on the homeless. I quickly began to snooze and made my way to the bedroom but when I got up for my evening's work Linda was quite upset, untypically so. The program on the homeless had distressed her mightily, so much so that she was in tears when she announced that our daughters might someday be homeless. She has rarely been truly alarmed in our long marriage, and after she went to bed I spent a couple of hours of brooding on ways to save some money. I had less than a firm notion of what I had done with several million dollars other than pay taxes. Our farm was now a hundred acres, the house was fine, we probably had two newish cars though new cars get old at a puzzling speed, and there was also the cabin, but no accumulated savings, stocks, bonds, suchlike. Joyce regularly gave me financial reports but I always squinted past the columns of nasty details to the bottom line which offered up how much I had to spend.

When it came to money I was shot through with comic insincerity. There were poignant details like you didn't have to pay taxes on borrowed money which made it pleasant. During the then recent marriage of our eldest daughter Jamie to her University of Michigan classmate Stephen Potenberg we had made a dent in the better bottles in our wine cellar, some '49 La Tours, '61 Lafites, '58 Yquems, and I had idly thought that they totaled in value more than I had made in the first few years of our marriage. Jamie, who had been self-supporting in New York City for a number of years working for Dean & Deluca and *Rolling Stone,* had actually hidden a number of fine bottles so I wouldn't swill them all during my melancholy nights. The facts of financial life that homeless evening became quite lurid due to a Dickensian sentimentality I absorbed from my father in whose life it was far more justified. There was the perpetual image of an early painting, *Orphan in the Storm*, or the London or New York street kid walking home in shabby knickers with a loaf of bread he had earned. Much more powerful were the images from reading Hamlin Garland or Steinbeck's *Grapes of Wrath*. The fact that all of this had nothing to do with my actual situation was irrelevant. Within the perimeters of the mystery of money I kept thinking of the biblical rich man wherein he is described as owning three camels, two horses, and a granary full of grain. The fact that a billion people in the world live on less than a buck a day does not seem to decrease the shower of tears coming to those whose worth was reduced in the plunge of the technicals from five hundred to two hundred million. When I received fifty times less for writing the work than the actor who performed it I had a fairly clear notion of the system that made this possible, but this was only a small detail in an economic life in which I definitely asserted my ignorance.

I have spent entire moments casting around for someone to blame. Why don't they teach basic personal economics in junior high? And, better yet, beginning anthropology so that fools might get an early inkling as to why they are fools. My parents, whose sole intent was to make the monthly paycheck last a month, could scarcely give their children advice in advance in the unlikelihood that an overflow might occur. My surviving brothers and sister, John, David, and Mary, found their careers in rather altruistic occupations, and we rarely have spoken about money except in quips and nervous smiles. I am forced, finally, to accept the idea that money isn't highly valued because I grew up in an atmosphere where money wasn't highly valued, a world that now seems antique and archaically ethical. Our past seeps into our psyches in absurd little glimmers. I'm not paying over two bucks for a pound of butter for my cabin but then forty dollars for a bottle of olive oil seems reasonable. Cranberry juice at four dollars is an outrage but a Côte Rotie at fifty is a deal. Now that I'm older I no longer mind the acute scrutiny I accept from others on this baleful matter. Never having filled out a check stub I have fun telling others to do so.

You feel real naked when they begin making movies you have written, much more so than when you publish a book. From the very beginning with books you have accepted total responsibility, and your tender emotions don't do that much waffling in their state of vulnerability. In a book you cease to worry whether your readers see the material the way you do because you'll never know, though you're tipped off in bad reviews that your efforts may have lacked universality. Good reviews that like you for the wrong reason are another matter. Movies, however, are a thoroughly collaborative art and you will clearly see how the director, producer, art director, wardrobe people, soundman, actors and actresses have understood your story.

My aide Joyce's husband, Bob Bahle, owns a small movie theater in Sutton's Bay, Michigan, so I was fortunate to screen "my" movies alone or with a few friends (and a few bottles of wine). Sitting there in the dark before the projector starts you have the distinct feeling you might be raped by an elephant or, if your imagination is running to the sea, a whale. Your milky brain is full of cursory banalities . . . your future depends on this blah, blah, blah . . . your bluff has been called, argh . . . why is it blamed on the screenplay? That sort of thing.

I had spent several days in Puerta Vallarta at the premiere party for *Revenge*, directed by Tony Scott (Ridley's brother) and starring Madeleine Stowe, Kevin Costner, and Anthony Quinn. I liked Mexico so much that I had neglected to watch the film. I had a few drinks and went swimming, or so I remember. Kevin Costner was still a fairly fresh face then and was a bit shy and unassuming. He was embarrassed in a cocktail lounge when I pointed out that he had received a dozen notes from surrounding ladies and I had gotten none. He kindly offered me several of the notes. Jay Maloney, a young Ovitz agent, was with us to keep track of Kevin. It is a sad memory because we had a fine time in Mexico and now Jay is dead from a suicide after an astounding success. For several years Jay was always going to visit me at my cabin or at our casita on the Mexican border. The plan was that I would drive him into the wilderness early in the morning, drop him off, then pick him up in the evening so he could "cool off." He never arrived though there were several misses. His death was at the same time dumbfounding and expected. It has struck me that Costner has also gotten chewed up by studios and agentry, with a rather obtuse selection of wrong projects after *Dances with Wolves*. There were a couple of good ones but a hot, bankable actor needs judgment plus balls of iron when it comes to refusing his agents, producers, and studios. Actors and actresses easily become overexposed and quite literally "used up" by the industry, and then consequently discarded. Nicholson had this in mind in his long and steadfast refusal to appear on television. The celebrity and sporting media are ruthlessly obsessive and single-minded. There are stretches of thousands of column inches on Brad Pitt, Gwyneth Paltrow, Tiger Woods, and Michael Jordan, as if there were no on else in the theaters, or on golf courses, or in the arenas. It is similar to the media at large a couple of years ago when we had months of dire portents about Y2K, and then nothing happened. You very much wished that pundits could be sent to separate desert islands to reread their babble.

You're sitting by yourself in the dark theater several rows away from your wife and perhaps a few friends who are nervously sniggering. You hold off on the wine, waiting for an emergency, and though you just put out a cigarette on the street you already want another when the first frame slides in a split second through the projector. The bottom line is that you're not even hoping for something great, fine, or even real good. What you are hoping for is something well short of bad.

Through a half-dozen movies I've been connected with, my first impressions, minute by minute, were that the films didn't look like they did in my head when I wrote them. Of course not. Nothing does. While I clearly didn't get raped by an elephant with *Revenge*, my own vision of the material was improbably darker and grittier than the director's. Everyone connected with the film should have read Octavio Paz's great book about the Mexican character, *The Labyrinth of Solitude*. When I mentioned this book while giving a conference to the Mexican press in Puerto Vallarta an attending Columbia studio rep had looked at me with bleak alarm. Mention a book! How dare you, you filthy writer!

My main problem with *Revenge* was the hundreds of lit candles when Kevin and Madeleine first made love in a cabin. Where did all the candles come from? No one owns that many candles except a candle store and we're in an isolated cabin in the Sonoran Mountains. O well. I thought the performances of Costner, Stowe, and Quinn were good and I especially liked that of a minor character, Miguel Ferrer. Naturally I have wondered what John Huston would have done with the material but I'll never know. Costner also edited a version he much preferred but I never got to see it.

I walked out of the Bay Theatre startled that it was still daylight, resolved to work even harder on my novels because any movie I contributed to would inevitably be out of my control. John Calley had once asked if I ever intended to direct but, for a change, my modesty overcame any ambition to be a big-shot director which must be a lifelong obsession. When I think of the good directors I've known, including John Huston, Orson Welles, Sydney Pollack, Federico Fellini (only for a long dinner), Hal Ashby, Robert Altman, Ed Zwick, Francis Coppola, Jim Brooks, Marty Ritt, Bruno Barreto, Mike Nichols, and Sean Penn, among others, I note that none of them were novelists and poets and part-time directors. It is a measure of our apparently genetic immodesty in America that so many Sunday painters think they can easily become actual artists, good home cooks become chefs, and rich men who like wine can say on starting a vineyard, "In ten years I'll make a wine that equals Lafite Rothschild."

* * *

Curiously there's another film, one I had written many years before with Tom McGuane, that came out abortively soon after *Revenge*. I absolutely refuse to ask anyone what the name of it is because there's still an ever so small abscess back in my brain over the matter. I have the ugly memory of my eldest daughter, who was still in high school at the time, walking up the driveway looking for the check that never arrived. I certainly would have murdered if I thought I could have gotten away with it, but then with my temperament I would have lugubriously confessed moments after pulling a trigger. McGuane and I have been the closest of friends for over three decades but we never should have worked together. The title for *Legends of the Fall* came out of one of our abandoned projects. Way back then we were both under the daily thrall of booze and various pharmaceuticals. I therefore, being of present sound mind, refuse to offer up the name of this movie.

Another of my films with the same viral resonance, a true celluloid Ebola, was the made-for-TV version of my novel *Dalva*. An old friend, John Carter, a curator at the Nebraskan Historical Society who has helped me on many projects, warned me on the phone, "Don't watch a minute or you'll dive under the bed and puke up a hairball like a house cat." I admit that I received three hundred thousand for the rights, which, after the bad news was revealed, had the effect of smearing Jergen's on a bullet wound, but then I was the one who sold his darling child for adoption. Maybe this constitutes sympathy for the devil. It often seems quite inscrutable because it takes essentially the same energy to make a bad film as a good one.

By the mid-nineties I had begun going to France twice a year because my books were doing better over there than they were in America. When certain nasty fellow citizens hear this they like to say, "Just like Jerry Lewis," but then in twenty or so trips to France I simply have never heard the name mentioned. France became a retreat and relief, and also good food had become a dominant solace in my life, so much so that I was writing a monthly food column for *Esquire* called "The Raw and the Cooked." France was also as far as I could get from my self-imposed Hollywood miseries. The entertainment industry, however, has become quite global, and I got a stomach jolt early one morning when my publisher Christian Bourgois and his driver Frank picked me up from Charles de Gaulle and there beside the freeway was an immense poster for the movie of *Legends of the Fall.*

I actually liked the movie. To love it was impossible because, once again, the film was destined to fall short of the resonance of my interior vision. There was the strong consolation that it was visually beautiful, and I had no quarrel with any of the casting. Aidan Quinn did particularly well with the unsympathetic part of Tristan's brother Alfred. I also thought that Julia Ormond did an excellent job as Susannah. She's English and has had a difficult time adjusting to our less subdued dramatics. All my real quarrels became rather remote and peripheral. Like Nicholson I thought the film should have been far grittier. It was also too short by a half hour, cheating Brad Pitt of his key madness scene on the yawl full of bloody elephant tusks. The other quite logical disappointment is I didn't make one red cent out of the film except for earlier property rights though the film grossed very well. This is hard for outsiders to understand but it's absurdly pro forma for insiders. I wrote the novella and the first two versions of the screenplay which would have entitled me to a partial credit but I refused to petition the Writer's Guild for moral reasons, thus losing possibly a couple hundred grand in video royalties. I refused because the real work was done by Bill Wittliff who also wrote the filmed version of *Lonesome Dove*. The Writer's Guild has never been able to come up with a broadly fair way of apportioning credit though it must be said that without the Writer's Guild Hollywood would be an abattoir of bloody writer carcasses.

When a project begins the creator of the material has an implicit partnership with the producer, director, and often the bankable actor. You may even become friends of a sort, but by the time the movie is released and the money toted up you're right on par with the guys who wash the pots and pans in the studio commissary. Your percentages are meaningless. Everyone's points, except for those of the studio, producer, director, and bankable actors, are as worthless as my Australian oil stock. Bob Schuster, a partner of Jerry Spence, was irked enough to look into it pro bono, to no avail. Of course it's almost common knowledge that Hollywood accounting practices make the Enron–Arthur Andersen mess look standard. You travel well past anger into a misty and quizzical zone where you wonder why people behave so dishonorably, but when you watch them closely you understand that it must be easy to endure contempt. No one murdered any babies. It's just business. Of course as our accounting scandals worsen from coast to coast you finally perceive that those at the top get all the money so Hollywood becomes less than unique.

I knew it couldn't last for reasons of exhaustion but between 1987 and 1997 I wrote dozens of drafts for various screen projects, plus the long novel *Dalva,* two collections of novellas, *The Woman Lit by Fireflies* and *Julip,* and a collection of poetry, *After Ikkyū.* I felt pleasantly secure with my publisher, Sam Lawrence, and when Sam died I felt even more secure with his protégé, Morgan Entrekin, who runs Grove/Atlantic. It's of inestimable value for a writer to feel comfortable with a publisher in an industry that has become more like Hollywood than it wishes to admit.

I gradually worked our way out of the homeless potentialities, had quit cocaine, wouldn't fish in Key West without my family, and had reduced drinking by half to two-thirds. It wasn't very dramatic. I talked to my home physician, Dr. Bob Johnson, and to a heart-specialist friend in San Francisco, Dr. Howard Kline. I have a little vodka now which isn't dangerous because I don't really like it. The saving grace was my growing affection for French red wine which was even more pleasurable when I cut out the whiskey in my life. The only possibly spiritual aspect happened in a period at the cabin when I dreamt I should always walk the sometimes precipitous edges of life. I began to fall more in love with the sheer moment-by-moment nature of consciousness and no longer wished to be drunk.

*   *   *

Recently, I spent a night in Portal, Arizona, over near the New Mexican border. This is a small mountain village where I stay in a combination motel/diner/grocery store when I wish to get away from it all. There are no phones in the motel rooms, which helped, but there are televisions and I was intermittently watching the Academy Awards for the first time in twelve years because our casita a few hours west of here has no television by choice. I missed most of the awards because I had to have my dinner pork chops, and then I had to see the end of the Lakers game, and then I had to have a nap. I wasn't exactly connecting because I hadn't seen any of the nominated movies. The closest theater is an hour away but on a video player recently I watched a splendid Mexican movie called *Amores Perros*, also *O Brother Where Art Thou?*, which had wonderful music.

In other words I'm out of date, and what's more, running out of time, scarcely a unique position. They say Nabokov wrote part of *Lolita* here in Portal when he was chasing butterflies as an impassioned lepidopterist. A very old local cowboy asked me if Nabokov had written *Lolita* "from life." I said as a hedge that everything is written from life but much of it's the life of the mind. The old cowboy wasn't satisfied and I don't blame him. Nabokov is dead and his sexual habits belong to the ages. I was recently irked when a famous feminist writer said that the very dead Allen Ginsberg was a pedophile. I knew Allen off and on for over thirty years and never saw any evidence of such behavior. They move the cutoff age around a lot but I didn't witness Allen interested in anyone under eighteen. What I'm really questioning is the urge by many to make well-known people smaller than they are, or were.

While looking at the awards I can't say I felt any emotions. I like good movies, not award ceremonies, the same difference in watching the improbable Michael Johnson run the four hundred meters or watching him climb the dais for the gold medal. The Academy Awards are a big one but in general you can scarcely keep track of the hundreds of movie, literary, sport, and other award ceremonies. Every small city in the Midwest seems to have a retail store called the Trophy Trolley. I went in one years ago out of curiosity. It was full of trophies of every size and price. There was a recent binge of lists that seemed to feed the same impulse wherever on the food chain. I even envisioned a list of "The Hundred Best Wines of South Dakota." We must police life, control it, order it.

Hollywood looked very large until my forties when it got quite small, and then it gradually reacquired its proper size. I wanted to make a living and be part of making a fine movie and pretty much failed on the latter, but then I'm certainly not going to let myself recast big people as small. I remember early on in New York when I was called by and had dinner with Luise Rainer, an early Hollywood escapee who starred in *The Good Earth* and *The Great Ziegfeld*. That evening she wore a kind of turban and diamond tiara. She carried it off in the same way John Huston and Orson Welles looked fine in voluminous black capes. She was physically only a normal-sized woman in the same way as Jeanne Moreau, whose voice alone could make your ears tingle. When Jeanne and I were trying to work together in New York I'd call before we met to see if she preferred a bottle of Cristal or flowers and she always said, "Both" with a resonant laugh and husky voice. I coaxed her into talking about one of my early heroes, Albert Camus, with whom she had had an affair. Once in Paris we went to a grand fete at the Louvre together at which every dignitary in the place made a bow before her presence, but then it was the work that made her permanent. The film *Jules and Jim* would have done it alone. When I was lucky enough to have dinner with Fellini at Elaine's it was pleasantly confusing because I was the only American at the table and everyone including Alberto Sordi, Giulietta Masina, and Mastroianni was mostly speaking Italian. Fellini like Henry Miller had leavened my despair in college so the evening meant a great deal to me. He invited me to come cook with him in Rome and I've always regretted not going.

Directors and painters are uniformly more interested in food than are writers. Once in Paris I was near Rue Brici looking for an oculist because I had sat on my glasses when I spotted Francis Coppola working at his laptop in a shabby café. He looked up and said without preamble, "I know where we should eat." He had been a little pissed at

me because I had refused to try to write a screenplay for Kerouac's
On the Road for the same reason I didn't want to attempt Gabriel
García Márquez's *One Hundred Years of Solitude* for John Huston. The
former lacked a coherent narrative drive while with the latter it was
partly modesty but also an unwillingness to be reductive with such
grand material. Both were classics and I didn't want to butcher them.
Despite this disagreement with Francis food was immediately more
important and the next evening we met at his apartment and went
to L'Ami Louis with a group that included Danny DeVito, Francis's
daughter Sofia, and Russell Crowe, who at the time had just gotten
warmed up in America with *L.A. Confidential*. Though it had been
recommended to me by various people, French friends, albeit food
snobs, had told me that L'Ami Louis was a "tourist" restaurant. If so,
that night the restaurant was full of French citizens, the kind you also
see on the Upper East Side of New York or in Beverly Hills. Like me
Francis is a food bully and insisted on ordering for everyone. Food
bullying is a kind of neurosis you have to fight against if you wish to
keep your friends as dining partners, but Francis plunged on, ordering
a platter of foie gras, a gross of snails, some roast chickens, and a leg of
lamb. One of our party, a young woman, was a vegetarian and the waiter
brought her a lovely selection of vegetables which seemed more and
more enviable as the evening progressed. It was a gluttonous mudbath
with me idly toting the bill as I counted eleven empty bottles of fine
wine. Crowe whispered to me that he'd like a beer and when I told the
waiter he brought a full bucket of various beers. I wasn't truly concerned
about the bill because if it came my way I would have bolted and swum
the Seine River. Francis and DeVito were quarreling about various producers and studios that had haunted Francis's contentious career. Danny
jumped up on the top of the banquet and did an admirable song and
dance to the applause of the French patrons. The check came and
Francis skillfully pointed at DeVito. A truly viable Hollywood tradition is that whoever is doing best that year picks up the check. I didn't
even avert my single eye as DeVito pulled wads of francs from various
pockets, left over from Cannes. The waiter politely shook his head no

to four thousand bucks (my estimate of the cash) and out came a credit card. Americans in Paris. Why not?

Another speculation arises when I think of people with a great deal of talent. Maybe the notion of "bigger" leads us astray like the woefully overused "great." Maybe they are like other people only more so, as if seven identical people could be contained within a single skin, and as a consequence there is a magnum amount of accessible vividness and emotional energy.

A producer named Douglas Wick saved my weary neck in my remaining years writing screenplays. Soon after my novel *Dalva* had been published, Melissa Mathison had come over to Nicholson's house and we spent a long afternoon trying to figure out if there was a viable movie in the book. Melissa had done well, a euphemism, with *E.T.* and *Black Stallion*, and I no longer wanted to try to adapt my own material. I was simply too close to it to make necessary alterations for a visual narrative drive. Besides, the only real fun in screenplay writing was the first draft of an original which simulated the pleasure of novella and novel writing. The consequent drafts are more like elaborate board games. I had heard from Mike Ovitz that I should write only a first draft, which would take full advantage of my storytelling, and then leave the following drafts and shooting script to those more skillful in the trade. Stanley Jaffe had said to me rather blankly, "I didn't hire you because you were a good screenwriter but because you can make up interesting people," a New York producer's reflection on the majority of screenwriters, expert on technique but short on character volume.

I was unnerved by the intensity of Melissa's structural probing, a problem I had later with my daughter Jamie who, when we were intending to write a script together, was far ahead of me before she had written a single line of script. While talking with Melissa I dully reflected on my deficiencies which, of course, I decided never to admit. By the time we mutually threw up our hands on *Dalva* and I had the drink I had been waiting for, Melissa asked, "My husband wonders if you might want to write a Western for him?" Being broke at the time I felt an urge to sail across the room, grab the phone, and call the number she gave me but I waited until she left. Shortly after, we met at Harrison Ford's ranch in Jackson, Wyoming.

On the phone Harrison had asked me if I had a producer in mind for our project and I said no, because I never had a producer in mind. He suggested his friend Douglas Wick with whom he had done *Working Girl*, which was nominated for an Academy Award. Our first meeting in Jackson was less than auspicious what with everyone but me coming down with flu though I suspected martini flu. Amy Irving was there and the evening got out of hand, to put it in its mildest terms, and I was accused of being an enabler for at least the hundredth time. The first meeting wasn't conclusive except that we decided to work together. I had already decided I wanted to set the film in the Sandhills of Nebraska in the 1920s. I quickly understood in a meeting with the top studio people at Columbia that this was a good idea because no one had ever been in the Sandhills of Nebraska, thus I was given a great deal of freedom of expression. Movie people are more likely to know Europe than our vast interior.

This project went on intermittently for seven years and seven drafts, which shows you the world *is* in balance. Wick and I enjoyed working with each other. Wick is an actual rather than an invented Yale graduate, witty like John Calley, and well read. He also likes to eat which gave us something very solid in common. Often while meeting he would call Orsini's to deliver lunch which I found to be a fine morale booster. He's married to the brilliant Lucy Fisher, whom I had met years before when she was running Coppola's company and who later provided the good sense in Warner's top brass. It took me years and three projects to wear out Wick. After we parted company as co-workers, though we remained friends, I envisioned him wanly hanging out around the Writer's Guild building hoping to meet a real and ordinary screenwriter.

*   *   *

During our abortive project with Ford (though I think at least three of my seven versions would have made fine movies, far better than some of his recent questionable choices), Wick and I were on a plane from Jackson to L.A. when I told him a story that piqued his interest about one late night at my cabin during which I had actually become a wolf.

Minimal research told me that the experience was an attack of lycanthropy, which, though extraordinary, was not all that rare, especially in the Middle Ages and among Native Americans. Wick, anyway, was intrigued but I was a little hesitant about going public with the experience, thinking it might be personal "medicine" in Native terms. My solution to the qualms I was feeling was to write the script with a New York City background and to leave out totally any material related to Native shape changing. There was certainly a strong enough European background to the material to give it a tinge of universality. Logically enough I called the script *Wolf*.

I had told Nicholson about the experience soon after it happened and a year or so later when I told him I was attempting a script he was interested. Wick wasn't overenthused with my first version, which was too broad, but by the time I finished the second we were ready to go. Nicholson, needless to say, is very hard to pin down and Wick had been pleased to hear that Jack and Jim Brooks, the director, had spent some time talking about the idea though Brooks deals with his own work exclusively.

I flew to Paris with the script and met Jack at the Plaza Athenee on his arrival from a vacation in southern France. We had lunch and dinner and then next midmorning when we met for a walk he said he had stayed up late and read the script. "Let's do it," he said. We celebrated for a few days and I flew home a bit deranged. The plane was off the tip of Greenland before it occurred to me that I had forgotten to stop by to meet my French publisher, Christian Bourgois. I had been close with Huston and Nicholson for *Revenge* but then I lost one and consequently the other.

* * *

Of course I should have known not to offer up my heart's affections. From my point of view the project began to disintegrate almost immediately with the choice of director. Wick and I discussed several who were acceptable to Jack, and Wick settled on Mike Nichols, who was a friend of both of them. Mike Nichols had directed a number of brilliant movies but I had doubts that he was appropriate for *Wolf*. I wanted him to be but he wasn't.

In the ensuing year I did three more complete drafts after extensive meetings with Nichols and Wick in New York City which had the palliative that I was close to my mind doctor, Sullivan. My nerves had become virtually peeled. The essential problem was that the story was Dionysian and Nichols's point of view was thoroughly Apollonian. Given the hero's problems in my versions of *Wolf* I thought it was a fine solution when his psyche changed him into a wild animal, an actual wolf. Nichols said he felt it was unbearable to give up Mozart, which I agreed with up to a point what with my being a Mozart obsessive, but then all the truly wild behavior I created for the character, and I know wild animals, was rejected by Nichols.

There was nowhere to go and one day I quit within what I thought was seconds from being fired. It didn't matter by then. Before I left New York Wick and I had a goofy breakfast of caviar and vodka, Dover sole and Meursault, something soothing. Jack offered on the phone to back out but I didn't think he should. I held on to the idea that there was still a good chance the movie would be good, and also Wick and I had become friends. A month before in Hollywood I had insisted that we all eat at Chasen's before it closed. Wick arranged to get Ronald Reagan's old table, which pleased me for captious reasons. Though Doug was a Democrat his father, Charles Wick, had been Reagan's head of the USIA. Harrison and Melissa Mathison Ford and Jim and Heidi Brooks joined Doug, Lucy, and me. The point here is that evening we all decided that Doug looked like he had recently emerged from Buchenwald. Our project was destroying his mind and body and that's one reason I wanted the movie to be made.

In recognition of my "goodwill" the studio gave me an unsolicited check and a thoroughly meaningless credit as an "associate producer," which was thoroughly misunderstood by my literary friends.

Good-bye to all of that. I ended up doing another version of my Ford Western to finance the writing of my novel *The Road Home*. *Wolf* was essentially the end of my screenwriting career. When Wick sent me the ensuing scripts by others I became so unhappy I couldn't bear to read them. I fixed on the smallest scenes, one of which I had discussed with Michelle Pfeiffer, in which she was on her hands and knees in a half-slip taking off Jack's handcuffs in a closet. Shot from the rear, of course. Mike didn't use it! My survival technique was to walk literally hundreds of miles over a period of months in the virtual wilderness of the Upper Peninsula though by then I was so tired I barely made more than five miles a day. At the beginning I mostly thrashed around but finally I walked.

"Let that be a lesson to you," we used to say. I didn't mean to go on at such length about my screenwriting but then it was my livelihood for twenty years, since I was unable to survive on the income of my novels. Now I can, with some journalism thrown in. Five years away from Hollywood I see all of my mistakes with painful clarity. Since it's essentially a director's medium I should have tied myself to a series of directors sympathetic to my writing. I went large when I should have gone independent and smaller.

Much of the difficulty is built in to the business and has been so long ingrained that it's incurable. The relationship between Hollywood and the writer is basically adversarial. The film business acts as if it wishes it could do without writers but it can't, and it has accepted the fact without grace. The traditions of storytelling are as old as humanity and the talent for doing it well is rare indeed. This talent is utterly undemocratic and is definitely not liberally spread among producers and directors. It's the writer who must create the story for the film and the dialogue for the actresses and actors. It has been demonstrated countless times that they can seldom create their own good dialogue. Meanwhile this pathetically adversarial relationship often makes writers act in defense like nitwits. It is one thing to brook no substantial editing interference in a novel, but then no one is spending fifty to a hundred million dollars to publish your novel. In the best filmmaking a balance between writer and director has been achieved but the best is a scant few percent.

When I left Hollywood our exhaustion was probably mutual but scarcely noticed by them. The industry is fortunate in that our culture has created at least a hundred thousand young people who want to write for the movies, doubtless some just for the money, but many in the same way I was obsessed beginning as a child. A bigger problem in Hollywood starts at the white-bread top among the few dozen people who can green-light a potential movie. The struggle to get where they are has narrowed their vision of American culture, thus the industry fails to represent the population. I keep thinking how cheaply a studio could hire ten black, ten Latino, and a few Native American novelists, give them a month's scriptwriting lessons, tell them to go for it, and send them home. A studio could do it for the price of an executive or two.

It's hard to sculpt the essential shapelessness of twenty years of life. To put Aristophanes in the past tense, "whirl *was* king." The most laughable word in our current culture is "closure." Closure is talked about before the blood is dry on the cement. Only ninety-nine percent of me has quit. If the remaining three hundred million brain cells came up with a startling film idea I'd probably go out there and pitch it. Meanwhile, it's unlikely that our daughters will ever be homeless.

BACK HOME

What is the meaning of a single human life? It is apparent that we don't really know. As to its events the haunting and consistent refrain is "Everything could have been otherwise."

We don't seem to remember one another very well. Perhaps part of the impulse in novel writing is to remember people who didn't exist in detail to reassure ourselves that such remembering is worth the effort, to reassure ourselves, too, that all of us were in a near miss with not existing. I had the disturbing experience before I began writing *Dalva* where I dreamt her into existence on two consecutive nights. Later, when I thought that matter over, I came to accept this experience as not so extraordinary. I had done a lot of research and had traveled a number of times to the Sandhills of Nebraska where I intended to locate the novel for a number of reasons, the first that it is relatively unknown and to me overwhelmingly beautiful with the grand Niobrara River bisecting the northern section. I was drawn to the rolling emptiness. The largest county, Cherry, is a hundred by fifty miles with a population of about five thousand. The landscape aches with an unknown mythology. Except for the late phases of the Apache uprising in the Southwest, the Sandhills, and just north to Wounded Knee, is the site of the last collision of Native cultures and our own. Because of the lack of population density the history of the area is quite naked, though history is only the skeleton on which we hang the hopefully living flesh of our stories.

With the character of Dalva I had the vague sense of the nature of her great-grandfather, her grandfather, and her father, before I discovered that "she would be a she." There was the Jungian question of what have we done with our twin sister whom the culture forces us to abandon at birth. In the first dream she was vividly naked in my studio, and in the second, clothed on a balcony in Santa Monica looking at the Pacific Ocean and thinking of home. Just before I begin a novel I am especially addled and have observed that the fuel, the mental energy behind the book to be written, is either unknown or not fully known. When her character arrived at my door I naturally wondered about the nature of my subconscious invitation. It is at this point in writing I'm most fearful of that "fugal" state I have entered several times wherein all the material I've invented, plus the entirety of my own history, marry and are filled with quite uncontrollable mental energy so that if I close my eyes hundreds of images whirl past. With *Dalva* I filled a couple of boxes of yellow tabs of images and then didn't need to look at them again because they were already part of my consciousness.

Back to the thought of nonexistence which translates to the fragility of our individual appearances here, the very slender and accidental lineages, the fatal interruptions of war and disease that denied so many existence. I have often thought while traveling in France how some earthen cellars might still be damp with the blood of World War II, and consequently the thousands who didn't exist because this blood had been so liberally shed. And in our own mundane lives the thought "everything could have been otherwise" keeps showing its face. Those of us who are married, divorced or not, remember the thoroughly haphazard and sometimes accidental way we met and married our mates, the days or hours, often unknown, when we made love, and then the singular sperm that met the singular egg that created so much of the nature of our children. In fiction, if you don't leave out the evidence, the nature of the story imitates the confusing nature of our own lives and, more remotely, the nature of nature.

My early novels and poems, like those of most writers, tended to depend on literary set pieces but beginning with *Sundog* I became quite impatient with anything I already knew. I became drawn to the idea of boarding a not clearly visible ship at night with no knowledge of its destination. I've wondered lately if it's for this reason that I've loved being in port cities like Marseilles, Vera Cruz, Vancouver,

B.C., or smaller ones such as Duluth, Minnesota, where the metaphor of arriving and leave-taking is visually alive. Maybe a writer is
always a stowaway. Hidden, and well off to the side.

In my Brown Dog series of novellas, three of them so far and
a fourth coming, a picaresque character emerged who lives as ran-
domly as the life he perceives around him. Living in some comparatively remote and economically poor areas I couldn't help but study
people who reminded me of the early van Gogh charcoal sketches,
The Potato Eaters, many of whom work very hard but earn only enough
to live the simplest of lives. They're always behind in their pickup
payments, everything they eat is fried, if they've been married their
wives have left for greener pastures, if they're horny a three-hundred-
pound barmaid is entirely suitable. My hero, Brown Dog, usually lives
in borrowed deer cabins. I'm aware that he's become almost a survival mechanism for me, a creature I envy and whose life seems an
alternative when I'm at desperate ends. My life at my cabin when
I'm not working bears similarities. I might wake early and take a walk
while my mind is still empty, which allows me to see the landscape
more vividly and, at rare times, holographically with the additional
illusion that you can see all sides of a tree or hill at once, the slightest filaments of time herself flutter in the air. After the walk I make
a peanut butter and jam sandwich as a negligent gourmand, and then
row my small blue-and-brown skiff counterclockwise around Au Sable
Lake, which can take up to four hours. The little boat is blue and
brown because they were the only colors the marine-supply store had
left. The motions of rowing are hypnotic and the mind's torments
slide easily away with the passing water. Once when rowing in a local
estuary I saw a bald eagle, two blue herons, a sandhill crane, the rare
piping plover, and an errant male loon who, finishing his six weeks
of nesting duties, tends to fly around several days wailing happily. Fully
accepting the unlikelihood of reincarnation I admire the idea of becoming a waterweed, a muskrat, a tree, or hopefully a plover in the
next life. The only problem with rowing is if a big wind comes up
the high gunnels and short skeg make battling the wind arduous. If
you're dumb enough to light a cigarette you lose a hundred yards. A

pint of the locally made ale at the Dunes Saloon after the hours of rowing restores drinking to a great pleasure rather than a stupid addiction.

I don't choose themes for a novel, as such, but I've noted how often new characters tend to inhabit the area around problems that have bothered me. For instance, my parents had a pretty good marriage and the same with my wife and me though it requires a large amount of ordinary etiquette and avoiding stasis. Throughout my life I've noted a certain kind of man, essentially a restrained bully, often someone who was early on a radical idealist whose life has been diverted into other pursuits. The woman, probably unassuming at the time of the marriage, misses the man who was the college idealist. The bullying is seen in hundreds of daily gestures if you watch these couples closely in restaurants, airports, and during social occasions. In *The Woman Lit by Fireflies* I envisioned such a woman abandoning her asshole husband at a rest stop on Interstate 80 in Iowa. She simply climbs the fence and disappears into a cornfield. Curiously, after this novella was published in *The New Yorker*, I received dozens of letters from women who had done something similar.

More recently in *The Beast God Forgot to Invent* I was speculating on the different perceptions of reality experienced by an idealized character who had suffered a closed head injury. The nature of the brain is so immensely various that a hundred victims of a closed head injury can each have a unique set of symptoms. I studied Harold Edleman's preposterously difficult *Neural Darwinism* and the books of other brain experts like Damasio. I was quite floored for a couple of months because so much of the material was professional and beyond my comprehension, though I was pleased to learn that the workings of the brain are utterly unlike those of a computer. Of course it's difficult to give a character absolutely fresh perceptions when we live in the thrall of our own habituation and conditioning. As I wrote I kept thinking of William Blake, John Clare, Christopher Smart, and an acute schizophrenic from Kentucky who wrote in his diary, "Birds are holes in heaven through which a man may pass."

* * *

If Yeats never got off his stilts, at least this is an option on a poet's path. A novelist, however, has to get down there with the raw meat on the daily floor. In the high range is the possibility I read in high school in Dostoyevsky's *Notes from the Underground,* "I maintain that to be too acutely conscious is to be diseased." The bulk of the work is in the midrange, but the low range can be comic and bathetic. The mind is delightfully errant. Your left foot hurts, possibly because you're a tad heavy and gravity is omnipresent. Thinking of your sore foot you feel lucky you don't walk on your head. You don't want to take a shower but you need one. Everything must be questioned. In the shower you want a martini and long for those fancy hotels with a phone in the bathroom where you could reach out from the shower curtain and order a martini or a fine expense-account bottle of wine. Life has been going poorly and you begin to think of it as basically aversion therapy. Perhaps in Lithuania women like burly men who have a fondness for anchovies and garlic. That sort of thing, all from the shower problem, not to speak of the complicated process of drying off.

To write novels you have to have an attention to detail, the "textural concretia" of life, ninety-nine percent of which you will never use. You make notes, occasionally in a journal which I think of as my image bank, and sometimes in the form of faxes to friends. Over the past few years Ted Kooser and I corresponded in the form of small three- and four-line poems, which we will publish jointly with Copper Canyon Press without attribution. Early this morning I wrote a fax to my friend Dan Gerber, which I'll keep just in case: "Up a canyon very early so Rose can avoid crotalids (rattlesnakes) because it's getting hot. Charged by three lovely yearling horses who swirled, jumped, and farted. I was the morning's excitement. Looked up to see a distant contrail making an abrupt U-turn. A tiny bug bit my nose tip. Rose pointed five quail who arose, desultorily. It's their sex season. More quiet. Saw a songless vermilion flycatcher in a mesquite where last year there was a bushel-sized evening primrose. None this year because of drought. Three empty migrant water jugs. Last night the moon fluttered like a round white butterfly."

*   *   *

I think it was Scott Fitzgerald who insisted we don't make friends beyond early middle age. This puzzled me when I was younger, and when older I found it to be quite untrue. It occurred to me that Fitzgerald may have said it in the tertiary stage of alcoholism when absolutely everything becomes self-referential. A plane flies over at thirty-five thousand feet and a man looks up and says, "What's this got to do with me?" An alcoholic in Michigan is resentful about September 11 because it detracts from possible sympathy about his problems, largely unworded.

Friends made in middle age seem to have a basis in mutual curiosity, where old friends are glued together by their anguishes, small triumphs, a lineage of travel, or hot afternoons and cool evenings when they did nothing whatsoever except be companionable. With Guy de la Valdéne, Bob Dattila, Jack Nicholson, Tom McGuane, Russell Chatham, my farm neighbor Nick Reens, Pat Paton or Mike Ballard in the Upper Peninsula, or Peter Matthiessen when we fish in Montana in September, we merely begin the conversation where we left off the last time. With Gérard Oberlé in France, Fred Turner in New Mexico, Peter Lewis in Seattle, it is all literature and food though I first met Peter Lewis twenty-five years ago when he was trying to help my friend Richard Brautigan survive. With some friends the mutual obsession is literary, also an aversion to shop talk: Eliot Weinberger, Robert DeMott, Doug Stanton, Jeffrey Lent, Colum McCann, J. Fier, Terry Schlais, George Quasha, Robert Alexander, Sam Hamill, Joseph Bednarik. I keep returning to Nebraska where I see Ted Kooser, the folk historian John Carter who helped me so much on research, Roger Welsch, Beef Torrey, and Bill Quigley up in Valentine in the Sandhills. There are also near misses because of time and distance and lives dense with work: Elmore Leonard, Mario Batali, Gary Snyder and Hayden Carruth, David Quammen, Timothy Ferris, Will Hearst. And certain long- and short-term friends fit into no category: Chuck Bowden, Jimmy Buffett, Peter Phinny, Terry McDonell, Bill Holm, Douglas Peacock, Jack Turner, Dan Lahren, Jimmy Fergus, my son-in-law Stephen Potenberg. I know I have forgotten some obvious ones but then my "senior moment" has been going on for several years. By contrast I

decided not to list my central female friends because it might be misunderstood, perhaps purposely, by husbands and boyfriends. It takes
years for a male to accumulate discretion and I don't want to discard
my own small measure.

The list seems long but I've always been fairly energetic and
intensely curious about how certain people lead their lives which is,
after all, the basis of friendship. I've never quite known how to clas-
sify my twenty-five year relationship with Lawrence Sullivan, which
is half professional wherein he throws me a rope to pull me out of
holes I've dug and fallen into, and the other half is about food, books,
family, the world at large.

Unlike the sciences literature is only slightly cumulative and this in
the misty area of influences, also the historical rendering of phases,
periods, fads, and movements where too much is made of the vagu-
est of contiguities. In a novel everything must be freshly brought into
question with the novelist pretending that the world has been previously undescribed. In a memoir, however, a writer is less likely to make
a case for his own unvarnished propensity for the varieties of truth.
There's nothing more wildly comic, if you remove yourself far enough,
than sex in a nontraditional society where some writers describe in-
tercourse in semiliturgical terms, and our sexualities are expected to
fill the lacunae left by a God who is said to have disappeared quite
some time ago.

All privacy is brought into question but not by my family and
many others. I've often thought my wife and daughters, Jamie and
Anna, got their sense of decorum from my father-in-law, William
Ludlow King, who though not snobbish was unyieldingly high-minded
like his grandfather in *Legends of the Fall*. My own mother when I wasn't
all that old was disgusted when her Swedish icon Ingrid Bergman was
flayed by the press on running off with Roberto Rossellini. Norma
Olivia Walgren Harrison certainly didn't condone adultery but she was
appalled by media snooping in the underwear drawer. When I told my
daughters that I was writing a memoir they fairly recoiled, and I coun-

tered teasingly that maybe I could send them to Europe the first two months after publication, a bribe offer that was considered pathetic. A month later I got the backhand permission, "Go ahead. You have to be honest." Of course I do but I wouldn't think it worth reading if Richard Nixon had had a long affair with Henry Kissinger. There are any number of good reasons to write about sexuality in a memoir when it's *au point*, such as in Mary Karr's splendid *The Liars' Club*, where her early experiences were raw and lucid and obviously had a part in forming her life. I'm pretty good at recovering memory but I don't recall anything similar in my own life. When we were mutually short-funded a few weeks ago my writer friend Charles Bowden and I mourned the fact that we had no evil priests in our past. I clearly remember the affectionate nature of certain Boy Scout leaders and maybe the lawyers will head for that area next.

The other day when I had begun to make notes about marriage and my immediate family, Linda and I nearly lost our home to a brush and forest fire that was stopped within fifty yards of our casita. A half-dozen local fire departments arrived in the area, helicopters released huge buckets of water, and other planes dropped dense clouds of pinkish-red fire retardant. It was a little dicey for twelve hours. We packed a few necessities including paintings and manuscripts, our prescriptions and my upper plate, a minimal amount of clothing, and, most important of all, the dogs. I was especially impressed by a young crew from the National Forest Service who cut the fence that crossed our creek, chain-sawed trees, and approached the fire directly, all in minutes. They seemed superlative athletes in a terrifying game.

It was especially upsetting because the closing on the sale of our home in Michigan was today and if we had lost the casita we would have been implausibly homeless. It's hard to count the one-room cabin in the Upper Peninsula which I find appealing but wouldn't do as a home. Most years because of the snow it's hard to approach until late April and you have to be out of there by mid-November. We've had the farm, though it has grown in size, for thirty-three years, but then the area has changed radically in that time from agrarian and commercial fishing to summer homes for the wealthy. This alone wouldn't have driven me away from the beauty of the area but a year ago when Linda, Jamie, and Anna went to England and Ireland together and the decision was made. At heart the move was planned out of loneliness for our daughters and grandchildren who live in Montana for the specific reason that that's where they vacationed as children, essentially the same ambience I was after when I found the U.P. cabin. Why not try to live, if possible, where you felt happiest and most free? McGuane was a little cynical when I told him the news in that we'd been talking about a move to Montana since 1968.

Living in Michigan and Arizona we saw our daughters and grandchildren only twice a year, on the September fishing visit in Montana and when they'd come to Patagonia in the winter to escape the cold. In some years there were summer Michigan visits but I sensed they were made without great enthusiasm. We're building a small house in Montana and hope to have enough sense to be unobtrusive the half year we're there. On my rather single-minded and obsessive arc as a writer in these later years I am more advised than I am offering advice to my daughters. I'm far from a Dagwood type but since they were about fourteen I've been a little timid about crossing their honest natures. McGuane once said about women, not totally in jest, "They all know we're assholes."

I mostly look forward to taking my grandsons, Will and John Christian, fishing when they feel up to going. When my daughters were in their late teens and early twenties I drove both of them quite batty with my fears for their safety. It was an illusion of control that they both ignored and defied, whether it was my insistence that when Jamie lived in New York City she have an apartment with a doorman, or when Anna was on one of her frequent car trips I had asked her to call me every evening. No way, as they say. Jamie has published three mystery novels so far dealing with Montana, and has recently finished a fourth set in New York City. Anna works at the Country Bookshelf in Bozeman, after doing her training at Horizon Books in Traverse City, Michigan. Jamie's husband,

Stephen, is a lawyer. They live a bit close to the bone because Montana isn't a litigious state. Anna lives with Max Hjortsberg, the son of an old friend and novelist, William Hjortsberg, after her first brief marriage to Matt Kapsner, a young novelist. My own marriage moves along fairly well as it should after over forty years of experience. Our only wars are Monday-night pasta wars when we make separate sauces. Our last major quarrel several years back was resolved when I had the bright idea of going into the front yard and throwing eggs at a large boulder. It was a very satisfying way to settle a quarrel and I recommend it to all of those experiencing marital spats.

My mother died in December 2000, which cut another tie to Michigan. Now only my sister Mary lives there with her husband, Nick, both social workers. My brother David lives with his wife Cindy on Bainbridge Island near Seattle where he is an aide to the new senator from Washington State, Maria Cantwell. My older brother John retired as dean of the libraries at University of Arkansas and now cooks and listens to his collection of thousands of operas full-time. His wife Rebecca writes poetry and children's books.

I visited my mother the November before she died and we drove for several hours on country roads that I hadn't seen for half a century but clearly remembered. She was a woman of maddening frugality and lived in a small house in a thicket on what little remained of her family's farm. Soon after my father and sister died in 1961 she had planted twenty acres with over seventy kinds of shrubs and trees. It was a magnificent thicket of the kind I favor myself, dense with bird and animal life and a small murky pond. When I arrived that November I poured out a half-empty bottle of wine I had given her months before. "Are you sure it isn't good?" she asked. When we had bought her a new car several years before she pointed out that she didn't need a car with a radio, and nothing I said could justify the radio's presence. She was a consummate self-taught naturalist and bird-watcher and still camped with her friends well into her seventies on their bird-watching trips throughout the United States. When she died she was facing double knee and hip surgery, which I doubted she would have survived at eighty-four, but then it was her insistent

announcement that she didn't wish to live unless she could walk properly in the fields and woods. I had to humor her when she asked if she
had been an encouragement to my writing. She wasn't particularly
because though she had a large intellectual capacity—our last quarrel
had been about the character of Kolya in *The Brothers Karamazov*—
she was of a practical frame of mind, doubtless from her impoverished
childhood. I told her that my work would have been impossible without her, and we both ignored the possibly silly backspin of this comment. I never could understand why James Joyce wouldn't pray with
his mother. I have knelt and prayed with Lulu Peyraud in France at
the grave of her husband, Lucien. I had to watch closely to see that I
crossed myself properly. I'd pray with any old lady who asked. Why not?
At the very least it demonstrates a reverence for life which I trust can
be found in my work. After our mother died my sister sent me a long
poem that my mother had written and hadn't wanted me to see. It was
an improbably detailed poem about what she loved about life.

I don't ask myself if I did what I set out to do. The calling was for a life
and the junctures between one work and another were often not that
explicit, the future only an abstraction we pull ourselves toward with,
once again, the false geometry of days and nights, months and years,
an illusion in the face of the continuum that makes up our lives. I'm
unsure about the character of ambition. As a young writer I wanted to
be well reviewed by Edmund Wilson, Randall Jarrell, and Malcolm
Cowley but then they were gone before I was truly started. Ambition
always reminds me of a dark time during which I'd walk my yellow
Labrador Sand (for Sandringham in England where she was born) on
the miles of deserted beach near our farm. Sand would chase the shadows of butterflies on the beach, scarcely ever the butterfly itself. Ambition for the breadth and resonance of the work itself is appropriate
but words like "victory" or "triumph" or even "success" seem better
attached to elections, wars, or sporting contests. Every writer knows
that nearly all of us disappear in the mordant collapse of our own generations. And I was slow to learn when younger that literary biogra-

phies lead us astray. William Faulkner was never "William Faulkner" to William Faulkner. What we think of as William Faulkner is an accretion of biographical details, not a little gossip, the specific arc and span of his work. We are privy finally to collective details and speculations that are quite aside from the life the man lived.

What I will miss in Michigan is the morning when a blue heron walked up our steps and down the sidewalk where it looked into the oval window of our front door. This is unlikely to happen in Montana but then it was very unlikely to happen in Michigan again. It was especially vivid because that morning I had been thinking again and making notes on the fact that in our evolutionary curve painful events are most memorable. We survive by learning from pain. This fact can easily be allowed to distort anyone's vision including a writer's. Once at a Westwood, California, newsstand I wrote down a précis of an article in *Scientific American*, "Hell's Cells. Miles underground, despite scorching heat, life thrives inside solid rock." What a descriptive metaphor, not only for rare bacteria but also for many lives. No wonder that so much work is the shyest literary pornography. Peek your face into certain areas of this planet and it's likely to be burned off. I keep thinking of two of Rilke's contentions: "The exposed heart is richest in suffering," but then comes "There's a point at which the exposed heart never recovers."

Easter eve in Patagonia and waiting for a full moon to rise at about ten o'clock, a hint of ruddy air in the first glow from the dust and forest-fire smoke in the air. Bright stars are there when your eyes adjust to the darkness. There are two observatories in the area because of the relatively clear air and lack of ambient light. Years ago when Peter Matthiessen was down here and we were studying the sky late at night with Fred Turner, Matthiessen said, "These are the stars of my childhood." I've always loved Lorca's line "The enormous night straining her waist against the Milky Way." A large image indeed.

I can readily imagine sixty years ago two little boys in the bathtub in a village in northern Michigan, probably fighting on the eve
of the holy Sunday, perhaps wondering what the word "rotogravure"
meant in the popular Easter Sunday song, or trying to imagine a
big parade to be seen in next week's *Life* magazine down the famed
Fifth Avenue, though up here the ground is still too frozen to make
holes to play marbles, and the ice on the local lakes has withdrawn
toward the shoreline where it's thickest. The first robin may have
appeared but that is less meaningful than the wild geese returning
from their trip south. Sixty years later life can seem like a long marriage of a poor-sighted man to someone he never quite knew in a
full sense.

In England for a writer all roads lead to London and even more so in
France it is Paris. In France it seems easier to go back to Paris and
start over than to move more laterally. In America for a writer no
longer do all roads lead to New York, or less so than in the past. To
be sure, most of the publishing still occurs there but I no longer sense
that New York City has the magnetic intensity it did when I moved
there at nineteen or taught near there in my mid-twenties. Maybe
like Paris, New York has simply priced itself beyond a young writer's
range, an economic variable I'll never quite comprehend. If my room
and a half on MacDougal cost forty dollars a month in 1957 why
should it be at least fifteen hundred a month now? Wages haven't
multiplied by forty times. Not even five times, in fact.

Every area now seems to possess its aggressive literary geopieties,
complete with active or burgeoning presses, often backed by universities. Maybe that's better than everything outside of New York being considered "regional." I'm unsure because it doesn't faintly matter
if I'm right on the matter. The middle class seems to be disappearing
and class lines are drawn more specifically. A casual look at the media
in general would make you think that there are the enviable rich and
then there's everyone else. At one time it was the town against the
gown, and now it is closer to the gown against the real world. Aca-

demic critics and reviewers tend to prefer work that reflects their own puzzling realities over any other kind. The recent controversy over the literary worth of Steinbeck makes one wonder if there is any academic awareness of what is still demonstrably our working class. In university writing programs metaphor can't be taught so it is held in disregard and in the thousand or so galleys I've been sent for "blurbs" in recent years I've noted a faux Victorian sincerity as the main direction. This misses me as I read novels for aesthetic reasons and if the writing isn't artful I stop at the end of page one. In my youth there was still a fading remnant, perhaps a mixture of the Romantic and the religious, that each of us has a personal destiny, something I haven't heard talked about in decades. Maybe that's a good thing. Last year when I wrote about Ana Claudia Villa Herrera, the nineteen-year-old Mexican migrant who died of thirst, I couldn't avoid the dominant perception of cruelty. In the arroyo, the dry wash where she lay curled, everywhere in the sand and rocks you see traceries of the water that was once there. The idea of destiny shrivels up to the size of the dead bug off the tip of your left shoe.

It may have been presumptuous but I didn't tell the stories within my stories in this memoir. Why would anyone care about my memoir unless they directly cared about my novels and poems? Anyway it's hard to stomach the egregious notion of the "master plots" we are force-fed in high school, and by Hollywood, and in bad novels. A novel is about what it *is*. Period.

Two years ago while fishing in Mexico I dreamt my body was the trunk of a tree and in my head there were billions of small shimmering leaves. The tree was out in the open rather in the thicket my temperament prefers. Life moved too fast this year and life usually moves fast only on television. There was the usual nearly insufferable roll and pitch of politics with a fresh war against the environment hiding behind a smoke screen of the justified war against terrorism. Politicians don't seem to care that their grandchildren will learn the good reasons for hating them. Among many difficulties were my potentially fatal blood-pressure attack caused by contraindicatory medicines; my dog Rose was lost four days in the wilderness during which I sobbed uncontrollably like the seven-year-old who still hides within me; I was lost, as I have mentioned; my wife's beloved "mind doctor," Mildred Newman, died; we had three months of nerve-wracking litigiousness over the borders of our farm in Michigan that we were trying to sell; and finally this week's fire that seared our brainpans. Perhaps shamefully I can hide in my work up to a point while Linda lives in the present. Another death looms in the background as a mountain, beside which our own problems diminish to foothills—my cousin's husband died in the World Trade Center, leaving three fatherless children.

I once felt enlightened when a scholar pointed out that when Dylan Thomas began a poem, "In my craft and sullen art . . . ," the "sullen" meant in the archaic sense "solo," although sullen and solo are emotionally frequently married. When a writer feels embattled the next step is paranoia which is only rarely justified. Two years ago in Marseilles I had a liberating nickel-ante satori. I was sitting in a room at a favorite hotel, Le Petit Nice, which is built on an *anse* protruding into the Mediterranean. I was supposed to be writing a small essay on literary reputation and xenophobia for the back page of *The New York Times Book Review* but, in contrast to the dark blue sea out the window, I was swimming in a mud puddle of conflicting notions. There was a strong antique sense of the dog in the manger. I had read Colin Wilson's *The Outsider* while I was a senior in high school. As a writer I had long felt like an outsider as opposed to the apparent "insiders" along the Eastern Seaboard, but when I met these supposed insiders they were always rather pleasant and welcoming. My thoughts wandered north and west to Les Elysies to a visit I had made in the Dordogne to the area of the caves of Lascaux and how at night at the Hotel Centennaire I had imagined the wandering prehistoric tribes in the area. If I live remotely and travel to New York City less than once a year, it is unlikely that I'll ever feel like an insider. I don't appear to be anonymous but in my entire career I've been asked to be on an award jury only once, although it is altogether natural that writers closer at hand would be asked. And doubtless thousands of writers in the East fashion themselves as outsiders. Of course the literary world as such is more tribal than it thinks, based on its peculiar social contiguities. It is a loosely formed guild and nothing is finally at stake except the destinies of each writer's books. There was also the thought that if I was doing as well in America as I had done for several years in France I would have to divide the year between British Columbia and Vera Cruz in Mexico for the grace of privacy. A French critic had told me that one of the reasons my books were well received in France is that American novels were usually about either the life of the mind or the life of action and I combined both.

In short, in Marseilles I knew that my essay on literary reputation was doomed, and *The New York Times Book Review* promptly rejected it with Charles McGrath, the editor, eventually telling me that the subject would require a book. They did, however, print a longish poem of mine called "The Old Days," which came out of my abortive attempt to cover the subject.

The Old Days

In the old days it stayed light until midnight
and rain and snow came up from the ground
rather than down from the sky. Women were easy.
Every time you'd see one, two more would appear,
walking toward you backwards as their clothes dropped.
Money didn't grow in the leaves of trees but around
the trunks in calf's leather money belts
though you could only take twenty bucks a day.
Certain men flew as well as crows while others ran
up trees like chipmunks. Seven Nebraska women
were clocked swimming upstream in the Missouri
faster than the local spotted dolphins. Basenjis
could talk Spanish but all of them chose not to.
A few political leaders were executed for betraying

the public trust and poets were rationed a gallon
of Burgundy a day. People only died on one day
a year and lovely choruses funneled out
of hospital chimneys where every room had a field
stone fireplace. Some fishermen learned to walk
on water and as a boy I trotted down rivers,
my flyrod at the ready. Women who wanted love
needed only to wear pig's ear slippers or garlic
earrings. All dogs and people in free concourse
became medium sized and brown, and on Christmas
everyone won the hundred dollar lottery. God and Jesus
didn't need to come down to earth because they were
already here riding wild horses every night
and children were allowed to stay up late to hear
them galloping by. The best restaurants were churches
with Episcopalians serving Provencal, The Methodists Tuscan,
and so on. In those days the country was an extra
two thousand miles wider, and an additional thousand
miles deep. There were many undiscovered valleys
to walk in where Indian tribes lived undisturbed
though some tribes chose to found new nations
in the heretofore unknown areas between the black
boundary cracks between states. I was married
to a Pawnee girl in a ceremony behind the usual waterfall.
Courts were manned by sleeping bears and birds sang
lucid tales of ancient bird ancestors who now fly
in other worlds. Certain rivers ran too fast
to be usable but were allowed to do so when they consented
not to flood at the Des Moines Conference.
Airliners were similar to airborne ships with multiple
fluttering wings that played a kind of chamber music
in the sky. Pistol barrels grew delphiniums
and everyone was able to select seven days a year
that they were free to repeat but this wasn't a popular
program. In those days the void whirled

with flowers and unknown wild animals attended
country funerals. All the rooftops in cities were flower
and vegetable gardens. The Hudson River was drinkable
and a humpback whale was seen near 42nd Street
pier, its head full of the blue blood of the sea,
its voice lifting the steps of people
in their traditional anti-march, their harmless disarray.
I could go on but won't. All my evidence
was lost in a fire but not before it was chewed
on by all the dogs that inhabit memory.
One by one they bark at the sun, moon, and stars
trying to draw them closer again.

In Patagonia I've been giving the seven cow dogs up here at Hard Luck
Ranch extra biscuits because I'm leaving in a few days. I'll drive to
Montana and leave our dogs with my daughters, then fly to Michigan
to help Linda pack up the farm for the move. I'll kiss the farm good-
bye in various places, a real big woman who has been kind to me for
over thirty years. In May I'll return to the Upper Peninsula to the cabin
in order to fish and see the budding of the thousands of acres of dogwood and sugarplum bushes and trees. When I return to Montana I'll
start a novel I've been thinking about for years, and explore the few
areas of the state I haven't visited, keeping my sharp single eye out for
fresh thickets for future use. I might need a thicket or two, though I've
come to think of rivers as moving thickets, truly lovely and safe places.
I don't feel an ounce of "closure" about finishing this memoir. I'll just
see how far this life carries me. There's a lot left to be described. My
life could have been otherwise but it wasn't.